Art in Action

Foundations of Expressive Arts Therapy
Theoretical and Clinical Perspectives
Edited by Stephen K. Levine and Ellen G. Levine
ISBN 978 1 85302 463 4

Principles and Practice of Expressive Arts Therapy
Toward a Therapeutic Aesthetics
Paolo Knill, Ellen G. Levine and Stephen K. Levine
ISBN 978 1 84310 039 3

Trauma, Tragedy, Therapy
The Arts and Human Suffering
Stephen K. Levine
Foreword by Shaun McNiff
ISBN 978 1 84310 512 1

Poiesis
The Language of Psychology and the Speech of the Soul
Stephen K. Levine
Foreword by Paolo Knill
ISBN 978 1 85302 488 7

Expressive and Creative Arts Methods for Trauma Survivors
Edited by Lois Carey
ISBN 978 1 84310 386 8

Art Therapy and Social Action
Treating the World's Wounds
Edited by Frances Kaplan
ISBN 978 1 84310 798 9

Using Expressive Arts to Work with Mind, Body and Emotions
Theory and Practice
Mark Pearson and Helen Wilson
ISBN 978 1 84905 031 9

Art in Action

Expressive Arts Therapy
and Social Change

Edited by Ellen G. Levine and Stephen K. Levine

Foreword by Michelle LeBaron

Jessica Kingsley *Publisher*s
London and Philadelphia

First published in 2011
by Jessica Kingsley Publishers
116 Pentonville Road
London N1 9JB, UK
and
400 Market Street, Suite 400
Philadelphia, PA 19106, USA

www.jkp.com

Library of Congress Cataloging in Publication Data
Art in action : expressive arts therapy and social change / [edited and co-authored by]
Ellen G. Levine and Stephen K. Levine ; foreword by Michelle LeBaron.
p. cm.
Includes bibliographical references and index.
ISBN 978-1-84905-820-9 (alk. paper)
1. Arts--Therapeutic Use. 2. Arts and society. 3. Art and social action. 4. Social
change. I. Levine, Ellen G. II. Levine, Stephen K.
RC489.A72A76 2011
616.89'1656--dc22
2010052927

British Library Cataloguing in Publication Data
A CIP catalogue record for this book is available from the British Library

ISBN 978 1 84905 820 9

Printed and bound in Great Britain

Contents

Acknowledgments

We would like to thank our colleagues and students at the European Graduate School (EGS) in Switzerland for their openness to extending expressive arts into the field of social change. The creative and dynamic environment of EGS has been fertile ground for this new development in the ever-evolving history of the expressive arts.

A special thanks to Gabriel Levine for his extensive work in copy-editing the manuscript and in helping us shape it into its present form.

Foreword

Eureka! Discovering Gold in a Leaden World

A group of diplomats from many parts of the world gathered near Dublin, Ireland in a workshop to problem-solve about one of the most intractable conflicts of our time: Israel/Palestine. They were no strangers to conflict. The challenge for us as facilitators was to move them out of the well-worn channels of reflexive statements, carefully devised political framings and limiting assumptions. For two days, nothing out of the ordinary happened.

Then we took a bus trip to Belfast where we looked down Falls and Shankill Roads, searching in a "pre-Good-Friday-agreement Northern Ireland" for ways to address intractable differences. Jostled in the bus, the previously restrained participants became multi-dimensional and a little more "juicy" to each other. They uncovered commonalities, shared passions, and began to play. As the bus headed back to Dublin following a group meal, people sang together under the comforting cover of darkness. Only after this excursion did conversations enliven, originality emerge and creative possibilities for shifting the difficult dynamics in Israel/Palestine begin to reveal themselves.

As I have spoken of this experience to colleagues over the years, it has generated questions: Should all problem-solving workshops include a field trip, preferably on a rough road? How can participation in conflict-transformation processes be structured or unstructured to invite creativity and innovation? What helps people step out of habitual perceptions and narrow understandings, allowing nuance and texture to enter into monolithic stories and linear analyses? How can we inspire people to do something other than traverse well-worn tracks of analysis and problem-solving when doing anything else seems risky or "different"?

Answers to these questions rest on obvious, hidden-in-plain-sight truisms. Everyone at this workshop had powerful gifts in common: they were in real-life bodies with creative capabilities and a love of play and beauty. Why state these obvious facts? Because that workshop – like dozens of others I have attended – was designed as if everyone existed from the neck up. As if brilliant analysis would flow directly from careful selection among a range of cognitive alternatives. As if those facilitating had only to nudge people to "think creatively, outside the box" and new spirals of fecund possibility would unfurl themselves, unfettered by previous inhibitions, perceptual habits or norms of doing business.

Just as the jostling bus ride and the stark reality of Falls Road interrupted the diplomats' patterns of behavior to yield creative openings, so have the visionary scholar/practitioners in this book revealed ways to transform conflict and catalyze social change outside customary practices. The world cries out for embodied, artful experience to invoke the pan-human capacity for creativity, even – or especially – in the midst of ashes. This book provides a window into how this can be done by leaders in the expressive arts field. From a firm theoretical foundation, the book offers insights grounded in case examples and is unafraid to pose questions. This is no rose-tinted window. It is as clear and unrelenting a piece of work as I have read in a long time. Stephen and Ellen Levine and their colleagues have done what many conflict resolvers and peaceworkers long to do: they offer ways to transform conflict, acknowledging its complexity while trusting mystery.

Reading this book was a "eureka" experience. It brings together inherited wisdom with the most compelling thinking I have encountered in a decade, addressing questions we in the conflict-transformation and peacemaking fields have been asking for at least as long. Not only does it address them, it does so with theory grounded in phenomenology, principles illustrated in practice, and possibility channeled into results. It does so in a spirit of partnership and deep respect for those with whom the authors engage, a spirit vital to the success of conflict transformation.

Ellen and Stephen Levine – with their contributing authors – have created a book that I hope every mediator, peacemaker, negotiator and social change practitioner will read. Why? Because their work in expressive arts – developed over the past 25 years – is a missing link in the field of conflict resolution and peacemaking. It not only introduces new and vitally important ways of thinking about conflict and its resolution, it provides clear examples of how these ideas actually work. Practitioners applying them may well find their work – and the results of this work – transformed.

M.C. Richards – a famous potter and artist – writes this about the complexity of imagining ways through conflict:

Can we imagine a kind of peace that includes the freedom to conflict, a kind of warmth that allows the freedom to withdraw, a kind of union that asks for free and unique individualities, a kind of good that grants the mystery of evil, a kind of life that bears death within it like a seed-force? (Richards 1998, p.234)

Art in Action addresses Richards' questions as well as many others from the conflict transformation/peacemaking fields. It is a carefully constructed collection of jewels that reveal how a visionary group of thought-leaders and practitioners discovered ways of addressing the following challenges in attempts to resolve conflict:

- Focusing on the issues in conflict often escalates disagreement, worsens relationships and deepens the conflict itself.

- Problem-solving and analysis are limited by parties' and interveners' perceptions and perceptual habits, assumptions and cognitive frames.

- Creativity is advised in addressing conflict, yet people in conflict tend toward narrowed perceptions, evaluating possibilities critically and negatively (even when they are asked not to), thus experiencing limited room for maneuvering.

- Durable solutions to intractable conflicts are elusive because the conflicts themselves change, and mysteries not amenable to logical problem-solving continue to emerge.

Given these challenges, how to proceed? This preface traces the genius of *Art in Action* in answering that question.

In the first chapter, Stephen K. Levine outlines the history of the field of expressive arts, identifying key ideas including intermodality. Intermodality – Knill's idea that arts practices engage different sensory capacities – helps us understand and conceptualize the body as a multifaceted perceptual, expressive and relational center. The creative capacity of the body as a vehicle where words and art come together is what Levine calls *poiesis*. He identifies humans' abilities to shape and be shaped by diverse worlds as *world-building* and *self-building*. The creative possibilities that arise from an aesthetic response to a situation or an issue generate change not only at the level of imagination but in lived, measurable reality.

By outlining an approach to conflict based in *poiesis*, Levine provides practical hope. He reminds us that it is precisely because we are capable of imagining our world in multiple ways that we feel hopeless when we are blocked from doing so. The work of the change agent in expressive arts, then, is to work with people to restore their capacity for *poiesis*. How is this done? The answer is both structured and emergent, bounded and open-ended. It involves a range of practices that magnify creativity, while steering carefully away from the more linear containment that too often characterizes conflict-transformation work. Levine shows us how art-making restores individuals' and groups' capacities for action and agency, giving up control in order to achieve mastery, as Paolo Knill has counseled. In short, Stephen Levine inspires while handing us tools to till ground we had feared barren.

Ellen Levine deepens the fertility of the book, relating her experiences in social activism and restorative work that led her to the vitality of expressive arts. Her memoir traces well-intentioned participation in social justice work that, in retrospect, excluded important parties. She powerfully relates an experience of visiting Israel during her teens in which she met the heroes of one side but not the other. Her dedication to being of service led her ultimately to "the community-oriented playfulness and joyousness of [expressive arts] work," attracted by its "emancipatory spirit of collective and collaborative art-making." This attraction shook the foundations of her clinical work, and caused her to step away from reductionist, deficit-oriented approaches. Levine's moving story traces how her work in visual art and clown performance changed the way she saw herself, yielding not only a new identity but also pointing to expressive arts as ways to expand possibilities in the world.

A leader in expressive arts and social change work, Ellen has partnered with Palestinians and Israelis to explore possibilities for shifting intractable relations and patterns. In doing so, she illustrates a full-circle journey from her early travels, partnering with others to create worlds whose peace includes the freedom to conflict and whose unity honors uniqueness.

One of the foundational ideas in this book is that our systems for analyzing and categorizing issues and problems are often too limited to yield effective results in a complex world. Karen Estrella situates the arts as transformative by nature and therefore amenable to holding multiple discourses and dynamics in coherent tension. In art-making, the goal of transformation is organically contained in the process itself. Estrella's definition of social action as including a broad swath of activities – from contemplative practice to reconciliatory work, from policy and coalition work to political action – opens a wide door for the application of expressive arts approaches. Crossing boundaries of practice while integrating intermodal arts methods is the fascinating challenge she poses. Conflict transformation practitioners – boundary-crossers themselves – will find much to inspire, provoke and assist them in her work.

Paolo Knill, a pioneer in the field, adds spark to the work by detailing his experience of childhood play during the bombing raids of World War II. He gives readers a glimpse of his early genius in transforming fear, as he traces his innocent attachment to underground adventures in bomb shelters. Knill's theoretical and practical work issues fluidly from these accounts. He patiently outlines the bones of his approach, emphasizing de-centering as a vital way of moving into unpredictable terrain and widening possibilities. Implicit in his work is the truism that conflicts cannot be solved by the same thinking – or the same kind of thinking patterns – that spawned them. Patterns need to be disturbed and stuck places unstuck for novel results to unfold. De-centering is a way to achieve surprise, to access what Knill calls the logic of the imagination.

He assures readers, "When we use the arts as a mode of interaction, the impetus for discovery balances the fear of uncertainty if we provide an adequate motivating space." Knill then sets out touchstones for expressive arts practice in language that ventures from aesthetics to kinetics. Emphasizing connections between emotional resonance and psychophysical experience, he demonstrates how art-making literally builds capacity as participants experience accomplishment and the satisfaction inherent in beauty. He illustrates how parties in conflict can step out of their ordinary grammar and conversational logic to discover individual and group resilience that they had not known before. Knill's work sent me looking for the nearest expressive arts group to experience de-centering for myself!

But I could not stay away from my reading for long. Knill's chapter is followed by another pioneer in the field, Shaun McNiff, who recounts more of the field's history and its roots in therapeutic models and practices. His awareness of the "alchemical dynamics of the therapeutic studio" led him to postulate possibilities for change in larger social spheres. Writing of the facilitation role, McNiff stakes out a strong position against relativism or imagined distance from the parties with whom we engage. He explains his conviction that people in the "change business" need to maintain rigor and be willing to take sometimes extreme positions in the social project of upsetting unjust or dysfunctional orders. In this, he acknowledges the shadow – the destructive part of individuals and groups that M.C. Richards writes about when she frames the inner work of peacemakers as acknowledging and loving our own inner lepers. Conflict resolvers can be stymied by a sense of moral elevation that distances them not only from parties but from their own human complexities. McNiff's acknowledgement that "in the truly creative space, the shadow and soulful expression are inseparable" underlines the labyrinthine nature of conflict and the ways it implicates all of us, and is a more complex map than many conflict practitioners have been using. Finally, McNiff cautions that the only thing we can do wrong is to plan what we do before we do it. He reminds us that overly scripted approaches are antithetical to creativity. Fortunately, McNiff's seminal work yields new choices beyond the familiar poles of purely elicitive and purely prescriptive work.

Part II of the book is a rich exploration of issues, held to the light in ways that show various hues of expressive arts work. These three chapters take us to a clinic for Iraqis in Jordan, a Bosnian refugee camp in Slovenia, and to Israel. From her work in Israel, Ephrat Huss shows how art created a vehicle for Bedouin women to express their social and geographic confinement, and in the process reclaim some of their agency. Stopped from moving in traditional nomadic patterns through the desert landscape, the women discover they still have motion, dynamism and fluidity in their lives, even though it is no longer sparked from migration.

Debra Kalmanowitz and Bobby Lloyd outline how constructing homes in the woods and a quarry helped express and re-story loss and bereavement for Bosnian refugees. Inner and outer domains form a counterpoint in which people whose homes were lost recover hope and agency in their creative acts and deep experiences of accompaniment in their grief. In their retold stories, the correspondence between the concrete and the symbolic dimensions is revealed to be a Möbius strip – continuous and without clear boundaries.

Finally, Shanee Stepakoff and colleagues explore how, in the aftermath of ethnopolitical trauma, the initial reclamation of speech in a clinical setting can translate into public truth-telling. Their work with Iraqis who took refuge in Jordan has particular resonance for conflict-transformation practitioners concerned with eliciting more complex, nuanced stories and images beyond the stark cycles of blame and retribution. They suggest that recovery involves constellating a new sense of self that encompasses the trauma but is not consumed by it. Their work with poetry powerfully evokes the healing archetype, as if the words themselves actively seek the rich loam of resilience when loosed from the desiccated soil of trauma.

Part III of the book chronicles projects where expressive arts have been used to re-animate, breathing vibrancy into geographies of loss. Carrie MacLeod takes us to Sierra Leone's crisis of youth in the aftermath of war. She describes her work using partnership language, with respect for the resilience and irrepressible spirit of people in Sierra Leone running through each word. This respect infuses MacLeod's methods, which resemble improvisation, not a fixed score. She uncovers powerful questions that frame inquiry and spark creativity in the midst of the turmoil of this post-war society. Her evocative language takes us to the heart of complexity, asking "What is peace?" while resisting easy formulas like "All arts heal." MacLeod challenges us to go beyond "givens" and examine the courage of those "who choose to live at the intersection where imagination encounters the unfathomable."

Gloria Simoneaux works with the canvas of the body, partnering with HIV-positive women in prison in a wash of color and passionate exploration that gives them tastes of fun – something largely missing from their confined lives. Her work also explores the terrain of intercultural collaboration as she details the confusions and challenges of working across contexts. Karen Abbs's piece on beauty in rough places is a meditation on contrasts: her words do not mute the horror of Darfur, yet they also trace ways that beauty seeps through the rough places. Her work is an account of quickening beauty amidst nearly unspeakable suffering: people who have lost their villages, their homes and family members find work in international agencies, only to find themselves vulnerable to new attacks. The partnership of Abbs and her colleagues must have come like a window in a concrete shelter, though one that could scarcely be big enough to light the dark corners of their layered losses. Her sensitivity to local ways of perceiving mental health and intervention underlines the gracefulness of her work; her focus on social change as well as critical incidents further deepens its impact. She writes, quoting Knill, of "aesthetic responsibility," and then describes how she discharged this responsibility with gentleness and attention to how expressive arts helped people de-center – to move away from the perceptions and experiences that kept them hurting or lost.

Sally Atkins takes us to Bolivia where the ongoing relationships she and her colleagues have developed have become a crucible for gift-giving. She powerfully frames her descriptions around Lewis Hyde's seminal book on gifting, sharing the spirals of giving and receiving that have characterized her involvement in Cochabamba. Atkins illustrates how expressive arts give her the confidence to engage without prescriptions, trusting that the inspiration for how to proceed in any given moment will come to her. And it does, revealing that the most profound gift is one of sharing presence beyond methodology or form. As presence is shared, social bonds are created, the kind of glue that enspirits people even in the midst of challenge. Atkins' work speaks to conflict prevention and transformation, posed as it is at the threshold of becoming, changing states in the midst of struggles.

The work of TAE Perú follows, where de-centering is described as a way of life. Again the reader encounters ghosts, this time the specters of thousands of disappeared and murdered people and their families, bereft. Again the reader encounters "othering," as we learn that the victims were largely Quechua-speaking peasants. The work of TAE evokes M.C. Richards when she writes of peace as a fusing of the opposites that overcomes the one-sidedness of violence. Richards elaborates:

> *In the psyche, violence creates trauma: consciousness breaks down. We lose our memories; we become deaf, dizzy, disoriented, disorganized, nonfunctioning. A violent emotional experience pulverizes us in the same way that an avalanche or a flood dissolves the structures of a lively town. But transformed from a ravaging force into a capacity for feeling, [this legacy of violence] is our warmth…[a]nd when it blows wildly and yet may be contained, it fills the forms of life with inspiration. (Richards 1998, p. 239)*

TAE's work in collage, in finding ways to dance with realities without being taken over by unchosen music, is an example of filling the forms of life with inspiration. It evidences daring and searing determination as it poses the challenge of living with our own contradictions and accepting those of others. TAE's work is not a denial of harsh realities; it is a work that sees squarely yet refuses to be cowed. It teaches a great deal.

Finally, Vivien Speiser and Samuel Schwartz describe their work with Ethiopian Jewish migrants in Israel. Detailing the harrowing circumstances under which many of them arrive, the authors explain how expressive arts were used to breathe life into "untold stories." Aware of the importance of assessment and relationship-building, they spent time listening and observing. Ethiopian post-army youth were identified as a group who tend to lose touch with Israeli society after their service. One of the most tangible – if unintended – outcomes of the workshops was increasing social cohesion within the Ethiopian youth community itself. Outsiders may not perceive the fissures within a community, yet generating new connections gave young people increased support in their quest for belonging in Israel. The authors' work is part of a patchwork of initiatives with vulnerable parts of the Ethiopian community, including middle-school students and single mothers. Their description of using arts for assessment and intervention raises new and interesting possibilities for conflict resolvers and peacemakers.

With Speiser's and Schwartz's chapter and the Afterword by MaryBeth Morand, the book ends. It is a book that I hope has a sequel; it is a book that offers answers to practitioners in social change work who know that the traditional approaches of identifying issues and problem-solving are often unsuccessful, and sometimes even escalate conflicts and worsen relationships. This book offers a series of exciting tools to address human myopia when trauma has made it even more difficult to see a spectrum of choices.

This is a book that knows that, in the end, we cannot know how to cross the threshold between defeat and resilience. There are no quick answers, no step-by-step guide to picking up pieces after the fragmentation of war and violence. Partnering is difficult: across chasms of privilege, we reach out to those who might not have limbs to grasp ours; whose hands have touched grief for which we have no corollary. Yet this book does not offer stories of paternalistic valor. The real heroes are clearly situated in each account: they are the people for whom the arts become routes out of despair, those who manage to weave even badly torn fabric into the beauty of new coherence. These people and the authors who write about them steadfastly refuse to accept tragedy as the only storyline. Instead, they gather and offer all the broken pieces to the crucible of expressive arts where a remarkable alchemy restores.

And so, to all who work to heal conflict, to those whose hope is frayed in diverse settings and broken places: here is a stream full of gold. The stream sparkles with surprise as it de-centers our assumptions about linear processes. It courses with possibility, carrying both gold and lead. The lead is the heaviness of understanding that linear processes of intervention are often too static and confrontational to yield transformative results. The gold is the realization that expressive arts theory and practice offer ways to find fertility even in eddies of desolation. Gold – ever more valuable than lead – is ours for the reading in this precious book. To Ellen and Stephen Levine, and to these authors, we owe deep appreciation for their gifts.

Michelle LeBaron
Vancouver, British Columbia
September 2010

Reference

Richards, M.C. (1998) "Separating and Connecting: The Vessel and the Fire." In M.J. Ryan (ed.) *Fabric of the Future: Women Visionaries Illuminate the Path to Tomorrow.* Berkeley, CA: Conari Press.

PART I
Principles

1

Art Opens to the World

Expressive Arts and Social Action

Stephen K. Levine

In this chapter I attempt to lay a theoretical foundation for the field of expressive arts and social change. In order to do so, I first have to conduct a brief survey of the development of the field of expressive arts itself.

As a specific discipline, expressive arts had its beginnings during the 1970s at Lesley College Graduate School (now Lesley University) through the work of Shaun McNiff, Paolo Knill, Norma Canner, Elizabeth McKim and others. At the time the field was called "expressive therapy." Shaun McNiff has explained in *The Arts in Psychotherapy* (1981, significantly revised as *Integrating the Arts in Therapy: History, Theory, and Practice*, 2009) and elsewhere that the word "expressive" came to him from outside, in the context of gaining support from initial funding sources. In some ways, the name is a misnomer, insofar as it has been taken to mean that art is "self-expression," the outward representation of inner feelings. This interpretation fit with the prevailing ethos of the times – "Express yourself!" – but it is not a helpful starting point for understanding the work of the arts.

Even at the time, it was understood that the arts do more than express outwardly what is felt inwardly, that in fact artistic expression cannot be reduced to pre-existing psychological states. Indeed, in contradistinction to the individual creative arts therapies, which usually begin from an established psychological framework, expressive therapy called for a "theory indigenous to the arts," a way of understanding that would be appropriate to aesthetic experience itself, not based upon another foundation.

The beginnings of such a theory were formulated by Paolo Knill with his notion of "intermodality." An obvious difference between expressive therapy and the creative arts therapies is that the former draws upon all the arts, rather than working only within one specialized form (be it visual art, dance, drama, poetry, etc.). *Minstrels of Soul*, Knill's first book in English, had the subtitle *Intermodal Expressive Therapy*, indicating that what is distinctive about the field is its intermodal character (Knill, Barba and Fuchs 2004). This character of intermodality makes sense once we realize that artistic disciplines are rooted in the different modalities of sensory experience. We can make visual art because we see; we can make music because we hear; we dance because we move, etc. And all of these sensory modalities are united in the common-sense experience of having a body. It is the same body that sees, hears, and moves. In fact, the separation and extreme specialization of the arts in modern times is itself a recent historical phenomenon. Art-making has traditionally been intermodal within the context of dramatic or ritual performance. Only the removal of the arts from everyday life has enabled practitioners to explore their specialized and formal capacities. As contemporary and post-modern art has developed, a renewed interest in interdisciplinary work has also emerged. Traditional artistic boundaries have been erased, and cross-disciplinary work is now common.

In addition, it was clear to practitioners of the expressive arts that the basic framework of the field had an artistic rather than psychological base. Both McNiff and Knill were artists (a painter and a musician respectively) before they were therapists. As the field developed during the 1980s and 1990s, the word "arts" was gradually placed between "expressive" and "therapy." The International Expressive Arts Therapy Association (IEATA) replaced the National Expressive Therapy Association (NETA) as the primary professional association in the field and deliberately included "Arts" in its title, as did many of the books that attempted to lay the theoretical foundations for the field (see Levine and Levine 1999, and Knill, Levine and Levine 2005).

This shift in nomenclature was significant. It not only rooted the field in its proper place, it also made it possible to extend this work in other directions outside of psychotherapy. IEATA opened registration to expressive arts educators and consultants as well as therapists, and programs were developed that included these new initiatives. At the European Graduate School (EGS), the doctoral program in Expressive Arts Therapy changed its name to Expressive Arts: Therapy, Education, and Consulting (including coaching under the term "Consulting"). It has now been extended to include the term "Social Change," indicating a further development of the field, of which the present book is another indication.

The evolution of a field is an interesting phenomenon, often reflecting changes in the wider society. If the field itself does not grow concurrently, it risks becoming outdated and irrelevant. During the past two decades psychotherapy has lost some of its cachet. Partly this reflects its professionalization: what was once an open, innovative (and sometimes undisciplined) field of practice has become codified, licensed, and restricted to those with licensed professional training. In addition, the concern with abusive practices, though important in protecting clients, has had the side effect of making therapists wary of trying anything not already approved or anything that could be considered "unsafe." To a great extent, the dynamic energy that had marked expressive therapy practice in the seventies has migrated elsewhere, to the practice of art itself, or to the new fields of coaching and consulting. Some practitioners became expressive arts coaches; others turned their attention to education and called themselves expressive arts educators. It became clear that although the work of expressive arts had begun in psychotherapy, the basic principles could be extended to other areas of practice. Most recently, this has included the field of social change. Under the direction of Ellen Levine, EGS began a graduate certificate program in Expressive Arts and Social Change (now developed into a full master's degree program in Expressive Arts in Conflict Transformation and Peacebuilding; see Chapter 2 in this volume). Students began to apply the work of expressive arts outside of the restricted settings of the clinic, school, or corporation to the wider world of communities and conflict-laden social groups.

We need to explore the theoretical foundation underlying this new development. What are the principles of expressive arts that open work in the field to broader social concerns? In order to understand this, we have to look at the basis of artistic expression itself. In several articles and books I have tried to formulate this through the use of the concept of *poiesis* (Levine 1997). The word *poiesis* is taken from classical Greek, originally signifying the act of making in general, and artistic making in particular. I go back to this word in order to make it easier to understand art-making from a different perspective than we are accustomed to, one that will perhaps shed light on the subject in a new way.

What is implied in the concept of *poiesis* is that art-making is not divorced from other forms of production. It is not a specialized activity radically separated from others; rather it is an extension and development of the basic capacity of human beings to shape their worlds. The human being is distinct from other creatures in that it is not pre-adapted to a particular environment. Instead it has the ability to build radically different worlds suitable (or not) to life in a wide diversity of surroundings. In building its world, the human shapes the environment, and as it does so, it shapes itself. *World-building is self-building*. This phenomenon accounts for the wide variety of cultures that exist in the world and the various ways that humans have changed their behaviors and world-views accordingly. If there is an essential quality of being human, it does not lie in a particular way of living but in this capacity to shape ourselves and others according to our needs.

Of course, this does not imply that all forms of world-building are appropriate. As we can see in our current understanding of environmental crisis, it is quite possible for us to mis-shape worlds, and ourselves with it. However, the very fact that we have made this world as it is should awaken us to the possibility of changing it. *Poiesis is always possible* (Levine 1999, p.31).

What role can the arts play in bringing about the possibility of social change? First we have to understand art-making within the broader perspective of *poiesis*. The arts are a particular form of making that differentiate themselves by showing themselves as having been made. Whatever else art is (and that is certainly a question without any agreed-upon answer), it *shows* something and it shows itself as having been made. We could say that, as something that shows, art needs to be seen; we could even say in this sense that art is always *performative*. Even visual art is "performed" in the viewing of it; it requires an audience in order to be what it is. This does not mean that works that have gone unpublished are not artworks. It only signifies that they have the capacity to be seen (heard, read) by others, even if that never comes to pass.

By showing itself in the mode of existing-as-being-seen, art indicates its quality of irreality, its ability to create an alternative world of the imagination. We know that the actor playing Oedipus does not actually tear out his eyes; nor is there anyone really murdered in *Hamlet*. Rather the work creates an imaginary world in which it exists. This quality of irreality does not make it any less effective; on the contrary, the limitation from realistic constraints means that the work can affect us on an even deeper level than the actual event that it depicts.

At the same time, this alternative world of imagination always takes place within the literal reality in which we exist. The imaginal world of the play, for example, happens in the real world of the theater. But more importantly, it always happens within the world in which we actually live our daily lives. *Hamlet* today happens in a different world than it did in Shakespeare's time. The production itself changes, even if we try to make it "authentically" Elizabethan. And we see it differently; it occurs within a different horizon of understanding than it did originally. We live in a different historical world and we are shaped differently by it; both our behavior and our perceptions have changed.

Because the work happens within our world, it has the capacity to affect us. The work "touches" us; we are "moved" by it. We call this our "aesthetic response" to the work. The term "aesthetic response" has often been understood in expressive arts therapy as the artistic response of the therapist to the client (e.g. by writing a poem in response to the client's artwork), but it properly means the client's affective response to what he or she has made. When the work results in an aesthetic response on the part of the client, we can say that it has been effective, it has touched what we can call their "effective reality." The power of art is that, although itself existing only in imaginal reality, it can nevertheless touch people's literal reality and have an impact upon them.

This experience of aesthetic response can also be seen as the proper psychological point of reference for aesthetic experience. Art is not self-expression; it does not merely give an outward form for what is already there in our inner worlds. This should be obvious from any cursory reflection on the arts. Can we think of *War and Peace* as an expression of Tolstoy's self? It's not even clear what that would mean. The excellence of the artist consists in his or her ability to transcend the self, to be able to imagine the experience of others and the world in which they live. Of course, *War and Peace* could only have been written by Tolstoy, but that does not mean it is a representation *of* Tolstoy's psyche. In fact the book is properly understood as an imaginative presentation of Russian society during the Napoleonic era in both war and peace. It was made *by* Tolstoy, but it is not a depiction *of* Tolstoy. This misunderstanding of the nature of art could only have taken place within a world-view shaped exclusively by the psychological perspective.

Of course we could say that the impulse to make art often begins with an inner psychic state. However, as soon as the artist begins to shape his or her material, that impulse becomes transformed. The work starts to shape itself, and the role of the artist is to allow it to find its proper form, rather than to force it into a pre-conceived mold. This is why novelists often talk about their characters having lives of their own which the author can only follow at their dictation. Certainly the artist must step back from the initial creative effort and make any necessary revisions, but this is a necessity to be found in the work itself, not in the mind of its creator.

We must get beyond psychological reductionism in order to properly understand the process of art-making and the artwork itself. The work does not express the *self*, it expresses a *world*. It starts with me, but it then finds its own shape which I can only follow. The proper psychological point of reference for the work is in fact in the way that it *affects* me, both in the making of it and in the experience of it once it is made. That the work is not an expression of the self does not mean that it lacks psychological significance. On the contrary, precisely because it goes beyond myself, it can affect me in a powerful way; it can touch me deeply and change my way of being in the world. This is what Rilke meant when, in his poem, "Archaic Torso of Apollo," in which he refers to viewing the fragmentary remains of a Greek sculpture, he speaks not about my experience of looking at the work but about the way in which the work looks at *me*. In the last line of the poem, the sculpture itself addresses the viewer and says, "You must change your life" (Rilke 1984, p.61). Of course, when we read this poem, we also understand that it is not only the poet but we ourselves who must change our lives.

To deny that the work is to be understood as self-expression, then, is not to take away its power but rather to make this power comprehensible. Otherwise, what possible effect would it have on myself for me merely to see what I am already feeling? Its power comes precisely from bringing me something new that comes to me as a surprise. To say that this new element comes from the "unconscious" does not help here; "unconscious" merely means "not known." To locate this unknown and therefore surprising thing in the psyche is merely to try to find some justification for our psychological prejudice. Unwittingly this prejudice makes the psychological impact of the work impossible to understand.

Moreover, not only does the work affect us emotionally, it also has the capacity to change our understanding of ourselves and of the world around us. The work can be a re-description of the world, a presentation of an alternative reality that helps us see ourselves and others differently. In the philosophical tradition, beginning with Plato, art is understood as semblance, as an imitation of what is already there, a poor substitute for the real thing. It may give pleasure but it cannot provide truth. This view of art only makes sense within a perspective in which reflective thought is understood as providing access to a form of existence beyond change. Eternal truth, in this view, cannot take sensible form but can only be understood by the intellect freed from the deceptions and changes brought about in sense perception.

Contemporary philosophy, beginning with Nietzsche, has rejected this metaphysical assumption of a second world of unchanging truth that lies beyond the senses and is only accessible to the intellect abstracted from the body and the world. For Martin Heidegger, the founder of this strand of contemporary thought, existence itself is temporal; being can only be understood within the perspective of time. Human existence is a being-in-the-world, a world that comes to be and passes away. The very characteristics that traditional philosophy attempted to deny are precisely what characterize the human being. We are sensible beings, we experience the world and others through our senses, and we *make* sense of what we experience. Any other view is an illusion based upon a metaphysical presupposition of eternal presence, what Jacques Derrida has called "the metaphysics of presence" (Derrida 1973, p.63).

If our existence is temporal, that implies that it is also historical. We are born into a world that we have not made; Heidegger even says we are "thrown" into this world. In this sense, we do not have the ability to make our world out of nothing, to act as omnipotent creators. Rather, we are already made by this world; I come into it at a certain time, with a gender, race, class, nationality, etc., that I have not chosen. At the same time I am not determined by what has been; rather I always have the capacity to *respond* to what has been given to me. In our own time, we have seen how extensive is our ability to change what we have been. I can embrace a different religion, move to another country, rise or fall in social class and even change my gender. Nevertheless I will always be marked by what I have been. There is no erasing the past, only different ways of living it.

History is what we make of what is made of us, as Jean-Paul Sartre's philosophy continually reminds us. Within the framework of expressive arts, we could say that *poiesis* implies the capacity to respond to the world in which we find ourselves. We suffer, both individually and collectively, when we find ourselves unable to respond, when this capacity for poietic action is restricted and we experience ourselves as being in a helpless situation. It is precisely because we are capable of making our world in a different way that we experience ourselves as helpless when we are unable to do so. The work of the change agent in the field of expressive arts, then, is to restore the capacity for *poiesis* that the individual or community has lost, and to help them expand the range of play within which they can act.

In this process, art-making can play an essential role. By creating an alternative world of the imagination, the artwork shows possibilities that are absent or dormant within our everyday awareness. Moreover, the work takes us away from this everyday world within which we experience ourselves as unable to act; we could say that it "decenters" us from this world (Knill *et al.* 2005, p.83). In so doing it frees us up for new possibilities that were not apparent within our limited horizon of understanding.

Art-making is itself a sensory-affective experience that gives participants a experience of their own capacities for action. Because it affects us through the body and the emotions, art-making can provide experiences that restore us to a feeling of being fully alive. And in making the work, by acting within the limited frame of the materials and the time and space available, we recover our capacity to be effective in the world, something that we have lost in the helpless situation in which we find ourselves.

Social change is only possible when people in a community have a sense of their own capacity to act, when they become aware of their resources and see themselves as able to re-make the world in which they live. The task of the expressive arts change agent is not to enter a community with a pre-existing plan, attempting to steer community action in an anticipated direction. This would be similar to trying to make a work of art by forcing the materials into a form that corresponds to an idea in the mind (a traditional view of art-making that even Karl Marx held).

Rather, the work of social change begins with trying to understand the world in which people already live. Only then can we see possibilities of responding to that reality. The role of the change agent from the perspective of expressive arts, like the role of the expressive arts therapist, is to help the community find its own resources and envision new ways of living together that draw upon them. By helping people engage in community art practices together, not only can they regain an awareness of their own poietic capacity, but they also can find new forms of being together, types of association that aid in reviving the sense of community itself.

When a social group is in a helpless situation, whether due to poverty, oppression, natural disaster, or other factors, individuals typically experience themselves as isolated and cut off from others. One of the things that the experience of making art together does is to restore the sense of a living community, of being part of a whole that is larger than oneself. This is "solidarity," the experience of being together with others

prison
soulcollage
project

that is an essential part of being in the world. This solidarity often takes place within a celebratory setting, one in which the joy of singing and dancing together can bind a social group in a mutual feeling of kinship, but the arts are also capable of holding the experience of mourning what an individual or group has lost. Mourning and celebration are two essential ways in which art-making can touch the essence of being human. Both our tears and our laughter hold us together.

The work of the social change agent in the expressive arts ultimately rests upon what Knill *et al.* call "aesthetic responsibility" (2005, p.138). We are responsible for shaping our interventions so as to help the people we are working with regain the capacity for creative action that they have lost. In order to do so, we have to be willing to go into a community without a prearranged agenda, to be sensitive to what we find, and to use our own imagination in helping others to transcend their limitations and, become aware of the unexplored possibilities that are available to them.

This process normally includes a liminal phase, one in which we are unable to predict or control what will happen. In this sense, we can say that our work is the opposite of the omnipotent and omniscient creator-god, who knows what he does and can control the outcome. Rather we put ourselves into the difficult state of non-knowing, "giving up control in order to achieve mastery," as Knill has often remarked in conversation. This requires a tolerance for chaos, an ability to improvise and a love of play. We do not know what will emerge, but we have the faith that it is possible for a surprise to come, for a solution to be found that was not envisioned by anyone, including ourselves. This faith is based on the belief, borne out by experience, that individuals, groups and communities have the resources to deal with their difficulties even if they do not recognize or acknowledge these resources.

Social change and social action require a humble and respectful attitude on the part of the change agent. We need to have an "appreciative curiosity," in Herbert Eberhart's words (2002, p.126) about the situation in which the community finds itself in order to help the members of the group become aware of their resources and to help them regain an awareness of their capacity for building the world anew. Human existence is essentially poietic. *Poïesis* itself happens only in the world with others. We have made this world together; this means that we can make it differently. The particular power of the expressive arts in the field of social change is to help us find our ability to make a new world together. Only by doing so can we leave to future generations a world which they will find worthy of response.

References

Derrida, J. (1973) *Speech and Phenomena: And Other Essays on Husserl's Theory of Signs.* Evanston: Northwestern University Press.

Knill, P., Barba, H.N. and Fuchs, M.N. (2004) *Minstrels of Soul: Intermodal Expressive Therapy,* 2nd edn. Toronto: EGS Press.

Knill, P., Levine E. and Levine, S. (2005) *Principles and Practice of Expressive Arts Therapy: Toward a Therapeutic Aesthetics.* London: Jessica Kingsley Publishers.

Levine, S. (1997) *Poiesis: The Language of Psychology and the Speech of the Soul.* London: Jessica Kingsley Publishers.

Levine, S. and Levine, E. (eds) (1999) *Foundations of Expressive Arts Therapy: Theoretical and Clinical Perspectives.* London: Jessica Kingsley Publishers.

Eberhart, H. (2002) "Decentering with the Arts: A New Strategy in a New Professional Field." In S. Levine (ed.) *Crossing Boundaries: Explorations in Therapy and the Arts.* Toronto: EGS Press.

McNiff, S. (1981) *The Arts in Psychotherapy.* Springfield, IL: Charles C. Thomas.

McNiff, S. (2009) *Integrating the Arts in Therapy: History, Theory, and Practice.* Springfield, IL: Charles C. Thomas.

Rilke, R.M. (1984) *The Selected Poetry of Rainer Maria Rilke,* trans. Stephen Mitchell. New York: Random House.

2

From Social Change to Art Therapy and Back Again

A Memoir

Ellen Levine

The extension of expressive arts therapy to the arena of social change has a particular personal meaning for me, one based upon my own history. It has become the thread that runs through all of my life, connecting the different parts. On another level, it feels like a re-emergence of an impulse for change that rose up almost 50 years ago – a time when we were playing with difficulties, helping voiceless communities find their voices through the forming and shaping of works of art, engaging non-artists in artistic practice, and bringing the work into the public sphere.

I can trace this interest back to my beginnings. I grew up in the 1950s and early 1960s in a suburb of Boston, Massachusetts where my life revolved around school, art lessons, and the synagogue, known as the "Temple." I attended religious school on Sundays and studied Hebrew there twice a week and later, as a teenager, became involved in youth group activities.

My parents, in reaction to their parents, had become Reform Jews. They rejected the binding laws and strictures of the Orthodox practice in which they were raised, a practice which encouraged separation, in favor of one that brought them into closer contact with the dominant culture. The services were conducted primarily in English rather than Hebrew. Every year there was an art show at the Temple and, when I was 11, I submitted an oil painting and won a first prize.

Our Temple was very small at the time, and until we had our own building we met for services in the local Unitarian Church. I remember my parents arguing heatedly with my grandparents about religious practice. Yet, throughout this period of doubt and transition, my parents always tried to articulate certain values important to the Jewish tradition, especially those of justice and fairness. We had a charity box at home where we were encouraged to put money every week and bring it to the Temple. This act of *tzedakah* or the giving of charity, based on the Hebrew word for righteousness, is one of the primary values of the Jewish tradition and one which my parents emphasized.

I remember feeling proud that my rabbi, together with many religious leaders, marched with Martin Luther King in Selma, Alabama. His social engagement was a model for me as a child, growing into adolescence. I felt his passion for social justice, which he articulated often in his sermons. This resonated with me very strongly.

At the age of 16, in the summer of 1963, I went to Israel on a trip organized by the National Federation of Temple Youth. With a group of 40 American teenagers, I toured the country in a bus and spent a few weeks working on a kibbutz, picking and packing fruit. This experience was pivotal for me. It was not the first time that I had been away from home, but it was my first experience of travel and of being in a different world. I was captivated by the spirit of the country, by what I perceived as the strength and tenacity of the people that I met. The life that they were living seemed in stark contrast to my sheltered suburban life.

When I look back now on this experience, I realize how much it excluded the reality of the situation – the experience of the other side. I met army officers and farmers, tanned and muscular men and women, all presented as heroes. I was shown the monuments to the wars; the rusted relics of tanks littered all the roads. Jerusalem was a maze of cordoned-off areas. It was not possible to go into the Old City. This seemed like a tragic situation that needed to be rectified.

The Arabs were depicted as demonized "Others," the ones who stood in our way. Our guides took us to hilltops to show us the great progress of the Israeli city building and were quick to point out the Arab villages right beside the cities where there were dirt roads and broken-down houses with goats and chickens in the yards. I was told that Arabs were "lazy and obviously did not care about their land."

I came back from Israel, finished high school in 1964 and left home to attend a small women's college in a rural part of Massachusetts. America was in the throes of major change. The Vietnam War and the Civil Rights Movement were becoming more and more intense and, at the same time, I was beginning to wake up. The self-satisfied slumber of suburban life was giving way to a sense of outrage about a war in a distant land that seemed more and more senseless. Many of my friends were in danger of being drafted into the military if they did not stay in school. Some friends were going to fight in Vietnam. Racism was increasingly being confronted with civil disobedience, and Northerners were going South to participate in marches and sit-ins. Among other tumultuous events 1964 was the year of the murder of three civil rights activists, Chaney, Goodman, and Schwerner. Goodman and Schwerner were white, and they were also Jewish. This made a big impression on me. At the same time a countercultural revolution was building momentum, based on the rejection of authority and a new sense of openness and freedom. I began experimenting on both a personal and political level and, most of all, I wanted to take some action in the world.

During college I joined together with several classmates to create a tutoring group. Every week we would hire a bus and travel to Roxbury, a black ghetto community near Boston. We arranged with the local public school to pair up with some of the children and visit them in their homes in order to help them with their homework. During the summer of my third year in college I connected with a Jewish social service agency in the South Bronx, working with children and families who were living in extreme poverty. I was a "junior social worker," entering chaotic homes where I witnessed great suffering. This was an eye-opening experience for me.

I studied philosophy and sociology in college, where my critical consciousness was activated by several important teachers and mentors. In college I encountered the work of the great continental philosophers in existentialism and phenomenology. I studied Hegel, Marx, Freud, Sartre, and Merleau-Ponty, among others, and wrote my undergraduate thesis on the philosophical roots of the New Left and the hippies, looking at Merleau-Ponty's notions of the "lived body" and "lived experience," trying to understand how his work could shed light on the actions and desires of the new movements for social change, with their stress on immediacy and directness.

At this point several impulses came together: I knew that I wanted to participate in the action of the times, to be of service in the world, and to understand what was going on all around me. I wanted to be able to articulate and to think about the movement of ideas, feeling strongly that ideas have the power to change the world, but I was primarily interested in changing the world – not only thinking about it but also acting upon it.

It was this convergence that led me to pursue training as a social worker in 1968. I went to the University of Chicago, where I signed up to focus on the Community Organization track. I had learned about the work of Saul Alinsky in the poor neighborhoods of Chicago and wanted to do that work (and get a degree). I felt that in order for change to happen it would be more effective to focus on whole communities, rather than individuals or even groups.

I arrived in Chicago in September of 1968, just after thousands of protesters had been beaten up and arrested at the Democratic Convention, my boyfriend of the time among them. At the same time I joined a movement to support Marlene Dixon, a sociology professor fired by the University because of her radical political views, and ended up at a 16-day sit-in in the administration building. I found that political activity was much more interesting than sitting in the classroom, and that the program in Community Organization was devoted to training people to be directors of social service agencies. It was definitely not the direction in which I wanted to head.

After spending one year in Chicago I went to New York City to study philosophy. I still had the sense that ideas were the key to understanding the world, and I was led by my desire to hone my thinking as well as to participate in social action. By 1969, when I arrived at the New School for Social Research, the countercultural and anti-war political landscape was very alive. I studied, but I also became involved in many demonstrations and actions against the Vietnam War and went to jail several times. I lived in a political commune and felt that I was part of a turning point in America, one in which I was being shaped by events at the same time as I was trying to shape them.

After 1971 I found myself in Canada, thinking it would be good to take a short break from the intensity of what had been going on in the United States. In a new relationship with Steve Levine, with a master's degree in philosophy and beginning a teaching career at York University in Toronto, I also felt the call to be of service. I found out about an art therapy training program and decided to investigate. Having been disillusioned by the Community Organization program in Chicago, I began to rethink the practice of therapy and to consider the emancipatory possibilities of individual work as important for change. I knew also that I wanted to understand myself and felt that my own therapy was the next step. Visual art had always been important to me; I had painted throughout almost my entire life, and the idea of combining art with therapy seemed intriguing.

It was this step into a psychoanalytically oriented art therapy training and a graduate course in Freud that launched me into working with the arts in therapy. I trained first in art therapy and then later in psychoanalytic child psychotherapy. At the same time, I began doctoral studies, focusing on the role of symbolism in psychoanalytic theory. At the time, the psychoanalytic lens seemed to provide me with a rich and complex understanding of the formation of the person. It informed and enriched the work and play that I was doing with children and provided a framework for understanding the "hidden order" of art.

Discovering the work of D.W. Winnicott provided a thread or link that brought together a number of my interests. His formulation of the transitional area of experience as a site for play, art, culture-building, and imagination excited me. I could see how political action and social change, particularly the activities of the 1960s, could also be understood as taking place on a kind of playground. Winnicott's work inspired me to think that all activity in which humans engage, if it is to have a transformative quality, should involve the back and forth movement of play.

After a number of years of practicing as a child analyst, a play and art therapist, I had the feeling that I wanted to situate my work in a larger context. I began to find private practice too isolating; again, the call to be of service was beckoning. I wanted to work in a social agency where I could collaborate with colleagues in other disciplines and to work with people who could not otherwise afford my services. I wanted to be in a more public situation.

After completing my doctorate I returned to school to finish the degree I had started in social work and began working at the Hincks Treatment Centre in Toronto. In addition to clinical work with children and parents, I have had the opportunity over the last 20 years to teach and train students in the disciplines of social work, psychology, and psychiatry, and to collaborate with colleagues in those disciplines. While at the Hincks I came to see how many of the psychological difficulties of my clients, often poor single mothers and their children, many of them recent immigrants, were connected with their serious social and economic problems as well.

As a recent immigrant myself, the move to Canada put my involvement in political activity mostly on hold; at the same time, the political movements for change began to subside in North America. Despite this, I continued to carry within me an impulse toward involvement in social action and social change. My work in individual and group therapy continued to absorb and interest me, yet I always felt there was something missing. The impulse toward action on a larger scale took the form of helping to shape the direction of an alternative school, which my children attended, and of becoming involved in an organization called "Parents for Peace." In addition, Steve and I did anti-nuclear workshops geared toward helping peace activists with issues of burnout in their work. These workshops used the arts, particularly visual art and movement, as a means of restoring hope and reinvigorating those engaged in political organizing.

However, it was ultimately the encounter with the field of expressive arts therapy that helped me to reconnect with my roots in the creative world of the 1960s in America. In 1985 I met Paolo Knill, Elizabeth McKim, Shaun McNiff, Stan Strickland, and others at Lesley College in Cambridge, Massachusetts. What struck me at that time was the community-oriented playfulness and joyousness of their work, how it came directly out of the arts, and how it embodied an emancipatory spirit of collective and collaborative art-making.

My connection to this new field began to shake the foundations of my prior training and encouraged me to begin to question several aspects of the psychoanalytic project. Psychoanalysis seemed problematic in several ways: first, in its emphasis upon the individual rather than the community, and upon deficits and pathology rather than resources; second, in its reduction of the person to a set of explanations deriving from the experience of the past; and third, in making a one-to-one correspondence between the artwork and the life or personality of the artist. By contrast, I found that expressive arts therapy placed the emphasis upon an individual's resources and capacities, and promoted a notion of the artwork as opening up to and as being part of the world, pointing to the present and to a possible future. In the expressive arts, the artwork is seen not as a mirror of the self or even primarily as an expression of the self of the artist. Rather the work always goes beyond itself and has a multiplicity of meanings.

By far the most important impact of my initial encounter with expressive arts was the reconnection with my own art-making, particularly with painting and performance. I began to paint again in a whole new way, to develop a style for myself. My painting had always been in an abstract style, often using organic shapes borrowed from the body or the landscape. As my work began to develop, my style changed, and I started to work with images of social suffering. I began incorporating newspaper photographs that had a strong impact on me into the paintings, extending their borders or framing and highlighting them with abstract forms. Many of the images have come from the Israeli–

Palestinian conflict or the wars in Iraq and Afghanistan. I have been particularly drawn to photos of men and women holding photographs of children and young people who were killed, missing, or lost. I have felt that the paintings with these photos embodied a sense of witness and testimony that has been part of my work in expressive arts therapy.

Years before this work with disturbing images of the suffering brought about by war and violence, I took classes in clown and began to develop my sense of the outrageous and ridiculous, another part of what it means to be human. The work in expressive arts has a comic as well as a tragic side; it encompasses the full range of our humanity. I ultimately started to perform with my husband as part of an old Jewish clown couple, "Max" and "Sadie," exaggerations of the most absurd parts of ourselves. We continue to perform together.

Working in the field of expressive arts felt like a homecoming – a return to my own art-making, which I had neglected on and off for many years, and which was just as much of a longing or need as my impulse towards social engagement and social action. I did not fully realize at the time how much this new field would begin to influence me personally, to have an impact on the way in which I conducted my work with children and families, and how I would ultimately connect it to the impulse toward change at the larger societal level.

Expressive arts therapy has play at its base. It stresses the centrality of play as a way out of the locked situations into which individuals, groups and communities often fall. In difficult circumstances, the range of play is constricted. Engaging in exploratory, experimental and improvisatory processes can open up the range of play and help people to envision new ways of being and acting. Play can also lead to imagining new ways of changing or shaping the world we live in.

Over the years, at the European Graduate School in Switzerland (which I helped found in 1996), we have developed a philosophical framework to underpin the field of expressive arts, drawing upon the idea of *poiesis*: the act of shaping or making in which all human beings engage. When human beings find themselves in "dire straits" situations, the experience of the capacity for making or shaping, for taking action and feeling effective, is lost. It is precisely the task of expressive arts to bring individuals, groups and communities back into the experience of *poiesis*, the capacity to take effective action in the world.

I began to see the work that I was doing with the arts in therapy as having an emancipatory quality, as embedded in the world and as world-making. I shifted my attention from focusing on the artwork as an expression of the self of the artist to seeing the work as pointing toward the world, as an expression of the human capacity for *poiesis*, and as an opening to the expansion of the range of possibilities. By engaging in the art-making process and by shaping works that have a life of their own – songs, dances, paintings, poems, plays, stories – human beings are also taking part in the fundamental work of being human.

It was this way of seeing the making of the work of art and the work itself that prompted me to begin to think critically about the exclusively clinical focus of expressive arts up to this point. Most of the students in the field were training to become therapists and to work in mental health settings. It seemed to me our principles and practices could be turned toward broader, more diverse, and more complex social issues.

Following this impulse, Steve and I began to work in parts of the world that had previously been foreign to us. For example, we had taught several times in Israel. Now we traveled to East Jerusalem, part of the Occupied Territories, to work with Palestinian students. I was so excited to be there that in my naiveté I began the workshop by saying, "I'm so happy to be in this part of Israel!" After a long silence, a voice rang out, "This is *not* Israel." Fortunately the students forgave us, and we had a wonderful experience with them teaching clown and playing together. The reality of the Palestinian experience began to hit home. I had already begun to understand the political situation in the Middle East differently, but getting to know those who had been presented as the "Other" on a personal level added a new dimension to my understanding.

Two years later most of these same students came to EGS and began to study in the masters and doctoral programs in expressive arts therapy. From 2002 to 2005 we worked with mixed groups of both Palestinians and Israelis. On both sides most of the students were working professionals: therapists and counselors. Some (though not all) were artists, but everyone was interested in the arts and in using the arts in their helping work.

In the first days of the first summer with these students, there was a tremendous amount of tension in my group (I was the leader of one of the core groups – a group that would stay together for the whole three-week period and take various courses together). While they worked and lived with Palestinians living in Israel (so-called "Israeli Arabs"), none of the Israelis had ever directly encountered a Palestinian who lived in the West Bank or Gaza. Nor did they fully realize beforehand that they would be studying with Palestinians in Switzerland. In fact some Israeli students expressed upset and distress at being in the same classes with

Palestinians. Both groups socialized, ate, and shared rooms separately. There was no interaction except in the classroom, and even then it was limited.

In the group there were Palestinian men who had spent years in Israeli prisons, who had bullets in their bodies, and who had experienced the loss of family members due to the conflict. There were Israeli women whose husbands, sons, and fathers had died in past wars and whose sons and daughters were currently serving in the army during that summer. There were some Israelis who could not even look at their fellow Palestinian students, let alone speak to them. There were Palestinian men who kept leaving the classroom to smoke in order to relieve the tension they were experiencing.

At the end of the first week the ice had been broken to some extent by my efforts to openly acknowledge the feelings that were present in the group, helping the students to begin to tell their stories to each other and encouraging them to work together on mutual learning goals and art-making projects in relation to the curriculum. However, the atmosphere was still constrained.

One night a few of the students organized a spontaneous gathering in our large community room. They brought out musical instruments, especially drums. Several of the Palestinian men began to play the drums. An infectious groove was established and everyone starting dancing. What was interesting was that both the Israelis and the Palestinians danced in a similar style – the typical hip movements of Middle Eastern dance, movements that resembled "belly dance." The dancing got more and more intense, everyone releasing the tension that had been held for so many days. Palestinian women danced with Israeli women. Palestinian men danced together in typical fashion (Dabka – traditional Palestinian folk dancing) and others (men and women) joined them. They proudly showed each other certain movements. All the students from other countries joined in, mixing everything up.

That night, the dancing went on for a long time and everyone danced until they were exhausted. The next day, I definitely noticed a shift in my group. It felt like something had been released or "cracked open." The tensions were not gone but there seemed to be much more ease in the encounters.

By the end of the three-week session there had been a dramatic shift between the two groups. Many of the Israelis were sad to leave their Palestinian fellow students. They knew that it would be very difficult to connect once they were back in Israel. Similarly, the Palestinians felt that they were going back to a very limited and confined existence. They were all looking forward to returning to Switzerland, a kind of "free zone" for both their bodies and their minds. Through the mediation of the dancing both sides were able to break through the impasse and come to live with each other despite the conflicts between them. Over the next two years the students grew even closer. There were love affairs and promises of continuing the relationships once they were back home. However, the difficulty of the political situation intervened and prevented these hopes from being realized. I can only wonder about the long-term effects of their experience together.

After working with and getting to know the Palestinian students at EGS I was invited to the West Bank to help set up a program for children, similar to the one in Toronto called the "Spiral Garden," an imaginative and lively summer art and garden project on the grounds of a large hospital for children with disabilities. My colleagues and I were initially sponsored by Doctors Without Borders to conduct a pilot project. We traveled to Ramallah, passing through several checkpoints and stopping on the way at Dheishe Refugee Camp. Although the project was ultimately abandoned, I received a first-hand introduction to both the difficulty of everyday life in the West Bank and to the daily humiliations that Palestinians had to live through as they tried to travel to their work and places of residence. Truly, these experiences have shaped me as much as I have shaped them, altering my way of understanding both the world and my work in it. Certainly, the messages that I received from my childhood Jewish education and my first trip to Israel as a teenager were contradicted by the reality of the situation that I encountered as an adult years later.

Subsequently, in 2007, I decided to open a certificate program in Expressive Arts and Social Change at the EGS. In the program we explored the ways in which the arts could be used to help communities in conflict, transition, and breakdown. Students came from all over the world to study and to take the learning back to their communities, seeing what projects already existed there which they could join, or where they could create new projects.

The certificate program has now been expanded and changed into a full master's degree in Expressive Arts in Conflict Transformation and Peacebuilding. This is the only graduate program that I know of that focuses on making the connection between the principles and practices of expressive arts, and promoting peace and justice. Students in this program are able to work in diverse situations both in their local communities and in international contexts. It is my hope that the impulse to change the world and to engage the arts will not fade away, but gain more momentum through the existence of programs such as this one. It is clearly the right time to be moving our work away from an exclusively clinical focus and opening up to the wider world.

Even as the problems of the world seem so intractable, I am convinced that we need to maintain our spirit of play and possibility. Perhaps this will continue to allow us to live in uncertain times without retreating into the safety of our own private concerns, and to keep us attuned to what we find in front of us as materials for transformation. I still believe we can play in the ruins of the old ways and see what new and more life-affirming forms will emerge.

3

Social Activism within Expressive Arts "Therapy"

What's in a Name?

Karen Estrella

The arts have a rich history of being used as a catalyst for social change. One has only to think of the protest and freedom songs of the 1960s and their impact on the civil rights movement, the poetry of the "personal is political" feminists, the impact of the Vietnam Memorial on a disaffected generation of veterans and family survivors, the street theater protests against the World Trade Organization in Seattle, or the role of the AIDS quilt or the graffiti art of Keith Haring in the AIDS activism movement, to recognize the power of the arts for consciousness-raising, empowerment, advocacy, protest, and provocation (Reed 2005). The expressive arts used within communities have even been said to be activist by their very nature, in that they radically expand our notion of who can be considered an "artist" (Cohen-Cruz 2002).

This chapter seeks to examine the interplay between social action and expressive arts therapy (or expressive therapy – these two terms will be used interchangeably). I will briefly examine the ways in which social activism within expressive arts therapy and expressive arts practice in community and education is a continuing tradition. Next I will describe the dilemmas of working within the system and outside the system – outlining how the therapeutic is political and the political is therapeutic. Finally I will discuss possible directions for areas of continued conversation and describe the importance of developing curriculum for educating expressive artists in social change principles.

SOCIAL ACTIVISM WITHIN EXPRESSIVE ARTS THERAPY: A CONTINUING TRADITION

For the past 35 years expressive arts therapists have been exploring the use of the arts for change within the context of mental health, community, and education. Early expressive arts practitioners emerged out of the countercultural energy of the 1960s and 1970s in the United States, encouraged by the emerging multimedia and performance arts movements, as well as the human potential movement, to break through conventional boundaries of self-expression and artistic expression and to bring an interdisciplinary arts experience into therapy, community, and education in a new way (Estrella 2005).

Many of these early artist-therapists were drawn to work in mental health in part out of a desire to be an agent of social change in their communities. The power of the arts to be a model for change was captured in *Poiesis: The Language of Psychology and the Speech of the Soul* when Stephen K. Levine wrote, "Expression is itself transformation, this is the message art brings" (1992, p.15). These practitioners saw their work as countercultural in that traditional mental health, community, and education settings, like society, had marginalized the arts and transformation. By making the arts a central feature of their relationships with those they sought to help, these artist-therapists asserted the radical notion that creativity is a human birthright and that the creative process is inherently linked with the movement towards growth, health, and life (Rogers 1993).

Artists, consultant / educators, and therapists

Unlike many of the other creative arts therapy disciplines (e.g. art therapy, music therapy, or dance therapy), expressive therapy has from its inception recognized the importance of arts for change and for community building both within the context and outside the context of psychotherapy. In 1994 a group of artist-therapists formed a new organization committed to democratic principles and the development of professional standards for expressive arts therapists. This organization, the International Expressive Arts Therapy Association (IEATA), also recognized the need to extend beyond the scope of psychotherapy to embrace the work of expressive arts-oriented artists and expressive arts consultant/educators. Even within early theoretical articulations of the practice of expressive arts therapy, the work of social action was prominent (Rogers 1993).

This willingness to embrace the affiliated uses of the expressive arts in studio, education, and community emerged in stark contrast to other creative arts therapy disciplines. These other disciplines have struggled over the years with ambivalence towards more arts-based approaches or less clinical approaches, and have often taken strong stances to distinguish themselves professionally by contrasting these other approaches with their more psychotherapeutic approaches. Within music therapy this was exemplified by its rejection of "music healers" or "sound healers" from its circle (Summer 1996). In addition, there has been a large debate within the field about the boundaries of music therapy and community-based music, and attempts to incorporate both approaches under the title of community music therapy (Ansdell 2002). Within art therapy this ambivalence was exemplified by an editorial in the journal of the American Art Therapy Association entitled "When the edges bleed..." (Wadeson 1996). In this article Wadeson examined the boundaries of the field by questioning the difference between "therapy and therapeutic," and argued that if art therapy is to maintain its professional integrity, art therapists must be in the business of providing "therapy." Similarly, within dance therapy, this move towards an identity based in psychotherapy saw its manifestation in a decision by their professional organization in 1998 to pursue affiliation with the National Board of Certified Counselors. This liaison allowed the American Dance Therapy Association (ADTA) to lobby directly for dance/movement therapy to be considered a defined specialty of counseling, and for members of ADTA to pursue licensure as National Certified Counselors (Cruz 2008).

Legitimacy through mental health counseling licensure

This trend towards affiliation with counseling as a road to occupational legitimacy has seen its zenith in the collaboration of many formal US educational training programs in the creative arts therapies with mental health counseling. Moreover, there has been a move towards reassessing credentials within creative arts therapy professions to align with those of state licensing boards in mental health counseling (Kapitan 2004). As with many of the other disciplines of creative arts therapies, expressive arts therapy has found a certain amount of professional legitimacy by partnering with mental health counseling and marriage and family therapy licensure as well. However, this shift towards licensure and the search for legitimacy has also left the field of expressive arts therapy with potential rifts that could be seen by some as fundamental.

While expressive therapy has become increasingly affiliated with traditional licensure in mental health counseling, IEATA has stayed committed to the principles of extending the practice of expressive arts to communities and education. This has resulted in an attempt to legitimize and articulate the practice of expressive arts consultation and education (see IEATA 2010a). According to IEATA, these expressive arts practitioners employ an interdisciplinary arts approach to "conflict resolution, organizational development, education, personal or professional growth, the healing arts, spiritual enrichment, and more. While this work may be of therapeutic value, it is not psychotherapy nor does this registration give recipients authority to conduct psychotherapy" (IEATA 2010b).

Critiques of traditional mental health

While some expressive arts practitioners are comfortable with expressive arts partnership with counseling and psychotherapy, others have questioned not only the practical limitations that working within these disciplines and structures have brought (e.g. are there communities and educational programs where therapy is less central to the work that expressive artists might do? or is there a place for the expressive arts within communities that reject "therapy"?) but also the theoretical limitations. Many expressive arts practitioners express concern that professionalization and affiliation with mental health professions in particular leave us at risk of becoming "handmaidens of the status quo" (Sue and Sue 1999, p.32). In this regard many of them echo the sentiment of Foucault as articulated by Rossiter:

> The human services professions created and were created by a kind of mobilized consent, which gave rise to systems that classify and categorize people. [Foucault] described these as systems of exclusion, which work to establish as normal and natural what has, in fact, been constructed through complex power relations... accounts of "what should be" are always effects of power; thus knowledge in human service professions is not innocent, but an outcome of power – an insight that obliges us to become intentional about how our work is constructed within power. (Rossiter 2000, pp.150–151)

In addition, the ethnocentric roots of psychology and counseling have increasingly come under scrutiny and question, as have the very conceptualizations of self, development, personality, normality, pathology, and treatment promoted by these fields (Nelson and Prilleltensky 2005;

Prilleltentsky and Nelson 2002). In light of the rise of various movements within psychology (community psychology, critical psychology, ecopsychology, feminist psychology, global psychology, liberation psychology, radical psychology, peace psychology, political psychology) it is evident that psychology and counseling are beginning to consider the role of power, context, community, multicultural factors, and global issues of domination, self-determination, injustice, and politics. But for many expressive arts practitioners this critique of the ethnocentric roots of psychology and counseling is not happening fast enough.

Expressive arts in therapy, community, and education: A continuum of services

While critiques of traditional conceptualizations within psychology have led to a greater focus on contextual forces within mental health counseling and the centrality of growth and development reinforced by strength-based intervention models (Eriksen and Kress 2006), expressive therapy for the most part continues to exist on the fringes of traditional counseling. Largely, there continues to be a lack of acceptance within traditional counseling towards arts-based approaches to mental health practice. In the United States this tension between traditional mainstream approaches to counseling and psychotherapy and the use of the arts in therapy has often attracted a group of practitioners not afraid to move outside of the status quo. These expressive arts practitioners have worked within a large continuum of services, from prevention and community development to medical-model based psychiatric hospitals.

Expressive therapy has been practiced within traditional mental health facilities, in community development organizations, in the context of healthcare, in schools, and in non-traditional settings – at times under the title of "therapy" and at other times under the title of "art." Expressive arts practitioners have partnered with communities, agencies, and institutions in ways that were models for activist and advocacy projects that promote social change today. At other times these practitioners worked within more conventional systems to promote social change from within – within themselves, within their clients, and within the system. But either way, the work of social change via the expressive arts is not new in practice, only perhaps in emphasis.

Expressive therapists have taken a critical perspective on traditional models of psychotherapy and clinical practice – a perspective that questions core concepts and that examines central ideas. For example, expressive therapists have long questioned the "authority" of the therapist. Expressive therapists have embraced the notion that the role of "expert" should not be exclusively claimed by the therapist or even by the clients or community, but that the role of "expert" should be shared through the very experience of creating and the very images that arise in the work (McNiff 1993). Expressive therapies have followed these dictates: Follow the image. Follow the client and the community. Meet the client and community where they are, and facilitate an environment in which arts-based inquiry and connection can take place, trusting that the process will take you to a place where suffering can be experienced, where feeling can be given form, and where the whole self (personal and collective, body, mind, spirit, and imagination) can be enlisted in the service of healing.

SOCIAL ACTION AND EXPRESSIVE THERAPY: WORKING INSIDE THE SYSTEM AND OUTSIDE THE SYSTEM

Social change processes can begin at the level of the individual, family, community, or society. Individual efforts to become more culturally competent and tolerant, more socially and politically aware and active, taking more personal responsibility for one's own behavior, or developing an inner contemplative/spiritual practice, are all potential forms of social action. Working within traditional systems, expressive artists may deliver direct care within an agency committed to advocacy and service that directly addresses social problems; they may work directly with clients/ consumers to advocate for greater change within the community, or they may work within a team committed to social policy change and greater political inclusion of all constituents. Working outside of traditional systems, expressive arts therapists and community practitioners may work directly as community activists and organizers via the arts. In this way expressive artists have always embodied the notion that "clinical work that is cognizant of the social implications *is* social action, and being politically active *is* doing therapy; these activities are understood to be interrelated processes" (Hocoy 2007, p.29).

Expressive arts in therapy and community work have always recognized social action

Within expressive therapy, social and political considerations have long been a focus. From its beginnings, expressive therapy has recognized the importance of self-in-context, the power of the individual in community, and the strength of the power of the image to give voice to cultural, universal, transpersonal, and personal meanings. It is the power of the image to mediate between the individual and the collective, to hold multiple meanings, and to bring into consciousness that which is unconscious, that has led Hocoy to propose that "images can concurrently heal personal-collective wounds while demanding a response to injustice" (2007, p.22).

Expressive therapy's willingness to embrace other forms of expressive arts-based practice stemmed in part from its international affiliations, partly from the lateness with which it came to credentialing, and partly out of desire to embrace a less hierarchical model that de-emphasized legitimacy through formal education. Since early on, expressive therapists have trained not only in institutions of higher education, but also within institutes and centers. The International Network of Expressive Arts Therapy Training Centres began in the 1980s as a network of training programs and institutes in Europe, Israel and North America. Programs such as the Tamalpa Institute (which has been training people since 1978) and the Person Centered Expressive Therapy Institute (PCETI) also trained expressive artists both in the United States and internationally.

The international use of the expressive arts for transformation amongst practitioners and educators reinforced a reliance on arts-based and aesthetic theoretical foundations, and less on Western models of psychotherapy as a foundation for practice. For many practitioners this has allowed for an easier transition to social justice agendas and has made their arts-focused work within communities more culturally consonant.

What should we call the arts' capacity to facilitate change?

Expressive therapy as a discipline is just now arriving at the place where it can look at itself retrospectively and begin to examine not only some of its roots but also some of its tensions. Unlike the related disciplines of art therapy, dance therapy, or music therapy, there is still relatively little formal scholarship, research, and literature that can help unify or establish a common language or discourse within the field of expressive arts. In essence, we are a profession of doers. The field has thrived for over 35 years in part because of its practical and enduring focus – namely, the facilitation of a relational context in which the inherently healing potential of the imagination and the creative process can be expressed, experienced, and exploited via the arts. We work via the arts to facilitate change. In so doing we also work to restore a fundamental capacity for imagination and play – surely something that is essential to bring into traditional mental health services. Levine writes, "…healing must be understood as the restoration of a person's imaginative capacity" (1992, p.41). We recognize that there is much in the world in need of repair, and that healing and constructive change are not tasks to be relegated to a group of specialized professionals. Rather, the work of personal, social, and restorative justice is a human imperative.

SOCIAL ACTION AND EXPRESSIVE THERAPY: WHERE ARE WE GOING?

Expressive arts' capacity to strengthen and support individual, family, and community resilience in the face of personal, societal, and global forces of oppression and injustice continues to be at the heart of expressive arts-based therapy and practice. It is the arts' capacity to give voice to suffering and to act on the hearts, minds, and souls of those who enter the sacred space of the imaginal realm that gives expressive arts practitioners hope and direction in their practice. While many expressive arts therapists work individually or with groups within traditional mental health settings, their training is not based solely on psychotherapeutic concepts but on arts-based principles. This frees expressive arts therapists to embrace a wide range of possibilities for practice. While some creative arts therapies have bristled at redefining their work to include community-based practices (Ansdell 2002), expressive therapy has from its beginnings defined itself not only as a practice of "therapy" but as a practice of social change via the arts.

I would encourage traditional educational settings that train expressive arts therapists and practitioners to include coursework and opportunities for students to learn about and engage in social activism. Curriculum should include the exploration of social action methods. I define social action quite broadly to include contemplative practice; consciousness-raising with both individuals and communities (e.g. raising public awareness); reconciliatory work; empowerment training; community organizing and development including group and team work (leadership and administration), program and organizational development, and social service delivery; partnerships including corporate and community partnerships, with their concomitant coalition-building potential; institutional change through small groups, through policy, through funding, and through coalition work; social inquiry and social research and evaluation through social critique and action research; political action through lobbying and government liaison work; policy analysis, advocacy, and change; and resource and fund development and evaluation via philanthropy, grant writing, and fundraising. These forms of activism and advocacy should be explored both within mental health contexts and within the arts.

Students should examine a range of social issues related to mental health counseling which are community-based rather than individual, group, or family-based, and explore ways the arts can be implemented as social action. This will allow students to gain an ability to recognize complex social issues and their roots in social policy, the environment, and the economy. These issues include such broad topics as environmentalism, including environmental initiatives and sustainability; globalization, including international cooperation, anti-colonialism, and global economics; health care; equal access to education; economic development; conflict resolution; engaged citizenry and participatory democracy; violence, including war, nuclear proliferation, domestic violence, and peace and justice work; stigma and prejudice, including advocacy and action related to issues such as racism, sexism, ableism, classism, heterosexism, etc.; human rights; and hunger and homelessness.

A course in expressive arts and social action should allow students to acquire an awareness of social action and its interface with expressive arts therapies. Students should be encouraged to learn more about community-based partnerships with local social action projects which utilize the arts, and to find the connection between these projects and mental health counseling and expressive therapies. One potential assignment for students could be to have them identify and interview an arts-based social activist in their community. The course should equip students with strategies, tactics, and methods used to advance social justice via the arts and to enhance social consciousness within the expressive therapies.

A final project could be to develop a proposal for an arts-based social action project. This could include developing a rationale; objectives which describe the arts-based social action intervention, and overall goals; resources needed for the project, including a budget; advertising or publicity that could be used to promote the project; and a summary with an accompanying bibliography. This assignment would allow students to develop their specific interests, gain confidence and mastery over some tasks that would allow the projects to get off the ground, and could allow for a range of projects that include the many varied forms of social action, and the many forms of the arts for change.

THE CHALLENGE AND THE CALL

Pluralism, improvisation, and experimentation have all been central to the practice of expressive arts therapy. As a result, perhaps expressive therapy's largest challenge to date has been the increasing tension with regards to legitimacy and professionalization. As Levine and Levine point out, expressive arts therapy's "interdisciplinary nature requires an ability to bring together disparate perspectives and practices without privileging any one of them" (1999, p.11). In the almost 20 years since Stephen Levine (1992) published *Poiesis: The Language of Psychology and the Speech of the Soul*, expressive therapy has thrived. While it has grown in practice and scope, it has yet to realize one cohesive approach. Expressive arts therapy in the US is still seeking equal status with other creative arts therapies by seeking membership in the National Coalition of Creative Arts Therapy Associations (NCATA). At the same time, the field is establishing a credentialing process for those members who seek to practice outside of therapy as consultant/educators. In addition, educational programs have recently been developed to focus on expressive arts and social change without the constraints of grounding in a psychotherapeutic approach.

Can the field of "expressive arts" continue to thrive without the coherence of a scope of practice? Is it enough to be grounded in the power of the imagination to give voice and coherence to self and community? Recent invitations to engage in dialogue around these issues (Levine and Antze 2008) represent a beginning answer to those questions; clearly more dialogue and investigation is needed. Those who practice the expressive arts in community and therapy need to step up and give voice to their experience. We need to tell others what we do in theory and in practice. We need to describe what is effective and what is necessary. We need to join together personally, professionally and theoretically – the expressive arts' capacity to facilitate change is a practice the world needs. We must lead the way by sharing what we know, what we do, and what we have borne witness to in our practice.

References

Ansdell, G. (2002) "Community music therapy & the winds of change: A discussion paper." *Voices 2*, 2. Available at www.voices.no/mainissues/Voices2(2)ansdell.html, accessed October 2010.

Cohen-Cruz, J. (2002) "An introduction to community art and activism." *Community Arts Network*, February. Available at www.communityarts.net/readingroom/archivefiles/2002/02/an_introduction.php, accessed October 2010.

Cruz, R.F. (2008) Personal communication, January 29.

Eriksen, K. and Kress, V.E. (2006) "The DSM and the professional counseling identity: Bridging the gap." *Journal of Mental Health Counseling 28*, 3, 202–217.

Estrella, K. (2005) "Expressive Therapy: An Integrated Arts Approach." In C. Malchiodi (ed.) *Expressive Therapies*. New York: Guilford Press.

Hocoy, D. (2007) "Art Therapy as a Tool for Social Change: A Conceptual Model." In F. Kaplan (ed.) *Art Therapy and Social Action*. Philadelphia, PA: Jessica Kingsley Publishers.

International Expressive Arts Therapy Association (2010a) "General Registration Standards and Requirements, Expressive Arts Consultant/Educator, REACE." Available at www.ieata.org/reace.html, accessed October 2010.

International Expressive Arts Therapy Association (2010b) "IEATA Registered Consultant/Educators." Available at www.ieata.org/main/become/rce.html, accessed October 2010.

Kapitan, L. (2004) "Cross-training: The case for creating the next generation of art therapy credentials." *American Art Therapy Association Newsletter 37*, 2, 1–2.

Levine, E.G. and Antze, P. (eds) (2008) *In Praise of Poiesis: The Arts and Human Existence – A Festschrift for Stephen K. Levine*. Toronto: EGS Press.

Levine, S.K. (1992) *Poiesis: The Language of Psychology and the Speech of the Soul*. Toronto: Palmerston Press/Jessica Kingsley Publishers.

Levine, S.K. and Levine, E.G. (eds) (1999) *Foundations of Expressive Arts Therapy: Theoretical and Clinical Perspectives*. London: Jessica Kingsley Publishers.

McNiff, S. (1993) "The authority of experience." *Arts in Psychotherapy 20*, 3–9.

Nelson, G. and Prilleltensky, I. (eds) (2005) *Community Psychology: In Pursuit of Liberation and Well-Being*. New York: Palgrave Macmillan.

Prilleltensky, I. and Nelson, G. (2002) *Doing Psychology Critically: Making a Difference in Diverse Settings*. New York: Palgrave Macmillan.

Reed, T.V. (2005) *The Art of Protest: Culture and Activism from the Civil Rights Movement to the Streets of Seattle*. Minneapolis, MN: University of Minnesota Press.

Rogers, N. (1993) *The Creative Connection: Expressive Arts as Healing*. Palo Alto, CA: Science and Behavior Books.

Rossiter, A. (2000) "The professional is political: An interpretation of the problem of the past in solution-focused therapy." *American Journal of Orthopsychiatry 70*, 2, 150–161.

Sue, D.W. and Sue, D. (1999) *Counseling the Culturally Different: Theory and Practice*, 3rd edn. New York: John Wiley.

Summer, L. (1996) *Music: The New Age Elixir*. Amherst, NY: Prometheus Books.

Wadeson, H. (1996) "Viewpoints: When the edges bleed…" *Art Therapy: Journal of the American Art Therapy Association 13*, 3, 208–210.

4

Communal Art-making and Conflict Transformation

Paolo J. Knill

PREAMBLE: THE MAGIC UNDERWORLD AS A COMMUNAL CREATIVE PLAY

They lived on Swiss territory on the German side of the Rhine during World War II. The neighborhood was a mixture of German NSPD members working on the German "Reichsbahn" (Hitler's Railway) under the Swastika, and Swiss citizens partially organized underground, preparing for a possible guerilla activity in an occupation by Nazi Germany. The Swiss Army had given up on this undefendable small territory. The tension and anxiety were high, and neither side dared to act out the conflict, fearing a later retribution. The kids we will focus on were between 7 and 13 years old. As the oldest of them, I remember that the relationships between those kids under the swastika were ominous. Restrictions had not been explained to us, and when we had some fun together, it was "talked away" by parents. The confusion reached its peak when the bombardments by the Allied forces started. The humming silver flocks of bombers crossed the blue sky, suddenly planting "Silver Christmas Trees" in the blue, and each time shortly after the earth shook like an earthquake. We rejoiced and they panicked, until they hit us for the first time, still with almost no damage. From that moment on, strong air-raid alarm rules were put in effect, and more and more time was spent in the improvised air-raid shelters, which every household had to build. In the public shelter, the kids were all huddling together wondering if we had been hit when the earth shook – or else just bored by the long waiting times and wondering how we could change this. A few of us, mainly under the leadership of my brother and myself, explored the fantasy of an underground world as a play space. Regardless of the political alliances of our parents, we started to construct furniture together, painting the walls and carpeting the ugly cellar floor of our private air-raid shelters. We assisted each other in building toys and selecting puppets or vehicles to go permanently into this underworld. After the first of the three devastating bombardments of our city and neighborhood, we had to spend more time in our "underworld" than above. When the alarm howled, we tried to arrange it so that we reached a shelter where we could all play out our stories. We had long-running stories with puppet protagonists, featuring ourselves in well-defined roles. Interestingly enough, the mothers did not interfere: they seemed to be relieved that the kids were taken care of, while they had to cope with gardening and civil service, maintaining the infrastructure of the city without husbands, who by that time were all in the army. By 1944 our "Magic Underworld" was so fascinating that we spent more time playing together there than outside; most of our toys, pastels, and papers joined us there. The kids of the two sides never enacted the political rift, even though we knew about the fate of the Reich and awaited the GIs with eagerness. Our great personal experience was our play in the magic underworld, and our sadness when it was over. My brother and I ended up having a good friendship with the German kids, and we went on using the password we invented to begin the play for many years more.

COMMUNAL ART-MAKING OR COMMUNITY ART

The term "community art" is a strange construct, considering that art cannot be thought of without communities. The word, coined by therapists and educators connected to the arts and creativity, stresses the "community" setting as something special and different from the usual one with individuals and groups. In the beginning, community art was done more or less in the tradition of "warm up exercises," to tune in or engage the audience. This happens with "scores" that are similar to folkloristic dancing, singing, or ethno-drumming, free dance, and voice improvisation. This style of community art is still used for communities that are put together for a short period of time, like audiences or transient communities in gatherings such as conferences, educational settings, festivals, reunions, and cruises.

I want to focus in this chapter on "community art" that is commissioned for conflict transformation or rehabilitation after catastrophic events, and therefore is shaped according to certain criteria. This kind of community art has as its objective to strengthen the resilience of the community to establish and regain well-being. Resilience is understood as the ability to activate resources and mobilize coherence (Schiffer 2001, p.11).

Although every act of art-making or creative play sets up an imaginary space which is distinct from the reality with its conflicts, restrictions, and inevitabilities, art-making and play is, so to speak, still part of the same world. Therefore we distinguish the difference by calling it an "alternative experience of worlding." Although this experience also has constraints posed by the artistic frame, the inevitable restrictions of material and the structures of the art discipline, these challenges can be overcome and act like openings to create a greater *range of play* beyond restrictions, even "beyond imagination" (Knill, Levine and Levine 2005, pp.81–88).

In the imaginary space of communal art-making, things are often surprising, unpredictable, and unexpected; yet after they are completed they are accessible in their genuine logic. Things happen differently than in the disturbing reality. For instance, people communicate with those with whom normally they may have little contact or shy away from.

A participant might play a leading role by contributing a new turn in a dance, while this person may be from a group with little influence in the community. People will get opportunities to act, move, and speak that they have not experienced with each other before. This difference expands the "range of play" of the dire straits situation, which in difficult times is experienced with distress.

There is usually something convincing and logical about the completion of a communal work of art, play, or ritual. Therefore reflections about alternative experiences of worlding through art do not offend the necessary logical and argumentative reasoning about experiences within the community.

To guide a community into an alternative experience of worlding and later back into the reality of a difficult life must be part of the score of community art. A characteristic of all the "ins and outs" of the alternative experience are aspects of "decentering" ("intermodal decentering") and "range of play" (Knill *et al.* 2005, pp.88–91).

By "decentering" we name the move away from the restricted experience posed by conflict and crisis, which had resulted in rigid reasoning and stressful, often destructive acting, marking the pressure around the "dead end" situations in a conflict. Decentering is a move into the opening of the surprising-unpredictable-unexpected, provided by the artistic experience within the logic of imagination. A centering follows the decentering, guided by the facilitator, who relates the two in an effort to find ease. It is helpful to validate first the artistic work resulting from the decentering phase, and the achievement of that work, before experiences are compared and/or consequences discussed.

By providing a "range of play," we contrast the situational restrictions experienced. The phenomenon of *play* is the "doing as if," the "open-endedness" in the timeless circularity in the here and now, that results in a freeing up from the pressure to achieve immediate solution under impossible circumstances.

> Melinda Meyer, who worked with Bosnian refugees and also conducted a longitudinal study over 13 years, reports how in early interventions the decentering into playful bodily experiences brought a basic relief – whether through communal imitation of culturally specific movement patterns, like the dance-like picking of apples, of other theatrical play like imitating animals or making faces. This freeing-up led to further steps to regain the physical shaping capacity necessary for the repatriation process, including documentary filmmaking and testimony. (Meyer 2007; *passim*)

COMMUNITY ART: A DECENTERING METHOD PROVIDING A RANGE OF PLAY

The complexity of the imaginary space in community art presents itself as concrete and "thingly." During the shaping process material interventions are concrete and very explicitly placed "on the surface." These interventions can serve the purpose of grounding, bringing participants closer to the here and now of the alternative experience of worlding. We may suggest to "dancers" to use more space and listen to the music, or ask the "musicians" to add their voices to the instruments.

The "in and out" to and from the decentering experience and the reality posed by it is discernible through the here and now of the artistic work, its initiation, its process of becoming, and its completion as a "thing." In its graspable presence it offers many options in helping to distinguish between the different realities. The distinction of stage, studio space, audience space, and the habitual experience of worlding is concrete and explicitly based in the body and the senses.

The idea of widening the range of play by engaging the imagination is a common concept in the practice of conflict resolution. Conflicts are seen in these practices as situations that lack choices, giving participants a sense of being locked into the matter of conflict. Community art gives a community an opportunity to leave the zone of conflict, with an opening to options for new actions and thoughts.

Systems theory argues that an intervention simultaneously perturbs the structure of interaction and widens the range of play. Even though this challenge may evoke some uncertainty, it is necessary to create a surprising autopoetic process of transformation. When we use the arts as a mode of interaction, the impetus for discovery balances the fear of uncertainty if we provide an adequate motivating space. Communal art-making can be seen as a discipline of play, where the probing of the participants is a kind of perturbation; self-organization happens within the range of play defined by the restrictions of the discipline and the frame (material, space, time, and means). The community art leader is a player in the system, who plays a game that is different from the troublesome situation of the community.

The limits that define the frame of an art discipline or play vary with respect to space, time, material, and method of shaping. They belong to traditions of art-making in every culture. Therefore, interventions with respect to limits and frame can be easily accepted and understood if they are sensitive to those traditions. These interventions made before or during the process of play may possibly restrict the range of play, but usually they do not restrict the act of playing and its content. On the contrary, they make the playing less threatening. Furthermore, those interventions help to distinguish between the realities of the habitual and the alternative worlding, as this develops during the decentering.

The accomplishment of art-making is literally enabling, and it has the merit of beauty, eliciting the "Aha!" of an aesthetic response. Communal art-making is thus also a learning experience, providing the individual opportunities for sociability, enabling, and situational coping. The effect of this experience is cognitive and physical. We can observe it in the change of behavior, emotion, mood, and tone of the participants. This coping process can also be seen as training, or as "exercise," to help cope with the situational restrictions and individual frustrations in the training of professionals doing relief work. Within a cognitive frame of reference, the coping experience in the communal learning process of community art means confronting entrenched beliefs: "We are not able to accomplish anything," "We have too few resources," etc. But a community art process goes beyond the level of solely cognitive argumentation:

- It is a rich exercise with repeated experiences of accomplishment. In a typical work-oriented practice of community art, a blues improvisation with a chorus is undertaken. With each repetition under a competent leader, participants get more and more excited, and get into the groove of it. It is a true repeated experience of accomplishment.

- It is a psychophysical concrete experience that allows emotional and cognitive reasoning.

All artistic experiences are concrete, and close to the psyche in their emotional resonance. In the above example, the blues will eventually have an improvised text that links to this experience. Under expert leadership, the discourse between repetitions is cognitive, even though it is focused on the communal art-making.

• In addition, the communal artwork can *touch* or *move*. All the senses are engaged and therefore it *makes sense* in its beauty.

Therefore the resulting work, e.g. the blues mentioned above, does not solely make sense in terms of the cognitive learning. It also makes sense in its beauty. It can be remembered as a touching, moving, regenerating, and nourishing experience – a kind of "soul food."

• It is also an experiential field of discovery that motivates curiosity. Discovery of this kind is one of the fundamental sensorimotor and cognitive learning experiences.

The method of community art, in its improvisational characteristics, is built on a leadership that engages curiosity and motivates discovery. The discovery of the blues riff, the words that work, and the rhythm that makes the community get into a dance, has many fundamental sensorimotor steps that will be reflected later in cognitive learning.

In the traditional understanding of coping, exercise has a fundamental position. The practice of repetition in community art is additionally guided by an attentive, supportive attitude toward a sensory acuity and openness to an aesthetic response. This openness gives what is hidden a chance to be met and to be utilized as resource. With these options come new perspectives, fantasies, ideas, and imaginations for alternative ways to act or respond (Knill 2000, pp.9–14).

COMMUNAL ART-MAKING AS A CONTRIBUTION TO THE CULTURE OF COMMUNITIES

When we look how Western task-oriented communities try to release some of their individual and social stress, we can usually find two offerings designed for that purpose:

1. entertaining that is somehow distracting, or "airing out" events

2. opportunities for counseling and reflection.

In the following section I will sketch the specific needs addressed in these two activities. Later I will elucidate the understanding of community art as a necessary part of culture, bridging these two isolated attempts at coping in everyday communal work. Community art then can be understood as a cultural necessity that fosters innovative thought and action by mobilizing resources and activating imagination across cultures.

Entertaining events

Task-oriented communities like companies and institutions have traditionally used entertaining events to ease the habitual hierarchy and protocol, and sometimes also to blur the boundary between workplace and private life. Such events range from bowling and soccer games to extended parties (New Year's, etc.) and company trips. These events are based in game-like social traditions. Therefore they offer the expectation of fun and distraction. They do not, however, provide an opening to an imaginative space that has a potential for new alternative experiences. The positive effect of such events in the life of a community should not be underestimated. What has proven to be lacking over and over again in these events is an opportunity for members of the community to reflect on their participation in their shared situation. To facilitate such reflection, in the second half of the last century companies and institutions hired consultants who had been trained in one of the group encounter or counseling techniques that became popular at that time. With their focus on "uncovering the pathological," they had little success in structural situations evoking crisis or conflict that needed more resourceful solution-focused methods.

Opportunities for reflection

In the beginning, confrontational models that had been developed for therapeutic or encounter group settings, such as group dynamics, gestalt therapy, and related styles, focused on conflicts and their root in the individual, personal biography. These confrontational models worked for groups oriented towards therapy, but they lowered the performance of the group in other tasks. Later, systems-oriented, person-centered, theme-centered, and similar approaches have been favored because of their focus on the social, cultural, and organizational aspect of coping in groups (Nellessen 1997, pp.66–72).

Toward the end of the last century the systems-oriented approach prevailed, often modified with a resource and solution-focused method. These approaches support the activation of resources as well as aspects of resilience. Therefore, they strengthened the system's coping mechanisms necessary to fulfill its mission.

When we consider the size of communities it becomes evident that these methods of reflection are limited to well-organized small clusters, groups or teams within relatively stable communities. In addition, the exclusive focus on words makes the process lengthy and cumbersome, especially with foreign languages, having the taste of "more of the same" and creating more misunderstanding then there already is. This is especially true for large, not very well-organized communities in conflict. We need to recognize, however, that the format of the resource and solution-focused method of reflection in the tradition of systems theory can have great merits when we reflect on community art projects. This has to be considered when we organize feedback in smaller groups and report back to the full community.

COMMUNITY ART AS A BRIDGE

The need for a bridge

It was soon recognized in work with communities that entertainment and distraction with opportunities for reflection, isolated from each other, are not very helpful in the attempt to create innovative solutions and resourceful behavior. Tension in the difficult situation increases: the fun of the event is over, and often issues become more severe in the tense atmosphere outside of the event, which does not provide space to work for a transformation of the conflict.

Attempts at bridging

In an attempt to connect an experiential event with a reflective opportunity, it became fashionable in the business world to offer "new games," "outward-bound," extreme sports, and similar activities combined with counseling, reflection, and coaching. Soon, however, the limits of these activities became evident. Although these attempts truly presented an alternative challenge, the outcome was never much of a surprise, and they were often out of cultural context. The game-like characteristics are often close to the problematic conflicting positions at hand. Even though games are different from everyday activity they have a predictable strategy for solutions. However, the complex characteristics of difficult situations around conflicts call for innovative strategies, rather than having to "win a game, without having a chance to invent it."

The bridge: Community art

In contrast to games, each individual art project undertaken by a community needs an appropriate spatial and temporal frame, selected materials, and envisioned directions of shaping. The act of creative forming in the arts includes innovative strategies and techniques of shaping, pursuing developments of the emerging, often surprising unforeseen product, and therefore necessitating a constant revision of the planned outcome. Each process becomes an innovative attempt to find the optimal response to a complex dynamic between resources, objectives, actions taken, and emerging patterns within a defined frame. This creates a feedback loop with shaping strategies, changing the structure of the material and the environment. All of this occurs in the frame of the discipline of artistic play, which includes the community as an audience, which witnesses and evaluates with feedback how the resulting artistic product works as a whole. The artistic product can be evaluated in various ways:

- It can be considered as "being on the way."

- It can be followed in its particular way.

- It is unique in its character and has a recognizable style.

- It contains surprises that belong to the sense-making logic of the work.

When we consider communal art-making in the context of decentering as explained above, we can recognize the parallels with the experience of a community. The complexity communities are confronted with in difficult times calls for innovative solutions that consider the dynamic interdependence of frame, material, structure, strategies, visions, emerging patterns, environmental patterns, and so on. The problems are unique in their characteristics and the way to solve them needs to be congruent to this uniqueness, although styles may be similar.

It is therefore conducive to use the artistic process rather than games as a decentering method, because it offers a complexity that games do not offer, unless we reinvent them each time and leave the envisioned emerging goals up to the process of completion. However, we would then need criteria for evaluation that most likely would also have aesthetic connotations, which would in essence be a kind of artistic process.

Community art therefore bridges the uniqueness of the complex reality of a community in its challenges to find transforming solutions connected to its conflicts, by way of the uniqueness of an artistic "time out" experience. Community art also offers some relief in the playful attitude of innovative explorations, which may be close to the pleasure of "entertaining events."

Like brainstorming, community art with its decentering characteristics circumvents the deadlock created by "more of the same" thinking, which is focused on the troublesome issues and patterned around "more of the same dead-end" strategies and approaches. The pedagogy of community art follows the potential for surprise in the intermodal decentering, bringing a range of play that steps out of the ordinary grammar and logic of conversational language. However, artistic shaping is also a kind of "language," a language that needs new words and ends in new conversations.

PEDAGOGICAL PRINCIPLES OF COMMUNITY ART

When we want to motivate a community to engage in artistic activities, we have to consider the ever-present respect–fear continuum in people faced with an art project. One way to confront it is by awakening the curiosity for an open understanding of art as it may be found in the culture at hand.

It is helpful to research folk and contemporary art in the culture of the community and identify people engaged in folk and/or professional art, using them as helpers in preparing scores that have an improvisational character and offer flexible possibilities of participation. Such research should in addition address questions like:

- What experiences or traditions of gatherings, events, and communal art already exist in this community?

- What is the organizational structure of the community, and what are existing formal and informal leadership patterns, especially with respect to communal events and artistic activities?

- How can I utilize these resources, within the contract I am bound to, using a process that includes community art?

- Concretely, what resources are available?

  ○ space and possibilities of usage

  ○ art materials, musical instruments, theater props, etc.

  ○ movable structures and technology (furniture, stage elements, lights, PA, etc.)

  ○ access to nature and its resources.

- Who are the people who have some experience, for instance as drummers, singers, storytellers, poets, dancers, actors, etc.?

  ○ Whom could I use in a pilot group to prepare and use later as assistants?

  ○ Should I bring or recruit somebody as co-leader?

  ○ What are the roles of co-leaders or assistants in the community art process?

  ○ In the preparation, we aim for an open score that includes enough space for improvisation. However, the time-frame has to be set clearly.

  ○ We also have to make sure that there is enough time to tune in, especially when we introduce community art for the first time.

The following principles are based on the assumption that the preparatory research was done carefully.

The two pillars of attention

The attention is given fully to the process-oriented learning, as it is understood in systems theory as self-organizational learning. The language used during the decentering community art, however, is purely in the tradition of the studio, the stage, or the atelier. This practice includes how we address the people and their activities, and also how we give feedback. We talk to the "company," "ensemble," "orchestra," or "choir," and address a "painter," an "actor," a "drummer," etc.

We guide or give feedback solely to the "surface" of the "artwork" or "process" in the way it presents itself as a sensory experience, and we abstain from superficial generalization or categories of meaning. The reflection in the artistic feedback focuses on the form and structure, the material, properties, techniques of shaping, etc. Individual psychological interpretation belongs to the personal private sphere, and space will be made for it in the so-called "harvest," the last part of the session, when everybody is free to share with whomever they need to.

THE FIRST PILLAR: "THE HERE AND NOW"

- *Where are we in "our arrival"?* We intend to anchor the community in our present time. We look to the calendar and consider the time of the day:

  - season, special holidays, day of the week, birthday, special events, etc.

  - morning, evening, midnight, beginning, ending, half-time, arrival, etc.

  We intend also to bring into the awareness the time-space continuum of the culture we are in:

  - customs, rituals, history, birthdays, anniversaries of the community or groups, the news, etc.

- *Where are we going to?* We look for possibilities to include this aspect of the envisioned goal, or what is approaching us:

  - the theme of the desired outcome of the contract (peace, a culture of tolerance, a conference topic, a cooperative identity, etc.)

  - the coming winter or spring, the coming graduation, the coming challenge, etc.

THE SECOND PILLAR: THE "I" AND THE "WE"

- *How will I structure space and time to prepare the individual participant for a communal working and shaping together?* The "tuning-in" and the "warm up" should focus on the physical and psychological preparation of the individual:

  - The awakening of the senses, especially those that will be the primary focus in the planned community art. An effective way of doing this is by guiding the attention toward what is concrete and physically present and what will later become part of the artistic process. It includes the space, the things at hand, the tools, the material, and the physical presence of the other members of the community. After this sensory awakening we need to guide the awareness of the possibilities of shaping planned for the actual community art score.

- *How do we motivate for the "ensemble"?* It is helpful to introduce the following:

  ○ The *ensemble* for music improvisations, the *company* for dance and theater, etc.

  ○ If such an ensemble or company is organized in such a way that every participant contributes equally, then the leader of the community art is in the coaching role of a *director, conductor* or *choreographer*.

  ○ The score can also ask for a *solo* or *soloistic small group* (*concertino*). In such instances those players will get additional coaching by participants and leadership.

  ○ In situations where one player, or a team of players, takes responsibility for a improvisational score, then this role would be considered to be that of an *arranger*. In this case the leader of the community artworks with the arranger, and the ensemble follows and participates in any artistic decisions.

The two levels of readiness

In addition to the two pillars of attention we have considered, the success of a piece of community art depends on keeping the participants on two levels of curious readiness.

THE FIRST LEVEL: A READINESS OF BODY AND MIND

- *Sensory arriving ("grounding")*: A kinesthetic awareness connects looking with seeing, listening with hearing, moving with being moved, in short, "sensing" with "making sense."

- *The shaping of the ordinary*: The ordinary will become interesting when we meet it in unconventional ways, revealing new sensory experiences.

THE SECOND LEVEL: A PSYCHOLOGICAL READINESS

- *We need to be aware of the participants' negative experiences with the arts resulting from cultural limitations, former educational experiences or group pressure, etc.*: We recommend staying away from formalistic jargon or abstract art specialists' language. The practice of validating activities with a concrete, simple language is helpful, especially if we are able to use it critically, though without judgment. The individual member should, whenever possible, also be addressed if the work concerns a common interaction.

- *"Low skill – high sensitivity": a principle in setting up "scores" for community art:* What we ask for should request a low level of manual artistic skills. On the other hand, we are demanding a high level of aesthetic competence. The sense for the material object and its properties to be formed or composed are heightened. Examples of contemporary and folk art with these qualities include contemporary installation art, traditional Japanese flower arranging, minimalist music, "art brut," collage, drumming circles, rapping, improvisational folk dancing, parades, carnivalesque theater, poetry slams, etc. Examples may be mentioned in a community to connect the work to our cultural moment and to raise the level of curiosity (Knill, Barba and Fuchs 1993).

Leading the process

In resource-oriented therapeutic work the clients are understood to be the experts regarding the problematic situation at hand. What, then, is the expertise of the change agent in a community art project? The trivial answer declares that it is their professional competency as a resource-oriented change agent. Yet when we consider that the resulting communal artwork is the healing agent (so to speak), then we become aware how much expertise the leader needs to lead such a process to a satisfying outcome. It is this success in the alternative contact of decentering through the arts that uncovers the hidden resources. We speak therefore of the "aesthetic responsibility" of the leader. This responsibility is also a guideline for interventions during the artistic activity. The leader ought to give utmost attendance to sensory perceptions, and give feedback that makes the experience of what presents itself concretely aware. ("Listen to the noise of your steps and sense the pressure on the soles of your feet, how it lifts you up step by step in a pulse…" etc.) The leader also needs the skill to use the principle "low skill – high sensitivity" to challenge and to give critical yet constructive feedback, always in a manner that facilitates the emergence and recognition of the work. The following guidelines can help:

- Guide always toward an opening for well-being.

- Intervene in an analogous way to the artistic process, directly in the moment and at the same time being careful toward the emerging work. Be attentive to what presents itself on the concrete surface of the forming and shaping process. Let others know when you see openings for new play ranges. Do not plan for a solution of the problem at hand, or else you are in a dire straits situation yourself.

- Always provide a challenging temporal and spatial frame as a window of opportunity. In this way curiosity motivates exploratory play. Be aware that the challenge must be of a magnitude that can be met. The art material and/or the possibilities of shaping must therefore be restricted in an optimal way, so that curiosity still finds an interesting play-range that serves the emerging work.

- The rule can be remembered with the acronym "less is **MORE**." Standing for: **M**aterial that is easily manageable, simple shaping **O**rganization, **R**estricted frame, give simple and clear directions for playful **E**xploration.

- As mentioned earlier it is important to give the participant a sense of aesthetic satisfaction and success that has its origin more in the sensibility toward the emerging work than in the virtuosity of artistic manual skills. This we achieve by following the principle of "low skill – high sensitivity." It is helpful to begin with an artistic interaction of improvisational character that is more familiar to the community, and from there awaken the curiosity for more challenging forms.

- In the performing arts we offer small time-frames in order to sketch the improvisational score toward an emerging work. We know this principle from jazz and rhythm-and-blues. We call the consecutive improvisations on the way to the eventual form "takes." Between the takes, the feedback about what works and what openings may be envisioned allows us to recognize the form that wants to emerge.

- The language we use should always be **SSP**, which means **S**imple, **S**pecific, and **P**articular. It should be simple in the way we formulate, specifically naming the shaping activity or thing that is present and particularly connecting to the person. Again we stay with the surface that needs to be dealt with and refrain from generalizations.

- I find it advantageous to stay in close contact with the participants while they work, and also demonstrate physically, sometimes illustrating my explanations or suggestions, and also to find the right rhythm of speaking when I guide a movement. This practice also helps to find the right words for instructions using my language from my sensorimotor awareness, rather than from an abstract strategic planning stance.

- Do not engage in long discussions between "takes." Ensembles get disconnected from their interactional flow of shaping, and may slip back into their everyday problematic behavior. It is possible to find decisions in a short time when we choose one of the suggestions on the floor, after a concise feedback, and we agree to try the other suggestions after a take and see then how to go on. Art happens in the act of shaping, not in the discussion about it.

- The motivational forces in the playful exploration of improvisational work are driven by *curiosity*. It is curiosity that helps to bring surprising forms and structures into the range of play. It is as if surprise and curiosity feed on each other. Yet there is another driving force that wants to repeat the surprising new form or structure. This force is the *functional satisfaction*; it is what pushes us to repeat an improvisational score in order to master it and bring it to its fullest beauty. It makes us ready for feedback and constructive critique. To keep a balance between curiosity and functional satisfaction is one of the tasks in leading a community art process.

- An artistic process can only get going when we are aware that it is our common work that is at stake; above all, it has to be our own *enthusiasm* that sparks off the process. We keep the enthusiasm going when we ourselves remain curious and attentive to what reveals itself surprisingly in the moment. The leader must, so to speak, seduce the community into their *yearning* for beauty or hope for an artistic work. Let's not forget, however, that we cannot just have hope: it has to be created.

CASE STUDY: MANAGING IN DIFFICULT CLIMATES AND TIMES OF CHANGE

The community

Twenty-five managers of UN compounds for refugees in war zones. The majority are from Asian and African countries. They were called in together for briefing and support, in a week-long conference at a center on the shore of Lake Geneva. They had two highly-trained, experienced UNHCR staff members as their facilitators.

Schedule

After a day of debriefing, with the objective of finding a common theme of concern, they were offered a day of community art with us (a team of two facilitators).

The contract

A full day of community art that addresses the common theme and provides a space for individual concerns. The objective is that each member can build on an outcome, which might provide guidance through and beyond the following week in his or her difficult work.

The "research"

We arrive the afternoon before. There is a small room that seats the participants in a circle, and a big room (120 square meters) furnished in conference seating, with tables of five seats each and state-of-the-art conference tools. There is some art material (paper and crayons), but the ordered piano is missing in these spaces. The participants all come from different "non-Western" cultures, are exhausted but in good spirits. We meet participants during the break and have a briefing with the staff during supper. The common concern all the members of the community shared can be summed up by the question: "How can we lead in difficult climates that do not change, while everything else is changing." Individual issues included overwhelming numbers of refugees, not enough space, staff or funds, and seemingly permanent changes of structure. We learned that the day before ended contemplatively in the small room in a circle, and that they had their notes from the day ready on the tables in the conference room.

The preparation (late at night)

We decide to meet the community on "the path" they were on, and bring a gift from our culture. We plan to meet first in the small room, in a circle, opening with a reading from Rainer Maria Rilke's "Letters to a Young Poet" (letter eight, the part about loving the difficult as something that needs our love). After the welcome, introduction, and overview of the day, we will change to the conference room, first using the set up to do a guided resource-oriented look into their concerns, and then change the space into a studio stage for the decentering. The same space will be used for the validation of the artwork. After a break we will restore the conference seating for the individual "harvesting" from the experience. We will end the day, as they did the first day, in the small room in a circle for a sharing and closure. We also want to keep the meal times constant, so the community can find a spatial and temporal ground during the week.

The sketched open score

The conference room had a full view (all-glass wall) of the mirror-still lake, with the gleaming, snowy Savoy Mountains on the other side. It was a sunny fall day, and a light mist veiled the yellow trees. This filled me with enthusiasm, and it was immediately clear to me that this must become the substance of the art project. It is elemental and universal in all cultures to respond to this. So it was decided to make the windows the upstage, and we would draw a line for downstage. Part of the preparation will be to move the furniture accordingly. While I meditated with this breathtaking view in the early morning, I was overtaken by the stillness of the water and the monumental mountains, and it came to me how the water moves from those glaciers until it finds the stillness of the lake. I will go with the movement: the water teaches us, from quicksilver-like and gushing to flowing and resting. It will be important to remember that we are not literally water, and don't need to try to be it: we just learn as dancers from its movement. So neither do we put mountains or rocks on stage, just things that might help. In this moment, the choreography of the interculturally sensitive great late choreographer Pina Bausch came to my mind (Café Müller),[1] and I planned to use chairs on stage. Also, I intended to use my flutes and a harmonica as musical resources.

The actual community art session

During *the opening* it became obvious that the poetry was extremely well received. People wanted to hear the text again, and were very motivated after the introduction to do the process.

In the conference room we guided the participants, who sat in sets of five, through resource-oriented questions and visions, starting from their personal concern about the general theme (managing in a difficult climate in times of change). This was done individually, in silence, while taking notes. The goal was to envision a possible outcome that is realistic about both the horrific situation and the personal and cultural resources brought to their renewed awareness. We end this phase by drawing posters about what they personally look for to create hope, without building any false hope about the situation.

In *tuning in* we explained our use of space as a studio, by walking through it and marking it with masking tape. We helped each other to move the furniture to arrange for an "audience," explaining that we will always use around three ensemble members as an audience to give feedback. We would take turns in being the audience, so that finally everybody would have a chance. When everything was ready, we stood in the audience space and looked at the wonderful landscape, which was now visible like a set. We asked for 30 chairs to be randomly distributed on the stage. I announced: "We all most probably know lower back pain, especially when we sit or lift a lot, and it becomes worse under stressful conditions. So let me give you some simple exercises which you might do for five to ten minutes twice a day." I asked them to sit on a chair on stage.

Through alternative sequencing between meditating on the view, giving attention to the landscape's water and our own breath, in order to focus the busy mind, and kinesthetic exercises with the chair, to get out of bad habits in standing up, sitting down and lifting the chair (adopted from the Alexander Technique, see Gelb 1996, and the Feldenkrais Method, see Rywerant and Feldenkrais 2003) the ensemble gets tuned in to the water as an image and to their own bodies. I made certain that the exercises were presented simply and concretely, using everyday language adaptable for their everyday stressful world. We ended by testing the results in grounding through walking. Focusing again on the view, we notice how the weight becomes a lifting force, up to the hips and to the head, making the walk into a swinging dance, and that it is possible to navigate without stress between dancers and chairs on the stage.

The project was now introduced: we want a celebratory dance dedicated to the landscape using the movement of the water from the peaks of the mountains to the lake.

1. First take

    We give the beginning and end and encourage them to leave the in-between open. In the beginning, when the music starts, dancers enter individually, little creeks gushing faster and faster around the rocks.

    At the ending dancers sit on chairs, stretch out still like the lake, the music ends. Dancers are trying to find the movement patterns that happen on the way, and the musician will find the music that dances with the ensemble. Three volunteers as audience.

    The feedback praised the density and the whirling effect of the river-like water, and also the sudden stillness. As an opening they suggested instead of trying to be fast, to take smaller steps and improvise longer in the river stage by following each other. Maybe the music could stay in motion, and then change into long legato much later to initiate the delta of the river. We always summarize the input in the second take by concise demonstration. We show that small steps with sudden turns look faster, and allow some time to try this. Dancers show they are having a lot of fun. The flowing by following also made sense. I decided to go to the harmonica when the lake phase is initiated.

2. Second take

    The dance starts to take shape. Evidently it becomes a pleasurable challenge, and the harmonica was helpful in finding an ending. The feedback also improves, gets concise and more specific, naming dancers and situations specifically. The summary focused on the end. The surface of resting water is horizontal, it was observed. Could we reach our arms out and try to touch hands? It would be a great image with the real lake on the set behind the stage, was the suggestion. This time we ask half of the audience to stay and give a comparative feedback.

3. Third take

    The difference is astonishing: the changes within the flow were more continuous and the ensemble produced choir-like synchronicities as well as individual extravaganzas as the water does when meeting obstacles or the wind. During the ending the ensemble moved delicately, a choir of dancers coming slowly to rest. As feedback I wanted to hear first the difference by asking: "Is the work on the way, and what makes you say it is emerging?" This time the main answer was that they find it touching, and that it is definitely on the way to becoming an improvisational dance piece. The audience had the suggestion that the ensemble could sing at the end, and that also while sitting on the chair they could reach out the arm and rest the head on the shoulder so it does not stick out of the quiet surface.

At this point we introduced an *in-between exploration* before going to the fourth take.

We envisioned a choir improvisation that could be used to end in a still pose. We chose a "cluster flow," because it produces a harmony that is not necessarily part of Western tradition. Each singer chooses a tone and holds its pitch no matter what its interval is with the others. The result is sort of a heterophonic "Ohm." We prepare it with breath and voice exercises, then sensitizing the listening and learning to melt voices together in different ways, until we produced improvisations with the cluster and learned to handle its intensity and color.

4. Fourth and final take

   As in most of our projects, the improvisational artists are by this time accustomed to their ensemble and to the improvisational score. This results in a more enthusiastic engagement, fed by the ability to hear and see themselves in the webbing of others and the work, without preoccupying themselves with playing the right thing. This was also the case with the fourth take. The new ending was strong, but considering its potential it was not yet fully integrated in the dance. There was too much preoccupation with doing it right. With the feedback of the audience about the surprising "otherworldliness" of this ending, the ensemble wanted to do it again and so it came to the last take.

   The final performance lasted eight minutes and held the attention of the audience and staff fully. The ensemble was engaged, and evidently gave their total attention to the embodiment of the imagery of water, coming from the wild melt to a peaceful rest in song. We saw wet eyes and waited a moment before we gave the releasing applause.

There followed the *aesthetic analyses*, the phase where we look at the work from the artistic point of view. We asked that everybody make individual notes. Our reflection followed, in the following order:

1. Open discourse about what makes this dance what it is. How is the form and structure special, and what stands out? It was mentioned, for instance, that it was a dance without a musical beat yet still was very rhythmic and exciting, that it was not just ending, it was also closing musically with a standing cluster, etc.

   We end this reflection by asking everybody to write up what they have gained in their perspective of the work through this reflective conversation, and what they did not see while being in the "production."

2. We ask them to write up what kind of inputs helped to accomplish the dance or song. We ask them to consider the feedback of the audience and our guidance. We start with positive questions like: "What was helpful in the provided structure? What measures have you taken for yourself, to master the work?" We end with the question about what was difficult or frustrating and ask: "What made you go on and not leave the process?"

3. We ask: "What are the surprises in the experience of the work, or the way you experienced your fellow dancers and the ensemble?"

4. "What could be a metaphoric title of the dance? And where are you now, compared with the state you were in this morning?"

All of these are individual notes. Then we offered a break to restore the
room back to the conference seating. Now we were ready for what we
call the "harvest." We find it helpful to return with the rich material of
the aesthetic analyses back into the space of the original concern. There
we sort out what notes may have an importance in connection with
the personal issue of the concerns they had envisioned in the morning.
Using the notes and using the poster about hope from the beginning, the
participants checked what jumped out at them, even though they might
not be able to spontaneously identify the connection. Then in a second
round we decide on one or two notes, to contemplate what they could
offer to the original concern. Only after this individual reflection would
the small groups share and help each other. Staff members circulated
between the tables as moderators.

There was a rich variety of outcomes, concerning each individual,
relative to his or her site and workplace differently. One thing that seemed
to run through all discussions was the experience that a permanent
change of structure was part of the Landscape (choreography) in which
the Water (dancer) had to find a way. What helped was the dancers'
attitude of "flow." This was only made possible by a movement-music
structure which was not on a beat or pulse (free rhythm), but flexible
and improvisational, allowing conflicts to be part of its nature. Also
it called for an ensemble attitude guided instantaneously by the flow
rather than by the "plan." Concrete measures were discussed in small
groups for steps toward a management by the choreographer in close
contact with the improvisational flow of the team.

Then came an *intermodal transfer to the closing*. As we noticed the
richness of the harvest and the "down to earth" character of future
steps the participants drew from the experience, we wanted to follow
their original positive response to poetry. We asked them to end their
harvest by choosing one of the words of their aesthetic notes that
became a key to the planned steps into the future. From this word we
suggested they write an acrostic, a poem that uses to start each line a
letter from the chosen word. We demonstrated by writing a community
acrostic. After each participant had created an acrostic they shared them
in the small groups around the tables. Each poem got specific feedback
about what worked well and where someone could see room for
further exploration. Here too, staff members circulated as moderators.
Analogously to the community project, we also suggested here to write
second takes and get feedback on them. We were taken by surprise by
the enthusiasm of the community in this communal poetry art structure.
We had to give additional time and postpone by 30 minutes the closing
circle planned in the small room.

Closing

We chose a ritualistic form, in which each member first read their poem, then said what concretely they would bring back to their compound from this experience if anything, and then give us feedback for the day. If they liked, they could end with the poem.

We were gifted with great poetry: everybody read twice, and also took away something that would help them to create hope in a hopeless situation.

This example serves as an illustration of what we have put forward as the principles of leading the process of community art. As one may notice, music is an essential part of leading in community art. Even though we might consider music to be an accompaniment, it is definitely more than that. It is part of the leading structure. The choice of music or no music, as well as what kind of music, always has an essential influence on what is happening in a space. It is not only the mood of the music or silence, nor is it noticed as present while we give a task of shaping. It is also the rhythm, the structure, the associations with the kind of music we have chosen.

When we ourselves feel comfortable enough to play, we are able to stay in close contact with the process; this is the issue I want to discuss here in the last section. Certainly there is the possibility of using recorded music. These days, with iPods and similar devices, I may have an almost unlimited repertory of music to chose from, and be able to lead flexibly to a much greater extent. This form of music in community art follows the tradition of using music as a basic score, as in the classical and contemporary ballet, while the synchronous improvisation of music in community art follows the idea of performance art.

The third option of using music follows the ensemble improvisational tradition in music, and guides the community to a communal musical improvisation.

In the following I will focus on providing spontaneous music while leading a community art process.

The music of community art

We need to think of music as being in a dialogue with the community art improvisation, with texts and/or visual art forms. Music is an equal partner and participates as such. To develop such improvisational skills as a musician, we might consider the following guidelines:

- Be attentive to the movement, acts, architecture, choreography, the light, the shadow, etc. Stay at the surface of what is formed and what you perceive. Do not speculate behind the things, do not explain anything and avoid giving meaning. Be a straightforward partner to the things, the dance, the theater, the poem or the performance. Remember, silence is part of music.

- Do not illustrate, just play with what emerges, go with it, go also counter to it (*contra punctus*). Music is just another player in the ensemble. Therefore you do not consciously lead or follow. Like anybody else in the ensemble, it may happen that you lead or follow or are totally in synch. If you get stuck in one of these positions (e.g. leading) you are deserting the partnership.

- There are many ways to practice music for community art. One way is to find a musical pattern, a figure, or a motif on an instrument that one feels comfortable with, as understood in the principle of "low skill – high sensitivity" (e.g. kalimba, flute, xylophone, piano, etc.). Repeat this figure, spinning it off until it develops, as a dancer explores the steps through repetition into a full movement figure, which develops into the choreographic element.

- The music may also find its form without any beat: one could speak of a "sound painting." When we use a pulse for a rhythm it is helpful to begin simply unless you can count on a good circle of drummers or a musical combo. Be careful that there is always enough space for others to offer new figures, and make sure the beat is alive, which means that it is not only driving or lagging, but breathing between the two like a communal organ.

The feedback culture

We describe what we observe concretely as it presents itself on the surface. We respond in ways that are perceptive for the community, and we raise the awareness, while reductionistic explanations suggest what is "behind" the observed. We offer help so that everybody can follow the feedback, and clarify any confusions or speculations that enter the interpretations. We move on when everybody is ready. It is possible to use metaphors as illustration, yet we are careful with them and make sure that these associations are understood as our own.

- Speak from your own declared perspective: I have seen, or heard, etc. Stay with the observed material, with its structure and form.

- Try to formulate in a positive way, from a position of aesthetic responsibility toward the emergent work.

- Anchor what "works" and validate experiments that failed. (What made you start again even though it failed, and what was it that then finally succeeded in this exploration?)

- The leader must be a role model in a culture of this art-analogous feedback practice.

EPILOGUE

Some of my improvisation scores come up again and again. They are like old friends that come as a helping hand. Yet they grow and each time mature in their ability to open up to the ever-changing difficult situations. Each time I meet them again they surprise me.

Let's embrace these open scores, inviting them with gratitude again on stage, and awaiting with curiosity what new works they may hatch on the communal stage. With practice you might get your ensemble of open scores to come to your assistance. Consider yourself like a minstrel with a caravan repertory company, having the capacity to create spontaneously in the communities you travel through.

Notes

1. A staging and choreography by Pina Bausch. The scene is set around chairs, like in a café. Music: Henry Purcell, Premiere: May 20, 1978, Opera House Wuppertal.

References

Gelb, M. (1996) *Body Learning: An Introduction to the Alexander Technique*. New York: Henry Holt.

Knill, P.J. (2000) "The essence in a therapeutic process, an alternative experience of worlding?" *POIESIS: A Journal of the Arts and Communication 2*, 6–14.

Knill, P., Barba, H. and Fuchs, M. (1993) *Minstrels of Soul: Intermodal Expressive Therapy*. Toronto: EGS Press.

Knill, P.J., Levine, E.G. and Levine, S.K. (2005) *Principles and Practice of Expressive Arts Therapy: Toward a Therapeutic Aesthetics*. London and Philadelphia, PA: Jessica Kingsley Publishers.

Meyer, M. (2007) "Reparation and Testimony," Ph.D. Thesis. Oslo, Norway: Unipub Press.

Nellessen, L. (1997) "Der Preis der Konsolidierung." In O. König (ed.) *Gruppendynamik*. Munich: Profilverlag.

Rywerant, Y. and Feldenkrais, M. (2003) *The Feldenkrais Method: Teaching by Handling*. North Bergen, NJ: Basic Health Publications.

Schiffer, E. (2001) *Wie Gesundheit entsteht, Salutogenese: Schatzsuche statt Fehlerfahndung*. Weinheim and Basel: BeltzTaschenbuch.

5

From the Studio to the World

How Expressive Arts Therapy Can
Help Further Social Change

Shaun McNiff

Expressive arts therapy is maturing into a comprehensive discipline of community building through the arts. Compassion and empathy for the troubling aspects of psychic experience and their imaginative transformation through artistic expression are the foundations of this approach to personal and social change. From the first days of practice our goal has been to make healing through the arts widely accessible, believing that service to others and to the creative process is in itself a mode of social transformation. This chapter explores the early influence of the therapeutic community model and its social principles on expressive arts therapy, the unique capability of expressive arts therapy to draw creative energy from difficulty and to transform life experience, and the ways that the alchemical dynamics of the therapeutic studio suggest possibilities for corresponding changes within larger social spheres.

THE THERAPEUTIC COMMUNITY AS A MODEL FOR MAKING CREATIVE SPACE

Expressive arts therapy was established during the early 1970s, at a time when social and institutional transformation permeated every aspect of the discipline and its desired impact upon the larger arts, health, and education domains. It was an era when significant numbers of people within the arts, psychology, mental health services, and education were seeking new ways of working, and nothing less than revolutionary changes in all sectors of human relations. The values that guided our work were focused on freedom of expression and accessing innate ways of creating that often displayed universal and cross-cultural qualities.

78

There was a sense that if a person could bring forth authentic inner contents and urges within the structure of artistic media, these processes and forms would engender insight, renewal, transformation, and a more general sense of health. A fundamental goal of practice was the making of creative spaces and community environments that furthered vitality and healing. From the start it was observed how well-being was strongly influenced by the way in which people supported one another within the overall social context of the studio. It was also clear that the sense of creative space established within expressive arts therapy practice was distinctly different from the environment of most mental health institutions and from society in general.

A primary political agenda was for change within the creative arts therapies themselves, which were at that time focused heavily on the use of artistic imagery for diagnostic evaluations that purportedly revealed the nature of a person's illness. In contrast, our methods, which never denied pathological conditions, were oriented toward the life-affirming and healing qualities of creative expression. The therapeutic process was aligned with the use of all of the arts to further a person's ability to communicate and construct experience, assisted by the inherent structures of artistic media.

A second social goal was furthering cooperation amongst artistic and professional domains, which then and now tend to be distinctly separate from one another. Professions, institutions, government, and even artists are often reluctant to span the boundaries of their specializations in search of common tendencies, more inclusive communities, and truly collaborative creation.

Our work espoused universal access to the arts and egalitarian participation within and between disciplines of expression. But the most pervasive inspiration was a belief in the natural, authentic, "home-grown" and spontaneous artistic expression of people everywhere. We found that if settings cultivating this kind of expression are established, therapeutic outcomes emerge organically from creative inquiry with others. In every respect the practice of expressive arts therapy adopted values and approaches to human relationships that suggested applications and interdependence with the larger social context.

At Lesley University (then Lesley College), where we established the first expressive arts therapy graduate program in 1974, a community-wide course focused on the relationship between personal and social change. Students of J.L. Moreno (1889–1974) were drawn to our community, which shared his commitment to creativity and spontaneity as fundamental aspects of well-being. Moreno, who always appreciated the social dimensions of the therapeutic experience, articulated how drama and creative expression "spring up in everyday life, in the minds of simple people" where lines cannot be drawn between the individual and the universal, art and therapy, theater and life, and where "Catharsis moves from the spectator to the actor and from the actor back to the spectator" (Moreno 1973, p.28). I believe that the same interdependence and reciprocity occurs between personal and social realms.

While prominently including the Moreno tradition in the Lesley training program, the high degree of control he gave to the psychodrama director in shaping individual creativity and group interaction differed from my core orientation, which was toward a more complete emanation of expression from the individual person and the group. When considering role models and exemplars for expressive arts therapy within the larger context of mental health and psychotherapy, I was inspired by Moreno's contemporary Maxwell Jones (1907–1990), who was also a medical doctor, a major contributor to the social psychiatry movement, and the most influential proponent of the therapeutic community model of treatment. Jones shared my inclination toward freedom of expression within group settings, and his approach to the structure and process of community relations corresponded to the essential dynamics that I experienced in the expressive arts therapy studios that I led. He encouraged a creative and "open system" of communication where sometimes "the process was more important than the goal itself" (Jones 1982, p.144). Intuitive reflection, rather than prescribed outcomes, was valued, and all members of the community including the director and senior staff participated in the process of criticism and learning.

Toward the end of his life, Jones applied the principles and methods of "social ecology" as developed within hospital communities to society as a whole (Jones 1982, p.155). Just as the conditions of people suffering from emotional disorders can be precipitated by societal dynamics, Jones felt that successful methods of therapeutic treatment could influence communities and organizations. He understood how every method of operation must constantly examine itself and stay open to its shortcomings and blind spots in order to build trust and encourage responsibility.

The therapeutic community movement, as with every form of therapy, has political qualities. But it set itself apart through a constant examination of its limitations, as manifested in various forms of bias, insensitivity, ineffectiveness, and the inability to tolerate open communication. For Jones, constant self-examination and sometimes "painful communication"

(Jones 1982, p.54) are necessary for change, and in preventing the institutionalization that he observed in the history of innovation and social experimentation (p.144).

The progressive and pragmatic positions advocated by Maxwell Jones resonated with my assessment of what was needed both within organizations and in all sectors of human relations. He suggested how creative expression and individual freedom could be supported within a formal social system, in which leaders provide a model of the behavior they profess, constantly receiving feedback from every sector of the community. This was opposed to the tendency of traditional authoritarian systems, from every part of the political spectrum, to insulate themselves from total assessment and communication.

I also understood from my observations of the operational structures of the hospital environment, and from my own early experiences in leadership roles, that negative experiences, complaints, misunderstandings, conflicts, mistakes, personal qualities that irritate others, and unfulfilled expectations were perpetual parts of group and organizational life. In Jones I found a model for dealing with these realities in a manner that corresponded to the dynamics of the expressive arts therapy studio. Both the creative space of the studio and the therapeutic community made use of problems and setbacks, viewing them as source material which can be universally transformed by creative and healthy systems.

For two years at Danvers State Hospital[1] I was responsible with a colleague for coordinating a therapeutic community within a section of the hospital. I did this in addition to my work with the arts in therapy, hoping to bring change to the larger environment of the hospital. We held daily community meetings where staff and patients communicated in a free way about the challenges they faced in working with one another.

Without question the ideals of the therapeutic community were more completely realized within the expressive arts therapy studio than within the actual hospital therapeutic community, where efforts to bring change were subsumed by the larger institutional forces and regulations of the state mental health system, which we could not influence. In contrast, the arts instilled imagination and emotion, allowing for concrete opportunities to act in new ways and make something different and creative from the difficulties that permeated institutional life within the mental hospital. Most essentially the artistic process involved action, doing something creative with a problem rather than just talking. It is this transformative power of artistic expression that has the most potential for amplification into institutional and social spheres. Our

Danvers experimentation reinforced the value of sanctuaries within larger institutional environments, where different ways of acting can be developed and then used as models for broader social application.

The most fundamental element that I took from the work of Maxwell Jones and applied to expressive arts therapy was his focus on the open circulation of the creative process, which spread through "contagion" (Jones 1982, p.146) rather than via conscious direction and control. We found that these principles were perfectly suited to the art studio environment, where they have been sustained for the past four decades. The community milieu where each participant is supported in establishing authentic modes of expression, all of which convey significance through their uniqueness and sincerity, has had a strong appeal to artists searching for a context where expressions are not judged and evaluated by institutionalized strictures.

This atmosphere of acceptance rather than judgment establishes a sense of safety and trust which allows participants to enter the unknown, express vulnerability, and explore the sometimes dark and unsavory aspects of expression and imagination, which are typically repressed in relations with others, and that must be engaged in order to experience significant change. A distinctive position that we continuously take in the studio is acceptance of difficulties and their place within our lives and creative expression, rather than projecting them on to others and various problematic conditions in society. The process turns inwards toward an examination of the negative aspects of power and control as manifested within ourselves. Attributing culpability and focusing on conditions outside our immediate experience with others takes us away from the vital source of creation and dilutes the transformative energy of people creating together.

The studio thus reinforces the belief that small communities of people can generate larger changes in society. As someone who has held a number of senior level leadership positions within organizations where it can be difficult and sometimes impossible to effect change, I have been buoyed throughout my career by the relatively reliable and forceful transformations that take place within these studio settings, which then inspire and inform my life and work in the broader social context. Setbacks to social change, beginning with those that I experienced within hospital and mental health systems, continue to motivate me and others to persist with studio practice where transformative change does reliably occur.

My experience suggests that the deep, complex, and most intractable problems of life cannot be solved or fixed through logical and linear thinking issuing from a particular point of view. As Nietzsche (1967) says, art appears as a savior when all else fails. These most difficult situations can only be transformed through the process of people working together with life-affirming intentions. The problems we face are themselves a complex of perspectives struggling to prevail over one another. From the creative process we know that entering and embracing this maelstrom – and of course acknowledging the presence and power of the negative forces, fixations, and antagonisms – is the way of transformation (McNiff 1998).

The overall creative space and actions taking place within the expressive arts therapy studio suggest concrete and reliable outcomes that shape the more general social lives of individual participants who in turn influence others. The process of social change is thus incremental on a micro-level of person-to-person contagion. In my personal experience, the movement from the creative space of the studio to daily life involves what I call walking between worlds. The course is forever circular, rhythmic, and unfinished, in that I must keep returning for renewal.

SHADOW POWER IN ART

The most significant factor in establishing the creative space of the expressive arts therapy studio, and the basis for a corresponding amplification to society, is the open embrace of difficulties, described here as the shadow – the often toxic and unacknowledged aspects of a person or group that accompany well-intended efforts to advance persons, communities, and societies. As C.G. Jung (1969) observed, all of us hold shadow forces, and when these elements are denied they become more destructive and harmful. Maxwell Jones felt that the same applies to social, community and group dynamics. The following discussion of how we engage this shadow aspect in the expressive arts therapy studio is offered as a basis for broader application to social settings.

Jung described the shadow as repressed flaws and instincts which generate a dark power, which in turn becomes a primary source of creative energy. My use of the term includes these features, as well as referring to how the particular social positions that a person or a group advocate, ostensibly positive objectives, have sometimes repressive dimensions that tend to exist outside consciousness. For example, I regularly observe how ideologies striving to improve the world can be controlling and restrictive in relation to the expression of others, manifesting Jung's view of the shadow as the unconscious opposite, an internal antithesis, of the face that we show to the world. The shadow can thus grow in proportion to the intensity we bring toward advancing a particular perspective.

The Janus-like quality of the shadow in no way diminishes my commitment to taking strong positions, and I do not encourage equivocation, ethical relativism, or the belief in a reliable middle ground. In keeping with Jung, I think that our efforts to serve and change the world need to maintain rigor, sharpness, and sometimes extreme positions – paired however with sensitivity to their shadow aspects, which as demonstrated by the creative process can be put to use.

As Jung advised, it is important to know these negative forces, and to have a more complete view of how our actions affect others and ourselves. The exponential ability of the unseen and unchecked shadow to cause harm has been all too evident in past history and in the world today. The humble expressive arts therapy studio, with its ability to mix creative expression with depth psychology and group understanding, may be a unique place for the practice of knowing and transforming shadow powers, and for establishing the basis for application to other sectors of society.

I have experienced the intensity of the shadow within my community of colleagues in the art therapy discipline. During the 1970s and early 80s, I was perceived by many as a *bête noire* in response to my advocacy for the healing powers of the art experience. This was a period when the dominant perspective favored the analytic reduction of artistic expressions to psychopathological labels and psychological constructs, when authentic and forceful artistic expression was nothing less than the shadow of art therapy. The ideology of psychological explanationism and personal revelation according to a particular theory could not tolerate uncertainty and the complexity of creative expression.

My efforts to keep the shadow in check have been informed by my mentor Rudolf Arnheim's warnings against psychological one-sidedness. I appreciate the fact that the arts communicate contents outside our immediate awareness, and that artistic expressions are typically a number of steps ahead of the reflecting mind. Precise clinical practice in my experience is wary of psychological absolutes and over-identification with a singular position rather than complementary relationships.

The discipline of mindful practice strives to stay open to the whole context, to correction and to conflict. It tries to listen with a true curiosity and willingness to be changed by what exists outside our current sense of what needs to be done, realizing that our lives and our influence on others may be completely different from our intentions. In this respect, life begins to correspond to the process of creation.

When the shadow is unacknowledged, it also tends to project its inadequacies into attitudes of moral superiority, manifested today by fundamentalist stances across the political spectrum, all claiming ethical superiority and correctness and prescribing their values for others while avoiding the crucible of creation. In this respect society begins to manifest and reinforce the dynamics which threaten well-being within individual persons. The outcome is a world of ideologies, all denying their shadows and doing their best to establish their points of view. As Maxwell Jones emphasized, the process of communication must be reciprocal, and critical communication becomes destructive when it issues from the emotional needs and bias of the critic.

In the truly creative space, the shadow and soulful expression are inseparable. Advances in civilization and healing are tied to the transformation of tragedy, loss, crisis, and the endless injustices and pathological conditions of life through acts of creative imagination. As stated above, the unique contribution that the arts make to this process of personal and social change is their ability to engage and even embrace the dis-ease, using the negative conditions as fuel and creating affirmations of life from afflictions, pain, and suffering. Some have dismissed this view as a new Romanticism; so be it, if this artistic term applies to doing something creative with the most challenging conditions of life.

When the arts promote a particular political position, they have a tendency to restrict imagination's ability to explore the total landscape of a feeling or difficulty, the perspectives of victims and those who inflict injury, villains and helpers, and the total collection of figures and characters operating in paradoxical and often inverted ways that permeate both drama and life. As I say to the participants in my group studios: be wary of literalism. The person who paints or dramatizes perverted or cruel scenarios or characters is not necessarily perverted or cruel. The nasty and unsavory images of imagination have their place within the individual and collective imagination.

In my personal practice I have been constantly challenged to expand my viewpoints and moral judgments, in order to further my ability to lead studio environments where the troublesome aspects of the psyche are welcomed as allies in furthering creation. We never introduce a specific psychological, social, or political theme. Rather, people are given the freedom to engage with what is most pressing in their lives, and this affirmation of individual inquiry and expression in turn creates a stronger group – another principle that can be amplified to society.

The environment is clearly structured in terms of purpose and group interactions (McNiff 2009), but the openness described by Maxwell Jones characterizes a person's freedom of expression within the group activity. The creative space is distinguished by the support and safety that is needed to risk engaging with shadow figures and elements of our experience, helping us move away from our habitual ways of acting and take on unfamiliar modes of expression.

I refer to the studio environment as a therapeutic community of images. This corresponds to Jones's emphasis on a constant re-examination of values, support for risk taking, respect for the diverse forms of individual expression, and the realization that group learning is a process that cannot be restricted by preconceptions. A creative environment thus supports non-linear and unexpected dynamics, leadership that vests freedom and responsibility in participants, a total atmosphere where therapeutic insight can occur through a vital circulation of expression and activity in keeping with the dynamics of creative imagination, and a place where therapists function as leaders who cultivate and hold the overall creative and healing space.

Within this context the shadow is most challenging when it goes contrary to our intentions, beliefs, and areas of familiarity. In keeping with the dynamics of creative expression, the most transformative art experiences are often those that break, fragment, annoy, and even destroy the leader's and/or group participants' frames of reference and expected outcomes. These moments are always difficult for me, even though I experience them with regularity and understand their necessary role within the creative process. This is in keeping with certain traditions of indigenous healing, in which the loss of soul is a necessary pre-condition to its restoration and renewal.

When asked to describe formative experiences that I have had with the shadow and the dark aspects of creativity, I recall the reaction that Paolo Knill and I both had to Thomas Moore's *Dark Eros* (1990), the little-known book that ironically preceded his major bestseller *Care of the Soul* (1992). Although we consider ourselves extremely liberal in our acceptance of different forms of human expression, we were taken aback by how the book challenged our limits and sense of creative imagination. It still does for me, as manifested by my hesitation and self-consciousness when mentioning and citing the subtitle, *The Imagination of Sadism*. Tom Moore caught me in acknowledging that there were areas of expression and imagination where I would not go. As he says: "the darkest and most perverted haunts of eros have a place in the art of soul-making" (Moore 1990, p.184).

The book also underscores this chapter's emphasis on how the dark aspects of creative expression are characteristically obscured by all of us when we focus only on the "light" and what we consider to be positive forces of change in the world, as contrasted to the more complex dynamics that occur in the psyche and group life. Problems might be better understood through compassionate embrace than through efforts to fix, fight, or eradicate them.

All too often, the pathological state or motive is exclusively attributed to others and we miss the opportunity for a deeper moral inquiry, replacing reflection with moralistic judgments that avoid the more complete examination of experience. When the shadow is cast onto others and aggressively battled, this process keeps us closely attached to it. Within the realm of interpersonal and social relations, I describe this as "taking the bait," which ties me at the hip to the things that I oppose. By doing this, I give energy to the condition and it controls me. As I mentioned earlier, the shadow is always with us, but we can give ourselves more breathing room in our relationship with it, more space for understanding, and perhaps engage with it in a more creative and mindful cooperation.

In *Dark Eros* Thomas Moore is not advocating literally sadistic and prurient actions and behaviors. Quite the contrary: he distinguishes the literal act in the world from the reality of the imaginal realm, giving the latter its necessary place within the psyche and more specifically within the development of morality and the ethical treatment of others. *Dark Eros* suggests that we "follow the lead of our symptoms in order to retrieve soul" (Moore 1990, p.160). It does not call for explicit sado-masochistic actions, nor advocate dark imaginings. Rather, it recognizes the existence of these and other socially unacceptable phenomena and suggests creative and moral engagement rather than denial. The same applies to the spectrum of pathologies and problems present in the world.

In keeping with the Imaginal Psychology of James Hillman, Moore sees the challenges we face today largely in terms of a deficit of imagination and a quick willingness to embrace literalism in its various guises. After spending over a decade opposing reductionist psychological approaches to pathological aspects of human expression, for which whatever a person creates is associated with some psychosexual problem originating in childhood, with the help of Hillman I began in the early

1980s to look with a more clinical and intrigued eye at the pathological expressions of human imagination. Rather than quickly judge, label, and attribute these expressions to a stock psychological type, as does common practice in many sectors of psychology and art therapy, or deny the existence of psychopathology, Hillman would ask, What is going on in this situation? What is the soul up to? What desires and needs are being manifested here? What is the expression trying to say about itself and my experience that I cannot see? These questions apply equally to personal and social phenomena, and (as suggested throughout this chapter) to practices that further creative change, imagination, insight, and understanding of ourselves and others within the expressive arts therapy studio, practices which can be applied directly to larger realms of experience.

Major changes in human history occur during crises and abnormal conditions, when worlds break apart and need to be transformed and recreated. Hillman asserts that, "The insights of depth psychology derive from souls *in extremis*, the sick, suffering, abnormal, and fantastic condition of the psyche" (Hillman 1975, p.55). He is apprehensive of how one-sided identification with the heroic ego, and moralistic positions in life, art, and therapy, limit the imagination and the full landscape of creative inquiry.

As I repeatedly see in my studio groups, horrific and frightening figures in artistic expressions are different from those that might appear within the actual world of experience. I have learned that these characters are often the ones who have the most to offer in helping us become more aware of feelings, personal concerns, and life conditions that we cannot or do not want to see. The malevolent image breaks through the barricades of perception to seize my attention and involvement.

I encourage people to accept these figures as characters within the most intimate sectors of their personal lives. The images are already present within us and repression only increases their power and destructive potential. The very chaos that people fear is engendered by efforts to overly control a natural process of expression. I emphasize how these fears are natural and that resistance is an appropriate reaction to what is perceived as a threat, but that it is something to embrace and understand rather than correct. I find that the best way to engage difficult contents is without external pressure of any kind.

Some have responded to this essentially positive approach to transforming difficulties as a denial of threats, and I am puzzled by how a full immersion in the pathological condition, working with it, and fashioning its energy and contents into another form of expression can be viewed as anything other than the most complete openness to its nature and the shadows we all carry. The dualistic mind cannot tolerate a mixing of elements – a creative and ennobling work with the base elements of life, a transmutation of substance which lies at the core of the alchemical process.

Edvard Munch described how those who are reluctant to relate creatively to suffering do not know "the essence of art." He recoiled when it was suggested that by painting sickness his art was itself sick: "my art is not sick… When I transform sickness into a painting, like *The Sick Child*, it is on the contrary a healthy expression. It represents my health. When I paint suffering, it is a healthy reaction to it – something others can learn from" (Tøjner 2003, p.208). Munch was troubled by the literal responses to images of illness when he felt the divine emerging from the wounded spirit. "Art" he said, "emerges from joy and pain. Mostly from pain" (p.135). He sought out subjects that aroused his emotions, furthered the study of the soul, opened the heart and enhanced communication with others (p.132). These characteristics apply completely to the work we do today in expressive arts therapy, where the artistic and healing processes are joined together in a shared commitment to transforming difficulties into affirmations of life.

In training therapists I emphasize the need for learning how to sit with a person who is expressing difficult emotions, how to suspend all inclinations to leap forward with suggestions, explanations, and solutions. In the expressive arts therapy studio we observe how depth of experience occurs when we are able to carefully witness and support the expressions of others, responding through attentiveness and empathy rather than judgment, explanation, and recommended solutions. Therapists need rigorous training in suspending conclusions, relaxing the ego and its opinions, respecting the shadow, holding the space for others, watching with fascination while withholding interpretative responses, concentrating on what is happening in the present moment, and allowing the scenario to unfold, to be seen from varied perspectives, and to transform itself.

If fear is accelerated or veers toward panic, I try and call attention to the breath and affirm how reflection on the act of breathing will restore equilibrium and protect a person within a safe group environment. Depth of expression tends to involve an ability to watch, listen, give compassionate consideration, and respond to situations. Our most common method of engaging frightening or dark figures in the expressive arts therapy studio is to witness and respond to them with imagination. One image begets another within an overall process involving ongoing movement and a circulation of creative expression. As Jung suggested, we imagine the process further, focusing on the discipline of "responding" to experience, which tends to relax the pressure to "initiate" something creatively significant in the presence of others.

Often the artistic process will get stuck, mired in expectations, self-criticism, or the inability to let go. In these situations I have found that the embrace of difficult conditions serves as the alchemical basis of their transmutation – sometimes through anger, humor, play, or persistent effort. Our relationship with a problematic figure can change by simply paying closer attention to it, asking it to speak for itself, and then learning how to listen carefully to what it might have to say about itself and its relationship to us, in other words, by becoming attuned to its expression (Kossak 2009).

A participant in one of my studios described how being witnessed by another person helped her witness herself and be more attentive to what she was experiencing. Others describe wanting their expressions to be viewed by others, but then feel a contradictory fear of being seen, all of which stems from a deep need to be appreciated and supported without judgment.

When another person responds creatively to our expressions, it can bring mutual benefits. Art and expressive arts therapist Bruce Moon recently described to me how the practice can "help you get out of yourself, move beyond your own boundaries to see how the other person feels. It is a vehicle for empathy. I can't be of much help to people unless I get a sense of how they view their own lives. It is a constant process" (Moon 2009). Artists receiving these responses are often moved to see how another person can be deeply influenced by their art, which they may have dismissed or taken for granted.

"THE NEXT THING HAPPENS": MOVING FROM THE STUDIO TO THE WORLD

As expressive arts therapy considers ways of stimulating social change, I encourage the discipline to act from the empirical and proven principles of practice that can be amplified to society. Just as the process of artistic transformation generates corresponding effects on the individual person, the same applies to the social context. The healing power of expressive arts therapy results largely from the process of creating a professional discipline committed to helping others. A similar sense of intention and practical capability needs to be applied to society. As we move toward this goal, I emphasize the importance of sustaining the unique features of the artistic experience as a mode of personal and social transformation, just as we have done in making a place for the arts in therapy.

The most fundamental of these features is art's unique ability to compassionately embrace uncertainty and difficulties without pre-established and ready-made plans for change. In the process of artistic discovery and transformation, we do not know the end at the beginning. However, this necessary immersion in the unknown is also the primary obstacle that we face in expanding participation on both personal and institutional levels. My experience – even in the most supportive studio environments with capable artists – indicates that most people find it challenging to spontaneously engage difficult and uncertain situations.

When I encourage people to work with the unknown, I say that the only thing they can do wrong is to plan what they do before they do it. Needless to say, this approach to unscripted emanation is not in sync with the current doctrines of both health and education systems. Yet this antithetical quality of the creative process may indicate expressive arts therapy's most significant impact on social institutions.

When I recently told the dance and expressive arts therapist Norma Canner about how her emphasis on making a movement, letting it go, and opening to the next gesture has influenced my work, she replied: "You do one thing and the next thing happens. You don't have to do anything else. It happens" (Canner 2009).

Since experience in the expressive arts therapy studio repeatedly affirms that the most profound changes in people occur spontaneously, it might be said that the best way to spread these effects to society is to just immerse ourselves in the work and let effects "happen." There is great merit to this suggestion, but artistic disciplines are more prone to paradoxical dynamics. Experience also indicates that we need to work at the process of expression, commit ourselves to it and struggle with its demands, in order to set the table for the most important discoveries and transformations that arrive in unexpected ways.

As I reflect in this chapter on the role of art and social change, I hope we can acknowledge and maintain core characteristics and powers that separate creative expression from more strategic and planned approaches to social engineering. We need to assure that creative spaces continue to offer the freedom to spontaneously explore expressive urges without preordained outcomes. There must also be support for engaging, embracing, and even befriending the toxins that need to change – or at least altering our relationships with them. These essential elements of the creative process tend to go against the grain of prevailing attitudes about social change, and this is precisely why they have so much to offer.

Notes

1. The hospital was constructed in 1878 in accordance with the Kirkbride Plan (Thomas Story Kirkbride, 1809–1883) for the moral treatment of mental illness, which focused on aesthetic and humane living conditions. Not long after its opening Danvers succumbed to the overcrowding which Kirkbride saw as a major obstacle to social healing environments.

References

Canner, N. (2009) Personal communication, October 3.

Hillman, J. (1975) *Re-visioning Psychology.* New York: Harper and Row.

Jones, M. (1968) *Beyond the Therapeutic Community: Social Learning and Social Psychiatry.* New Haven, CT: Yale University Press.

Jones, M. (1982) *The Process of Change.* Boston, MA: Routledge & Kegan Paul.

Jung, C.G. (1969) *Collected Works of C.G. Jung, Vol. 11, Psychology and Religion: West and East,* ed. and trans. G. Adler and R.F.C. Hull. Princeton, NJ: Princeton University Press.

Kossak, M. (2009) "Therapeutic attunement: A transpersonal view of expressive arts therapy." *Arts in Psychotherapy 36,* 1, 13–18.

Levine, S. (2009) *Trauma, Tragedy, Therapy: The Arts and Human Suffering.* London and Philadelphia, PA: Jessica Kingsley Publishers.

McNiff, S. (1998) *Trust the Process: An Artist's Guide to Letting Go.* Boston, MA: Shambhala Publications.

McNiff, S. (2009) *Integrating the Arts in Therapy: History, Theory, and Practice.* Springfield, IL: Charles C. Thomas.

Moon, B. (2009) Personal communication, July 21.

Moore, T. (1990) *Dark Eros: The Imagination of Sadism.* Dallas, TX: Spring.

Moore, T. (1992) *Care of the Soul: A Guide for Cultivating Depth and Sacredness in Everyday Life.* New York: Harper and Row.

Moreno, J.L. (1973) *The Theatre of Spontaneity.* New York: Beacon House.

Nietzsche, F. (1967) *The Birth of Tragedy and the Case of Wagner,* trans. W. Kaufman. New York: Random House. (Original work published 1872.)

Tøjner, P.E. (2003) *Munch: In His Own Words.* Munich: Prestel Verlag.

PART II
Issues

6

A Social–Critical Reading of Indigenous Women's Art

The Use of Visual Data to "Show,"
rather than "Tell," of the Intersection
of Different Layers of Oppression

Ephrat Huss

INTRODUCTION

This chapter will analyze impoverished Bedouin women's artwork and their narratives explaining their work through the prism of third-world feminist theory, which demonstrates how the intersection or collaboration of different cultural, national, and gendered types of oppressions severely limits the women's spaces, both symbolic and physical. More specifically, the intersection of patriarchal Bedouin norms, the actions of the Israeli state in political conflict with the Bedouin, the limitations of poverty, and the context of a culture in overall transition, will be analyzed in terms of their collaborative impact on the women's lack of agency. At the same time, the women's artwork shows how the women themselves constantly struggle against these limitations. However, the 'web-like' quality of the "collaboration" of oppressions, patriarchal, state and cultural, makes them hard to unravel and fight effectively. "Showing," rather than "telling," this through visual means can be understood as a form of indirect resistance. Art, as a spatial medium that portrays experience in terms of space, can access the women's experiences of body in space, or subject in context of background, rather than through abstract and pre-determined concepts of the therapist or researcher. To elaborate, the pictures, explained by the women who drew them, describe their experience of rapid cultural transition – common to indigenous populations living in Westernized countries – in terms of the inside and outside spaces that they live within, and especially, as poor and marginalized women, in terms of the lack of spaces, both physical and intellectual, and the lack of mobility between spaces. On this level, art becomes a symbolic reclaiming of space, or a speech act that shows their lack of space.

LITERATURE SURVEY

The following cultural changes have impacted the spaces within which Bedouin women live: The Bedouin Arab community in the southern part of Israel, due to enforced sedentarization, has been dealing with cultural transition in the context of gross neglect by the national funding bodies. This has resulted in a decline of collective family support and funds, and in an externalization of social responsibilities to state authorities, who invest limited resources and cultural competency in their dealings with the Bedouin community (Barakat 1993; Kapri, Roznik and Budekat 2002; Meir 1997; Perez 2001). The consequences of the oppression and impoverishment of the Bedouin community as a whole for female Bedouin women includes intense interconnected poverty, social, and health problems such as depression and anemia, difficulty accessing health care facilities for women, and the ensuing problems of children bought up in poverty and social stress (Cwikel, Wiesel and Al-Krenawi 2003). Due to this enforced cultural transition, children, as well as women, have lost their financial power within Bedouin society, except in terms of receiving welfare for children. The sedentarization process has also impacted the spaces within which the Bedouin women live. Hijab (1988) describes how outsiders to the Arab culture assume that Arab women have no power if they lack legal rights, as they cannot choose their husbands or control the family's finances. However, in fact Arab women play central roles in the family, especially in rural communities where they work alongside their husbands and are economically productive and mobile within the tribal area (Afkhami 1995; Cohen 1999; Yamini 1996). Bedouin women traditionally expressed power relative to other Arab women, rather than in comparison to the male public arena. However, the cultural and demographic shifts described above have resulted in a dramatic change in the social and spatial organization of Bedouin women and children. Abu-Lughod describes how Muslim men often embrace modernism while projecting traditional roles onto women. While men enjoy the freedoms of modernity, women remain constricted, serving as a symbol of spiritual and cultural "purity" or authenticity (Abu-Lughod 1993, p. 10). For example, due to the forces of modernization, women are no longer busy with agricultural work but are in a small house alone rather than in a network of women. Polygamy has risen due to modernization as men desire a more educated wife or wish to enhance their declining sense of power (Al-Ataana 1993; Cohen 1999). Additionally, poor women's ability to travel within Western spaces is limited, as they are not permitted to travel alone in public transport due to values of modesty. The decline in the role of the extended family has made it harder for women to find accompaniment when they want to move outside their settlement (Meir 1997; Tal 1995). This is in contrast to the experience of middle-class Bedouin women with access to cars and to education, for whom more mobility and options are opened due to the cultural transition. These women have been much described in the literature, also in terms of their experience of being split between two cultures (Levi-Wiener 2004).

We have seen how race, culture, and poverty work in a synergistic manner to limit women's agency, as expressed in terms of lack of space and lack of mobility (Mohanty 2003). Similarly, the voice of impoverished indigenous women is often left out of research spaces (Tal 1995). Bowler (1997) describes the difficulties she found in using questionnaires and interviews, both of which stress Western-style verbal articulation, as a research method with poor Asian women. She found that the women try to give the "right" answer or to be polite. In-depth interviewing was also conceived of as a strange and foreign way of constructing and exploring the world for these women. As a result women in these studies are often mistakenly conceived of as "mute" because they are not educated to express themselves within Western norms (Bowler 1997; Lawler 2002). Goldberger *et al.* (1996) describe how within Western society verbal and abstract intelligence are dominant, while in other cultures different types of intelligence, such as spatial, musical, or visual intelligence, are often the dominant ones. Indigenous and feminist methodologies stress the research participants as experts, and emphasize the need for multi-lingual texts (Denzin and Lincoln 2000; Huss 2009a; Huss and Cwikel 2008; Tuhiwai-Smith 1999). On this level, art, in which the woman's phenomenological explanation of her own artwork, rather than diagnostic meta-theory, is the primary interpretive level, doubles her voice, in that she both expresses the contents and then interprets them.

METHOD

The group of Bedouin women used in this study included 20 women, ranging in age from 20 to 40, with all except two women wearing traditional dress and veils, and most of them living in townships. The women all spoke a minimal level of Hebrew. They belong to groups – jointly run and organized by the Department of Welfare Services and various non-governmental organizations (NGOs) – which are private franchises for impoverished Bedouin women with the aim of empowerment. The groups usually work in small tin huts, club-rooms, or the basements of houses, out of the public eye. The researcher provided the art materials used in the sessions. The groups were led by the researcher as a participant observer, and by the Arabic-speaking social workers who run the group. Each art session started with a short discussion of what each participant was thinking about that day. The women then had time to draw or sculpt, and each woman presented and explained her work to the group. The focus of these groups was using art in a 'diagrammed' fashion, as a trigger for words and as self-expression rather than as therapy (Huss 2009b). The art was analyzed first according to each woman's explanation of her own artwork, as in phenomenological art therapy, so that the women both provide the data and also analyze it as a group. This intensifies the expressive and interpretive voices of the participants within the research. The group discussion adds a peer-group interpretation of the pictures, highlighting elements common to the women's circumstances. The second level of analysis is undertaken by the researcher, who helps connect the work to the social reality described above, and to the influence of the position of the researcher as a participant observer from outside the culture, representing the dominant culture and its power position. In terms of ethical considerations, the use of art was negotiated with the women themselves, to serve their own self-defined ongoing group aims of self-expression, and to offer support for issues that concerned them. The anonymity of the women was protected by the omission of the names of the townships that the women live in, and by not describing the women directly. The women at their request were not videoed or transcribed, and women could choose to participate in the art sessions without being named (Malchiodi and Riley 1996). The categories presented in this paper are all concerned with the experience of spaces, such as houses, natural spaces, mobility, and the distances between people.

DATA PRESENTATION

The data will be presented according to the theme of space defined above.

First, the women describe their difficulty in reaching real, rather than idealized nature. Rather than drawing traditional symbols of nature (such as sunsets in the desert), the women chose to draw modern spaces in nature such as a swimming pool, the sea, or a car traveling, and their yearning to reach these spaces. Due to their poverty they cannot reach these spaces through cars, and due to cultural norms they cannot reach them through public transport.

The following woman drew her wish to go to the sea. She explained:

> *I wish to go to the sea, I have been to the sea and I love the sea. I wish to go more to the sea. I want to learn lots of things, also to drive, and then I can also go to the sea.*

We see that this sea described above is not symbolic or aesthetic, but rather a realistic depiction of an Israeli "beach" in which people are physically present and bathing. Similarly, in the next example, the creator explained her wish to take her children to swim in the pool:

> *I'm just drawing my dreams, to go to a pool. I want to go to a pool like this and to have all the children swim in the pool. Now I want to dive into that pool. I went there once but I cannot take my children to such a pool because I can't drive.*

In the above two examples, the first difficulty is gaining access to outside spaces. This is stressed both in the art and in its explanation. The use of the term "dream" to describe the pool situates the act of taking the children to a pool as an impossibility, or as a "dream" for the impoverished woman. The issue of learning to drive, as a key to mobility, and to reaching "nature" is described in the narrative below:

> *She described how she has after many failures completed her theory driving test, but must now find the money to learn to drive before the theory test expires, as that already happened to her...*

Conversely, the women describe their traditional childhoods as taking place outside, rather than inside:

> *...I remember going out with the sheep, I loved going out with the sheep – and also staying in my grandmothers tent...*

Compared to the above difficulty in mobility, this woman's childhood memories are situated within more mobile physical experiences, such as wandering outside with the sheep and being in a tent, which is a more flexible space in terms of access to inside and outside. Within the tent she is with her extended family, as compared to the following "inside" pictures in a township.

While a lack of mobility makes it hard to access the outside, we see that for poor women, poverty can make it difficult to access the inside:

> *My hut has broken windows, a few mattresses on the floor, one room. We don't have enough blankets. Last night we couldn't sleep – all of us we were so cold and the wind blew through the broken window. But it's my hut and it gives me safety. I'm glad I have it. My dream is to fix it, to plant flowers, to make it nice, to give each child his space.*

However, we can see from the woman's explanation of her house that even when defined as basic protection, the house moves beyond this to become a symbol of ownership, private space, and aesthetic and nurturing space. Here, the difficulty of maintaining this is described as financial, while in the next example the difficulty of owning a house intersects with political oppression:

> *My marriage house was taken away from me, and now I am in my parents' house, it has no permit. I am bored. I am like on an upward hill – trying to get back my house [cries]. This is a hill. I have no building permit, I feel I am on a steep hill, going up, and never reaching the top. I build my house, they break it. I am always climbing up [cries].*

The struggle of this single widowed mother for a house is described by her as more than just a financial struggle. It extends to cultural and national struggles against both the dominant Israeli culture, which on a political level does not give her house a permit, and the Bedouin culture, which on a cultural level expects her to live with her late husband's relatives.

However, even when a house is owned, as shown in the next example, the house is also experienced as a constricting space, due to its loneliness and the prohibition of leaving it, or the lack of mobility.

> *Participant 1 [crying]: I have a big house but I am lost, I am lonely in it. I sit and watch TV all day – I feel like an ant in that house.*

Thus the houses are also wished for, on the level of poverty, but also constricting and lonely, on the level of cultural norms and sedentarization.

DISCUSSION

In terms of both inside and outside, we see that the women's overall experience of the cultural transition from nomadic lifestyle to sedentary townships, as described in their artwork, is similar to that described in the literature (Al-Ataana 1993; Cwikel *et al.* 2003; Huss and Cwikel 2005; Lewando-Hundt 1976; Meir 1997; Perez 2001). However, the mapping of inside and outside areas into drawings, and the discussions about these drawings, reveals the interacting oppressions of poverty and culture. The women experience these oppressions as social, rather than as filtered through Western psychological conceptions of identity, such as depression or low self-esteem. The women do not have spaces of agency, whether inside or outside. They are caught between two cultures, and left with no spaces or no financial recourses (such as cars, education, etc.) to use the new spaces opened up by cultural transition. They cannot be either sedentary or mobile (Mills 1997).

This experience is described by Spivak as:

> *[Being] shuttled between different levels of oppression...disappearing not into a pristine nothingness, but into a violent shuttling which is the displaced figuration of the third world women, caught between tradition and modernization. (Spivak 1993, p.292)*

In other words, the experience of the women is enfolded within the spatial devices that they utilize to tell their story. The drawing of space thus becomes a "political" act that resists the lack of spaces available to the women due to the interconnection of cultural constraints and poverty. In his book on political geography, Soja writes, "Class struggle must encompass and focus upon the vulnerable point of the production of space, the reassertion of space in critical social theory" (Soja 1989, p.92). The art and its explanation show these different levels of oppression, the lack of space that is the "displaced figuration" and the ambivalence or duality of being "caught between tradition and modernization." The content conveyed through the arts enable the reader to experience this reality. Thus, as Spivak argues, the place where these women's "speech acts" can be heard is not in historical and political writings that are male-dominated, but rather in the areas of symbolic self-expression where resistance does not directly threaten the central male discourse, as it is removed from reality (Spivak 1987, pp.197–219 and 241–268).

Artistic expression becomes a way to show the problem in its social context, or within spaces that construct it (Mernissi 2003). The problem is shown to be "outside" rather than "inside" the women. Once the lack of spaces has been concretized and made visible to self and others within the art, it can be a base for creating what Freire and Macedo (1987) call "social consciousness." While the women in the study may not define themselves as feminists, or have read these theories, the use of spatial categories illuminates and thus resists their lack of power. It shows their struggle to both gain a house and to resist constriction within that house, by making these lacks visible and not hiding behind rhetoric (Wang and Burris 1994). On this level, the arts-based method put forward in this paper is a form of indigenous research that uses the nomadic Bedouin's spatial "ways of knowing" rather than imposing Western abstractions. Implications for social and group empowerment, while not developed in this chapter, are created by the discussion in a group context around the page. This in itself acts as an additional symbolic space to redefine new social avenues for self-expression and communication, which are the basis of creating meaning, a stable identity, and a knowledge base out of the rapid transitions that the women are undergoing.

References

Abu-Lughod, L. (1993) *Writing Women's Worlds: Bedouin Stories*. Berkeley, CA: University of California Press.

Afkhami, M. (ed.) (1995) *Faith and Freedom: Women's Human Rights in the Muslim World*. London: Taurus Press.

Al-Ataana, M. (1993) "Connection between marital status of Bedouin women and her self image and psychological well being." M.A. thesis, Bar-Ilan University, Faculty of Humanities and Social Sciences, Department of Psychology.

Barakat, H. (1993) *The Arab World, Society, Culture and State*. Los Angeles, CA: University of California Press.

Bowler, M. (1997) "Problems with Interviewing: Experiences with Service Providers and Clients." In G. Miller and R. Dingwall (eds) *Context and Method in Qualitative Research*. London: Basic Books.

Cohen, M. (1999) "The status of Bedouin women in Israel: Economic and social changes." *Maof Vemeaseh 5*, 229–237 (Hebrew).

Cwikel, J., Wiesel, R. and Al-Krenawi, A. (2003) "The physical and psychosocial health of Bedouin Arab Women of the Negev area of Israel." *Violence Against Women 9*, 2, 240–257.

Denzin, N. and Lincoln, Y. (2000) *Handbook of Qualitative Research*. Los Angeles, CA: Sage Publications.

Freire, P. and Macedo, D. (1987) *Literacy, Reading the Word and the World*. London: Routledge.

Goldberger, N., Tarule, J., Clinchey, B. and Belency, M. (1996) *Knowledge, Difference and Power: Essays Inspired by Women's Ways of Knowing*. New York: Basic Books.

Hijab, N. (1988) *Women-power. The Arab Debate over Women and Work*. Cambridge: Cambridge University Press.

Huss, E. (2009a) "A case study of Bedouin women's art in social work: A model of social arts intervention with 'traditional' women negotiating Western cultures." *Social Work Education 28*, 6, 598–616 (Special Edition: Cultures in Transition).

Huss, E. (2009b) "Bedouin women negotiating the cultural spaces of childhood: Arts based research within a welfare training course in early child-care in the Negev." *Gender and Education* [publication pending].

Huss, E. and Cwikel J. (2005) "Researching art, creating research: Applying arts based research to Bedouin women's pictures." *International Journal of Qualitative Methods 4*, 4, 1–16.

Huss, E. and Cwikel J. (2008) "From putting pain in the body to putting pain on the page: Somatism and self expression within Bedouin women's groups." *Archives of Women's Mental Health 11*, 2, 81–169.

Kapri, H., Roznik, R. and Budekat, B. (2002) *Welfare services in the Unrecognized Settlements.* Israeli Ministry of Welfare Study Project (Hebrew).

Lawler, M. (2002) " Narrative in social research." In T. May *Qualitative Research in Action.* London: Sage Publications, 242-259.

Levi-Wiener, N. (2004) "In between two worlds: A narrative analysis of the Druze women and higher education." Paper read at the Conference on Psycho-Social Challenges of Indigenous Societies: The Bedouin Perspective, July, Ben-Gurion University of the Negev.

Lewando-Hundt, G. (1976) "Conflict styles between Bedouin women." *Notes on the Bedouin 7*, 15–30.

Malchiodi, C. and Riley, S. (1996) *Supervision and Related Issues.* Chicago, IL: Magnolia Street Publishers

Meir, A. (1997) *As Nomadism Ends.* Boulder, CO: Westview Press.

Mernissi, F. (2003) "The Meaning of Spatial Boundaries." In R. Lewis and S. Mills (eds) *Feminist Postcolonial Theory: A Reader.* Edinburgh: Edinburgh University Press.

Mills, S. (1997) *Discourse, the New Critical Idiom.* London: Routledge.

Mohanty, C.T. (2003) "Under Western Eyes: Feminist Scholarship and Colonial Discourses." In R. Lewis and S. Mills (eds) *Feminist Postcolonial Theory: A Reader.* Edinburgh: Edinburgh University Press.

Perez, H. (2001) "My skin is my only protection." *Notes on the Bedouin 34*, 34–50.

Soja, E.W. (1989) *Postmodern Geographies: The Reassertion of Space in Critical Social Theory.* London: Verso Publications.

Spivak, G.C. (1987) *In Other Worlds: Essays in Cultural Politics.* New York: Menthuen.

Spivak, G.C. (1993) "Interview with Spivak: 'Subaltern Talk-concerning Sati' 29 October, 1993." In D. Landry and G.M. McLean, *The Spivak Reader.* London and New York: Routledge.

Tal, S. (1995) *The Bedouin Women in the Negev in Time of Changes.* Joe Alon Center for Bedouin Culture (Hebrew).

Tuhiwai-Smith, L. (1999) *Decolonizing Methodologies: Research and Indigenous Peoples.* London: Zed Books.

Wang, C. and Burris, M. (1994) "Empowerment through photo-novella." *Health Education Quarterly 21*, 172–185.

Yamini, M. (1996) *Feminism and Islam.* London: Garnet Publishers.

7

Inside-Out Outside-In

Found Objects and Portable Studio

Debra Kalmanowitz and Bobby Lloyd

A BOSNIAN REFUGEE CAMP IN SLOVENIA, 1994

Many of the one hundred children spontaneously drew and painted houses, but the repeated outpouring of such images seemed to provide little relief. On observing this for some time, we decided to "extend the art groups beyond the confined space of the art room/bedroom as well as beyond the intensity of the camp itself and into three-dimensional form in the environment surrounding the camp. Twenty-five children queued up to join us and so we decided to select five older children at this stage whom we took to the nearby town dump in a disused quarry to physically construct a symbolic house" (Kalmanowitz and Lloyd 2005, pp. 116–117). On returning after a break to find the house knocked down, the children formed a human chain to pass rocks "from the quarry to the ruins of the house to create a stronger structure. While making the house, one of the girls spoke of her home in Bosnia being destroyed. The process was fraught with physical effort, controversy, and discussion. It led to the adaptation of what had been a two-room space into one shared room as well as the taking of photographs with the children posing with the pots and pans, vacuum cleaner, stove, and other objects they had by now collected both inside the structure" (Kalmanowitz and Lloyd 2005, p. 117) (Figures 7.1 and 7.2).

The next day the same children revisited the "house," which "had again been knocked down. Rather than walk away, the group of children poignantly chose to stay at the site and make drawings of the rubble and surrounding landscape. We walked back through the wood and discovered that the gateway structure they had constructed had also been knocked down. It was upon this that one of the girls laid flowers. We followed the impetus of the children generated by the first house by facilitating other 'houses' in woods on the hills around the refugee

Figure 7.1 Rebuilding the house

Figure 7.2 Children posing in the house

camp with these same children over subsequent days. These seemed to offer scope for adaptation and change. For example, two days later the group built with us a series of structures in a pine-wooded area. Here there was a dispute between Belma and one of the other girls about the building of a 'house' that each laid claim to. Both became tearful. For Belma it emerged that this was the first time she had cried since news of her father's death. The two struggled to resolve their quarrel and ended up building a house together, planning and planting two garden areas in the front and inviting us in as guests for coffee" (Kalmanowitz and Lloyd 2005, p. 117).

"While we worked with the group of children in the quarry, the volunteer supervised the play of three of the little girls in the woods behind the camp as they constructed little 'shrines' containing small constructions made from found objects (Figure 7.3). These they then surrounded with twigs, which acted to demarcate each construction, one from the other. One of these girls later that evening used a cardboard box to create a house. The next day these same children extended their activity by fetching blankets from their rooms and physically climbing into the small demarcated spaces they had made, asking us to photograph them one by one" (Kalmanowitz and Lloyd 2005, p. 118).

Figure 7.3 Collection of objects made from found objects in the woods

Although these activities took place in the quarry and woods and involved the physical making of houses and other spaces, it seems that they provided an opportunity for re-storying and the expression of loss and bereavement, as well as allowing for symbolic representation. It seemed possible that some of the children could experience a valuable process, in which mourning could begin to take place in relation to their multiple losses. Over the next two weeks, we continued to work with these children using art materials at the camp.

INTRODUCTION

The above narrative represents a decisive moment in our practice. It also provides the central focus of this chapter: the use of found objects and the notion of portable studio in contexts of political violence and social upheaval. The dynamic between *inside-out* and *outside-in* is one with which we suggest it is essential to engage, and is alive in our exploration of found objects. Of course this must be seen as part of a whole; in the latter section of this chapter, "inside-out: portable studio," we revisit the art therapy studio in which these found objects are being used and explore briefly some further thinking about our concept of "portable studio" (Kalmanowitz and Lloyd, 1997, 1999, 2005).

"Inside-out" is a phrase commonly used to describe the inside of an object, a piece of clothing perhaps, turned to the outside, while the outside faces in. In this chapter we explore the need to be able to move comfortably between both (inside and out), physically, psychologically, symbolically, and metaphorically, while remaining focused and clear. As is apparent from the journal extract above, attending to both inside and outside seems to have the potential to create energy where this is lacking. This ability to shuffle things around while still maintaining a firm ground can allow for surprises. We explore in some depth the way in which found objects operate within this dynamic, as well as, more briefly, the ensuing and necessary adaptation of our art therapy studios, taking a look, for example, at contemporary art practices of installation and site-specific art.

Traditional psychoanalytic therapies encourage the verbalization of the client's thoughts, and the uncovering and interpretation of unconscious internal conflicts, using such methods as free associations, fantasies, and dreams. A humanistic approach to therapy is concerned not so much with the unconscious as revealing pathology, but with the inherent human capacity to maximize an individual's potential. One of the tasks of a humanistic therapist and indeed of an art therapist could be seen as working to create a relationship between the environment and the individual – an environment which has the capacity to facilitate growth, and within which the potential of the individual may flourish. Given the complexity of each individual person, their varied life experiences and complex socio-economic, political and cultural circumstances, the internal world cannot be viewed in isolation from the external world; indeed, these are inseparable. As is evident in the work in the town dump in Slovenia, the theories from which we draw are not simply theoretical constructs, but are embedded in our work. We have also found that there is no single paradigm suitable to responding to situations of this nature: our work pulls on many threads only touched upon in this short chapter, threads that are intimately inter-connected.

For the first weeks of our stay in a small room in one of the army barracks that nestled into the Slovenian hillside (Figure 7.4), we worked indoors and offered art groups to children and teenagers, parents (largely mothers as most of the fathers were fighting in Bosnia), and grandparents, adapting the groups to meet their different needs. The mothers, for example, seemed to prefer embroidery as their primary medium, while the grandparents were comfortable making portraits of each other or producing carefully annotated drawings of their home village in Bosnia. Children made up half of the camp population and worked with us in small groups depending on age. As the days passed we noticed that many of the children drew and re-drew houses, often appearing dissatisfied with their images, and limited by the materials and the four walls within which we worked. In addition, while the barracks clearly provided a welcome and essential shelter – and indeed continued to do so over several years – they also seemed to reinforce the fact that the majority of these children and their families were stuck there for the foreseeable future with nowhere else to go. We had become familiar with the camp surroundings and aware of the innate resources they had to offer. The decision to take these children outside the camp and into the woods, into the landscape and the disused quarry, and to invite them to make use of the physical environment and the natural and manmade materials they found, was therefore significant. The shift from inside to outside, both physically and emotionally, seemed to free the children and contain them at the same time. While we judged that this was an appropriate response, we also struggled with the breaking of the traditional therapeutic boundaries we were accustomed to using in other settings. Despite this,

Figure 7.4 The army barracks nestled in the hills, Slovenia

we were acutely aware that we needed to find a viable way of working with these individuals. This was true not only in Slovenia, but also in other contexts of political violence and social change where traditional models are often neither possible nor relevant.

THE PARADOX OF CHANGE

Our work began in Bosnia, former Yugoslavia, a country devastated by war. Our parents and grandparents remember the region for its beautiful coastline, but we recall pockmarked buildings housing displaced people, constant streams of UN trucks, and struggling NGOs. The war forced change upon the people we met. This change was all-encompassing, affecting personal lives, family networks, social structures, physical space, personal space, communal space, and impacting the emotional, cultural, and spiritual aspects of the individual's life.

Berman writes about her experience of using art therapy in a changing South Africa: "[Like the art therapy course] the structure of change is open ended, determined by the needs and opportunities of the environment, and the goals of correcting the effects of the past" (Berman 2005, p.175).

One of the hardest things to do in the face of extreme events, great loss and suffering is to remain open. Our instinct is to shut down, to try to banish the memories from consciousness, in order to protect ourselves. This is evident in the extensive literature (Herman 1992; Van der Kolk 1987; Yule 2003, to name a few) and in our experience with survivors of trauma and torture. Individuals may become rigid and inflexible in their attempts to avoid the pain and deny the event.

Levine discusses Heidegger's idea that we are in the world as beings trapped in time, and as such we cannot master this world:

> *Our task is to enable it to show the possibilities that are hidden in what is past. Thus the work arises not from mastery but from an attitude of openness to what is given, a receptivity that lets the world be what it can be. This attitude of Gelassenheit or "letting-be" is not a mode of passivity. (Levine 2009, p.33)*

This notion of openness is one that we cannot deny in the context of change. Change is open-ended – we do not know where it will lead. But there is also a persistence to change, which is not an aspect of change we ordinarily consider. There is a French proverb that expresses a sentiment of change which seems to ground this openness and articulate its paradoxes: "The more something changes, the more it remains the same" (Watzlawick, Weakland and Fisch 1974, p.2). This is because all perception and thought is relative, operating by comparison and contrast. Watzlawick, Weakland and Fisch (1974) write that, in a universe in which everything is blue, the concept of blueness cannot be developed for lack of contrasting colors. Indeed, in Bosnia, a country which was once a beacon of culture and was extensively damaged and changed, lacking "contrasting colors," the internal lives of many Bosnian individuals held different degrees of persistence, from wholeness and resilience to trauma, embodied in part by memories, both personal and collective. This paradox of persistence versus change can be very comforting. Instead of beginning from the vacuum which is so pervasive, we as therapists can hold onto this notion that where the one exists, so must the other. Indeed, part of our primary responsibility as art therapists is to hold onto this potential, and to facilitate art-making and this attitude of "Gelassenheit," "letting be," or openness.

OUTSIDE-IN: FOUND OBJECTS

The psychoanalyst Christopher Bollas speaks of transformational objects as capable of altering self-experience: "Not yet fully identified as an other, the mother is experienced as a process of transformation… The memory of this early object relation manifests itself in the person's search for an object (a person, place, event, ideology) that promises to transform the self" (Bollas 1987, p.14). He continues:

> *I think we have failed to take notice of the phenomenon in adult life of the wide-ranging collective search for an object that is identified with*

the metamorphosis of the self. In many religious faiths, for example, when the subject believes in the deity's actual potential to transform the total environment, he sustains the terms of the earliest object tie within a mythic structure. Such knowledge remains symbiotic and coexists alongside other forms of knowing. In secular worlds, we see how hope invested in various objects (a new job, move to a new country, a vacation, a change of relationship) may both represent a request for a transformational experience, and at the same time, continue the "relationship" to an object that identifies the experience of transformation. (Bollas 1987, p.16)

Indeed, Bollas's emphasis on a process of transformation is in itself significant to our art therapy work. Found objects become meaningful through the attention we give them and relationships we create with them, often through transforming them into something else. Art theorist Margaret Iverson describes the role of found objects in related terms. She writes:

The object found as if by chance is situated at the point of connection between external nature, perception, and the unconscious, and thus has a peculiar, elusive relation to vision. The space occupied by the found object is carved out by traumatic experience, defined precisely as an experience that has failed to achieve a representation, but on which, nonetheless, one's whole existence depends... this object calls attention to itself by creating a hole in the fabric of normal perception. (Iverson 2004, p.49)

Bollas speaks about what he calls the "unthought known" (Bollas 1987, p.17) in relation to his transformational objects. The "unthought known" sometimes causes individuals to repeat aesthetic experiences through which they can remember their origins on an existential level. Accordingly, Bollas writes that to seek an object may be to recollect an early experience, to remember, not cognitively, but existentially.

While we of course cannot know the meaning of the objects for each child on an individual level, we suggest that the transformation of the found objects into a house (in our example above) served to bridge the conscious and the unconscious, the elusive or intangible and its opposite, the concrete. And yet as concrete as the objects are, in their transformation they seemed to maintain an important capacity to hold symbolic meaning or significance for the children. This is another paradox with which we work: the concrete can also be symbolic, and can allow the finder to discover unrealized and perhaps surprising significance in the object itself, or in the object once it has been transformed or incorporated into a work of art.

When using found objects with children newly arrived in East London from other countries, as well as with students and arts therapists (in the UK, Middle East, Europe, and Hong Kong), it was most often the act of finding in itself, and the act of incorporating the found object in something new that was empowering. Poignantly, one of the participants in one of our found objects workshops explained that her found objects allowed her the possibility of finding something she did not know was wanted. Another explained that all his senses were activated by the process, while a third said that bringing something in from the outside gave her a greater sense of freedom as well as more direct access to her internal world than starting from a blank piece of paper. It was through working with these objects and with other materials that powerful connections began to be made on a conscious level. Circumstance, place and time were often embedded in the object, leading to a sense of history and connection to place. Lost history, fantasies, and early childhood memories were regularly explored. Personal narratives were symbolically held in these objects. These findings, often only fragments, helped us to understand the weight that objects can hold, both personal and collective (Figure 7.5).

Figure 7.5 Artwork made from found objects, workshop, Israel

We are aware that for some, using discarded fragments of objects in art therapy could connect with issues of displacement, despair, rejection, abandonment, fear, uselessness, or feeling unwanted and unvalued. It might mirror or feed into the individual's own feelings of loss and worthlessness. Alternatively, we have observed how these feelings can be explored and worked with: the processes of seeking, hunting, and discovery; of sorting, re-using, adding to, mending, and reparation. An eight-year-old boy, recently arrived in the UK from Pakistan, was clearly disgusted by the idea of picking up discarded objects from the wet playground and struggled with the feelings this evoked. Interestingly, when reviewing his artwork overall, it was the green landscape made from sweet packets, twigs, a plastic bottle, and paint that he singled out as his most important artwork

FOUND OBJECTS AND MEMORY

The literature on the use of found objects in art therapy is not extensive (e.g. Berman 2005; Brooker 2010, 2011; Davis 1999; Kalmanowitz and Lloyd, 1997, 1999, 2005; Moon 2010; Yeh 1997). However, much has been written about the role of found and salvaged objects in art history and contemporary art practice. Artist Susan Hiller, for example, describes the making of her piece *After the Freud Museum* (2000). Drawing upon Freud's analogy between the psychoanalytic process and digging on an archaeological site (Freud and Breuer 1974, p.206), she writes about her five-year process of gathering objects, artefacts, and materials which seemed to carry for her an aura of memory or meaning – often fragments or rubbish as well as reproductions and souvenirs (Hiller 2000).

An art residency on a regeneration project in a neglected and deprived multicultural neighborhood in East London included Bobby Lloyd's act of gathering several hundred discarded objects from the former hospital site and photographing them individually. These now valued objects have been re-presented back into the site in the form of a large photographic/ceramic wall within the new, mixed-occupancy housing development. Each of these often discarded fragments, without obvious value, evokes an emotional, historic, or aesthetic quality, and/ or a precious life of its own; when placed together, the objects form multiple narratives and connect across layers of history and social and cultural experience. This model of gathering objects and reframing them has proved useful in a massive regeneration program in Doha, Qatar in 2009: the "found objects project" there has helped provide a framework for salvaging, naming, locating, and preserving objects and artefacts, which would otherwise be subsumed by the demolition process, and further making them available to artists to use in their work (Figures 7.6 and 7.7).

Figure 7.6 Photomontage of found objects, London

Figure 7.7 Salvaging objects, Doha, Qatar

The word salvaged comes from the Latin *Salvare*, to save. The "primary meaning is associated with compensation for saving a ship or a cargo from the perils of the sea, or for lives and property rescued in a shipwreck" (Digby 2006, pp.174–175). Indeed in the above examples, it took the curiosity, search, documentation, digestion, and reflection of an artist's eye to reframe these objects and understand their potential. Without this understanding of the potential of that which is "salvaged," the objects would be buried and forgotten.

As prevalent as the use of found objects in art has been over the past century (Duchamp, the Surrealists, Picasso, Beuys; Dion, Lucas, Hiller; the list of contemporary artists is vast), it has been suggested that the historical origin of art can be traced to the discovery of "found objects" by prehistoric man who subsequently made them the central elements of numerous works of art (Fairbairn 1938). A very early example is the three-million-year-old Makapansgat Pebble (University of Witwatersrand, Johannesburg), discovered in the Transvaal in 1925. Zoologist and surrealist painter Desmond Morris, in The Human Animal series (1994), suggests that the pebble, with its striking resemblance to a face, was found, collected and brought back to a favored dwelling place as a "treasured possession" and is the earliest example of an art object or *objet trouvé*.

Small portable objects carried intact as precious items give us further clues to the significance of found objects for individuals experiencing displacement or dislocation. These objects manage to transport and transform the space into which they come. In our work, we have seen that objects carried by the individual from their previous lives, or alternatively searched for as part of the art therapy work, contribute to the individual experiencing a sense of safety, even home. We observed that a number of Bosnian refugee families in the camp in Slovenia had with them their traditional coffee grinder amongst the few possessions with which they had fled, and were able to continue the routine of making coffee at intervals throughout each day, as over an extended period of time the refugee camp became their new long-term residence. Other authors have explored the role of objects, reaching similar conclusions. For example, Mehta and Belk interviewed adults of Indian origin in the United States and found that objects they brought with them from India reminded them of a prior life and were "an important symbolic source of security and cultural identity" (Mehta and Belk 1991, p.407).

Geographer Susan Digby writes movingly about her own grandfather's experience of collecting objects or souvenirs in a small box which he called his "casket of magic" and which helped him on his journeys far from home in the early years of the Second World War. These "*salvaged-object souvenirs*" or "*salvaged encountered* objects" are those "objects to which individual meanings are attached, often seemingly of the everyday, plucked from anonymity or destruction" (Digby 2006, p.175). Digby suggests that for mobile people, travellers, and refugees, such objects are particularly valuable for the stories attached to them, their placement helping to establish a person's identity within a space and therefore the construction of home.

Archaeologist and anthropologist Nicholas Saunders (2003) has researched extensively how ordinary soldiers, prisoners of war, and civilians across numerous wars and conflicts have found objects on the battlefield and made artworks out of them which have served to embody their individual responses to war, as well as to act as important social documents. In Vietnam, Northern Ireland, and Korea, and in earlier wars such as the Crimean War, the American Civil War, and the Boer War, soldiers have picked up shrapnel, shell castings, and other fragments to rework into often intricately formed and engraved art pieces and artefacts. Most notably, these objects, known as Trench Art, are connected to the First World War, and were made by wounded soldiers during convalescence to send home to family or to sell. Saunders describes how, between 1919 and 1939, many bereaved family members themselves set off on battlefield pilgrimages and returned with objects intended to keep alive the memory of loved ones. He also suggests, interestingly, that these objects are somewhere lodged in the back of our memories, as well as literally stored away in our attics and homes. They have also been avidly collected and displayed (Figures 7.8 and 7.9).

Figure 7.8 Aeroplane. Collection of Bill Howell

Figure 7.9 Brass aeroplanes. Collection of Bill Howell

We have ourselves been interested in the objects that have made their way into our art therapy groups or workshops and the ways in which they operate. Such objects seem to have served as a social document or "salvaged encountered object" (Digby 2006) for the finder. It has not been unusual to hear comments like: "This reminds me of an object my grandmother brought from Germany," or "of a tea set I used to play with at my auntie's house." These objects, or social documents, serve to trigger personal memory and may point to the way in which things have changed. Sometimes this change is inevitable, sometimes it is desired. Sometimes the memory leaves a hollow sense of loss, while at other times it conjures a welcome feeling of comfort and belonging.

THE PHOTOGRAPH AS OBJECT

Art Refuge UK was founded primarily to support newly arrived Tibetan children, first in Nepal and then as they move on to Dharamsala (India) in transit to a new life, far away from family and home. At the center of the program is an art room in each location within which vulnerable children and young people can paint, play, and take stock of their experiences in safety, supported by Tibetan staff and volunteers. In 2008 we were invited to help train the staff in Nepal in the sensitive and safe use of art-making in the context of their work. The center is a stark place, with cold interiors furnished with iron bunk beds and neglected outside grounds. Even discarded objects are hard to find. With the cameras we had brought with us as tools, the children were invited to photograph objects in their environment as well as an object they had brought with them from home. One boy asked to be photographed holding his object – a photo of the Dalai Lama, banned in his homeland. Other photographs that emerged were of a suitcase, a shoe, the hand of a friend, and of the Tibetan flag which fluttered in the wind around the center, the possession of drawings of which are an imprisonable offence in Tibet. The photographs were reworked into collage, paintings, and drawings by the children. Like found objects, they provided a presence in the "here and now" (Figures 7.10 and 7.11).

Figure 7.10 Collage with photos of suitcase and self, holding image of the Dalai Lama

Figure 7.11 Pastel drawing with photograph of the Dalai Lama

We have observed that when there is an apparent absence of objects, there is most often an absence of relationship to context. The environment in which we are working is likely to feel alienated and un-owned. In the absence of objects, photography has created a tangible frame of reference. In our experience, photographs can, like found objects, aid in restoring a sense of lost identity, both personal and collective. When forced to abandon one's home, as with the carrying of objects described earlier, some people take photographs which become "portable sites of remembrance" (Zijlmans 2009, p.221) and as such, "a substitute for the real place... Taking a photograph means taking a piece of somewhere with you" (Zijlmans 2009, pp.227–228).

Having said this, however, in the art room in Nepal, reflection or even triggering of memory by the staff or ourselves would be premature. The reception center is a place of transit, a place of survival, in which a reserved and exhausted celebration of freedom was most graphically expressed in the previously suppressed images of the Tibetan flag and the Dalai Llama.

In London, in 2007, a Romani Gypsy family of 65 adults and children who had lived on the same caravan site for over 40 years were relocated as a result of the 2012 Olympic building program. This once mobile community whose ancestors had moved through the area for five centuries had been forced to live on a fixed "legal" site due to laws against stopping by the roadside. Now the enforced process of moving – 12 different dates, packing and unpacking – led to at times overwhelming feelings of individual and collective loss and anxiety in the community. As part of an ongoing project,[1] photography seemed to provide a means whereby this anxiety could in part be held. Throughout this stressful period, children and parents photographed things that would soon be lost to them – their beloved wendy-house, the troughs of flowers, the view from their caravan, the site as it was dismantled. The controversial plot of land chosen for the new site was formerly the local children's playground, which the Gypsy families had shared amicably with other local families. With the old site soon bulldozed and buried under a mound of rubble, and the families finally moved, the photographs served to connect the past with the present. They were initially held in albums, and later formally exhibited in the family's new residence as a public witness to their experiences and lost home. The photographs provided for the processes of mourning, reflection, and remembering described above. For some, they led to an acceptance of the inevitability of their new and changed situation (Figures 7.12 and 7.13).

Figure 7.12 Children looking out from the original caravan site at demolition in progress, East London. Copyright © On Site Arts

Figure 7.13 Child looking at photographs exhibited in caravan on the new site, East London. Copyright © On Site Arts

INSIDE-OUT: PORTABLE STUDIO

The use of found objects in art therapy does not take place in a vacuum. The collection of objects and images has a time and a place. It is the beginning of a relationship. This may not, however, be a psychodynamic relationship in the traditional sense: between client and therapist, or in the case of art therapy, between client, therapist, and artwork. The relationship about which we are speaking is between individuals and their environment, such as a town dump, a new arrivals center, a regeneration site, a refugee camp dining room, a Gypsy site, or an inner city center for asylum seekers.

As art therapists we are not alone in dreaming of, and often striving after, the ideal studio, but in reality we seldom work in environments which are "perfect." We know that the optimal condition for therapy is a confidential, reliable space free from interruption from the outside world. So the work-spaces we have described could potentially cause great anxiety in the therapist, unless we find a way to understand the characteristics and limitations of each environment. Working in these imperfect spaces demands thought and conscious choices, but does not need to compromise our ethics or practice. Much of the work is done by the therapists themselves, in that there may need to be a great deal of internal work to maintain the studio space.

Not an "inert box"

The Portable Studio came into being as a response to our work in the field and our realization that the art therapist often needs to take the initiative that transforms a less than perfect space into one that facilitates art-making. The Portable Studio is based on the premise that the internal structure we carry with us as art therapists can allow for work to physically take place in a wide range of settings. It is this internal structure that makes it portable. This includes an attitude to the art and the individual making it, a central belief in the individual as possessing internal resources, resilience and a culture from which to draw, rather than being a powerless victim for whom the therapists hold all the answers. In addition, the internal structure includes an attentiveness to the images in the understanding that they can hold multiple meanings, and that the therapist in his/her attentiveness can hold these meanings and potential (Kalmanowitz and Lloyd 2005).

We have pondered over this challenge of physical space for a number of years, and found that Gaston Bachelard's words reflect our experience. In 2005 we wrote:

> Indeed when the individuals became immersed in their art making, the "studio" in which they were working was not static and lifeless, not an "inert box" (Bachelard 1994 [1958], p.47) but for some was dynamic, active and absorbing and seemed to allow for some degree of reflection and internal movement. It seems that despite the external and internal destruction, the art therapy studio was able to hold these paradoxes and retreat from the world, while attending to it. (Kalmanowitz and Lloyd 2005, p.111)

The art therapy studio model has been used by art therapists since the origins of the profession. Different art therapists have tried to define its essence, and the accumulation of the sentiments they express holds its multiple potentiality. All of this informs the Portable Studio. Moon (2002) summarizes different attitudes to the studio beautifully:

> Kramer (1994) identifies the healthy studio environment as a place where there is "space for improvisation, openness to the unexpected, acceptance of the eccentric" (p.92). Allen (1995b) identifies the primary attitude of a studio setting to be energy, while McNiff (1995) describes the studio as an "ecology of mutual influences" (p.181) and Henley (1995) believes

the effective studio provides both inspiration and sanctuary. (Moon 2002, p.72)

Moon writes that the spirit of the studio and its practice are possible anywhere, "smacked down, dead center, in the middle of life. Against all the odds, and perhaps because the odds are against us, we make art" (Moon 2002, p.71).

In our experience, individuals have tended to work with whatever was available in the external environment, and at times despite their external environment, and this has not precluded their ability to become absorbed in art-making. Importantly, many have been willing to engage in the "art therapy studios" while maintaining an ambivalent attitude towards us as therapists.

An example of this is an open art therapy studio set up by Debra Kalmanowitz in contemporary Hong Kong, a context within which asylum seekers and refugees are among the most vulnerable groups, belonging to a community which is often transient, unmotivated and disempowered. Over a number of years, Kalmanowitz has worked with one of the only NGOs in Hong Kong which offers psychosocial services to refugees. This is a small organization, which functions on a shoestring budget and offers some much needed support; asylum seekers can for example attend English lessons, eat three meals a day, use the computers, participate in various groups, be referred to counselors or art therapy. It is within this context that Kalmanowitz set up an open art therapy studio. This model of working seemed one way to provide support within this constantly changing environment.

With few resources, and a revolving-door of volunteers, with the "art therapy room" being shared by everybody in the center, with the near impossibility of keeping the door closed for the entire session, with attendance being erratic and the organization frequently changing management, it was difficult to keep the space consistent. Kalmanowitz came to consider this open art therapy studio in terms of portable studio. Indeed, the lack of external order mirrored the lives of the people who used it, and despite the fact that this art therapy studio took place indoors, it often felt as tenuous as the woods in Slovenia. In the art therapy studio Kalmanowitz created, her attitude became a key to forming the space, and it turned out that no matter how the room looked on that day, nor how many interruptions there were, art materials were chosen and a silence descended upon the room. This straddle between the internal and external worlds of the participants was embodied in the structures or paintings that emerged, with the therapist acting as a witness as well as an external reminder of the capacity for internal support and of the participants' own humanity.

The studio as installation

Returning to Slovenia, we have pondered the emotional power and significance that the structures made by the children seemed to hold – the house making in the quarry, the spontaneous making of dens and the arrangements in the woods made of gathered objects (Kalmanowitz and Lloyd 1997, 1999, 2005). It appeared that these children were making use of healthy play and art-making as well as the witness of adults. In addition, the shifts and changes occurring within each episode of house building, as well as from one house building activity to the next, seemed for some to serve the purpose of self-preservation, restructuring and potentially healing. In retrospect, what we struggled with was not the actual form that the art-making took, but with the placing of the art within a frame: the art-making was taking place outside our traditional work settings, outside physical as well as temporal boundaries, but it still seemed to be a poignant expression which held significance for all the groups in the camp.

Moon triggered in us a moment of clarity. She writes: "If we are to cultivate an artist's identity in all aspects of our work, it makes sense that we use the artistic sensibilities to re-conceptualize our work spaces..." And further, "Architecture, interior design, environmental sculpture and installation art all have relevance for us when we begin to think of our physical spaces as works of art in and of themselves" (Moon 2002, p.83).

Installation art is site-specific and may provide a frame of reference with which to understand our studios, including those in Slovenia, Hong Kong, and London. It is sometimes described as an environment, often in the form of a construction made up of multiple media, designed for a specific place. Sometimes the artwork occupies an entire gallery-space or room, and in order to engage fully with the artwork the viewer must walk through and into it. The environment, the objects, and those interacting with the artwork co-exist.

Using installation art as a frame is an imaginative way of conceiving of the art therapy studio, certainly some distance from our traditional models, and certainly not suited to all settings. In the types of contexts of political conflict and social change we are exploring in this chapter, however, this frame allows us to re-vision our "studio" spaces into viable working environments. In addition to broadening our perceptions of what the "perfect studio" is, it has allowed us the reflective distance to see beyond the difficulties of workplaces, and to work within as well as with what we have.

Philosopher Michel Foucault (1986) maintained that space in our contemporary world is mainly experienced and understood in terms of "sites," a jumbled mass of elements. If we take on board Foucault's thoughts here, then we need to consider an installation art not only as an art form, but one which addresses our experiences with the spaces in which we live, work and play.

An art installation, or the houses in the Slovenian woods, are/were actively constructed within, and in response to, an environment, and as such move between actual and perceived space. The physical form that the installation takes is often an expression by the artist of an internal or imagined place. So the installation may be a passage between an internal and external space, which we experience when we step into its orbit.

This play of internal and external, inside and outside, is the world we straddle in working within these contexts of social change. As art therapists, we do not have the luxury of simply concentrating on one – either inside or outside – but are constantly alert to both, where they intertwine, and what emotional responses they could be eliciting. We also keep in mind that not all installations are harmonious: some may cause a tension between what is given and what is evoked, some may stimulate memories or thoughts that amplify a sense of dislocation. Site-specific art can therefore refer to both losses and gains (Westgeest 2009). These are important observations if we are to utilize our environments in the same way as we do found objects and photography.

CONCLUSION

In our work in the context of political violence/conflict and social upheaval we are constantly reminded that the external destruction points to internal destruction too, but that many individuals can be stronger and more adaptable than the buildings that they lived in. Often the people we worked with seemed to possess a capacity to live with tremendous pain and loss while at the same time having the potential to move beyond it, despite their compromised circumstances (Kalmanowitz and Lloyd 2005). Part of our work is/was to help the individual to emotionally inhabit the space available to us/them, whether through using the space, or working in spite of it, for a given period of time. Gaston Bachelard writes that "inhabited space transcends geometric space" (Bachelard 1958, p.47), and understanding this is essential if we are to facilitate the move between inside and out.

We began this chapter with a narrative from our work in a Bosnian refugee camp in Slovenia in 1994, and went on to examine the role of found objects and the adaptation of our art therapy studios in seemingly unlikely and often unstable contexts. By using found objects and re-visioning our studios, we allow the opportunity to open up to the multiple layers of an experience without things falling apart. It seems that both the studio and the object have the capacity to provide a shelter and make a place for representation and presence, between the internal and external, inside-out and outside-in.

Notes
1.   Delivered through "On Site Arts" with the Traveller and Gypsy communities in the London Olympic area, 2004–2009.

References
Allen, P.B. (1995) "Coyote comes in from the cold: The evolution of the open studio concept." *Art Therapy: Journal of the American Art Therapy Association 12*, 3, 161–166.

Bachelard, G. (1994 [1958]) *The Poetics of Space*. Boston, MA: Beacon Press.

Berman, H. (2005) "Transforming objects in South Africa." In D. Kalmanowitz and B. Lloyd (eds) *Art Therapy and Political Violence: With Art, Without Illusion*. London and New York: Routledge.

Bollas, C. (1987) *The Shadow of the Object*, New York: Columbia University Press.

Brooker, J. (2010) "Found objects in art therapy." *International Journal of Art Therapy: Formerly Inscape 15*, 1, 25–35.

Brooker, J. (2011) "The Therapeutic Use of Found Objects." In N. Zhvitiashvili (ed.) *Innovations in Art Therapy Practice: Britain–Russia*. St. Petersburg: Russian State Museum.

Davis, J. (1999) "Report: Environmental art therapy – metaphors in the field." *Arts in Psychotherapy 26*, 1, 45–49.

Digby, S. (2006) "The casket of magic: Home and identity from salvaged objects." *Home Cultures 3*, 169–190.

Fairbairn, W. (1938) "The ultimate basis of aesthetic experience." *British Journal of Psychology XXIX*, 167–181.

Freud, S. and Breuer, J. (1974) *Studies on Hysteria*. London: Penguin.

Foucault, M. (1986) "Of other spaces." *Diacritics 16*, 1, 22–27 (based on a lecture delivered by Foucault in March 1967).

Henley, D. (1995) "A consideration of the studio as therapeutic intervention." *Art Therapy 12*, 3, 188–190.

Herman, J. (1992) *Trauma and Recovery: From Domestic Abuse to Political Terror*. London: Basic Books.

Hiller, S. (2000) *After the Freud Museum*, 2nd edn. London: Book Works.

Iverson, M. (2004) "Readymade, found object, photograph." *Art Journal 6*, 2, 44–57.

Kalmanowitz, D. and Lloyd, B. (1997) *The Portable Studio: Art Therapy and Political Conflict: Initiatives in the Former Yugoslavia and KwaZulu-Natal, South Africa.* London: Health Education Authority.

Kalmanowitz, D. and Lloyd, B. (1999) "Fragments of art at work: Art therapy in the former Yugoslavia." *Arts in Psychotherapy (special issue) 26*, 1, 15–25.

Kalmanowitz, D. and Lloyd, B. (2005) *Art Therapy and Political Violence: With Art, Without Illusion.* London and New York: Routledge.

Kramer, E. (1994) "How will the profession of art therapy change in the next 25 years? Responses by past award winners: We cannot look into the future without considering the past and the present." *Art Therapy: Journal of the American Art Therapy Association 11*, 2, 91–92.

Levine, S. (2009) *Trauma, Tragedy, Therapy: The Arts and Human Suffering.* London and Philadelphia, PA: Jessica Kingsley Publishers,

McNiff, S. (1995) "Keeping the studio." *Art Therapy: Journal of the American Art Therapy Association 12*, 3, 179–183.

Mehta, R. and Belk, R.W. (1991) "Artifacts, identity and transition: Favorite possessions of Indians and Indian immigrants to the United States." *Journal of Consumer Research 17*, 398–411.

Moon, C.H. (2002) *Studio Art Therapy: Cultivating the Artist Identity in the Art Therapist.* London: Jessica Kingsley Publishers.

Moon, C.H. (ed.) (2010) *Materials and Media in Art Therapy: Critical Understandings of Diverse Artistic Vocabularies.* London: Routledge.

Morris, D. (1994) *The Human Animal.* New York: Crown Publishing.

Saunders, N. (2003) *Trench Art: Materialities and Memories of War.* Oxford: Berg. Available at www.tate.org.uk, Glossary, Installation Art, accessed December 2009.

Van der Kolk, B.A (1987) *Psychological Trauma.* Washington, DC: American Psychiatric Press.

Watzlawick, P., Weakland, J.H. and Fisch, R. (1974) *Change: Principles of Problem Formation and Problem Resolution.* New York and London: W.W. Norton.

Westgeest, H. (ed.) (2009) *Take Place: Photography and Place from Multiple Perspectives.* Amsterdam: Antennae Valiz.

Yule, W. (ed.) (2003) *Post-Traumatic Stress Disorders: Concepts and Therapy.* New York: John Wiley and Sons.

Yeh, A. (1997) "Exploring the lost and found: The use of found objects in art therapy." Unpublished master's thesis, University of Chicago, Illinois, quoted in Harriet Wadeson (2000) *Art Therapy Practice: Innovative Approaches with Diverse Populations.* New York: John Wiley and Sons.

Zijlmans, K. (2009) "Place, Site and Memory in Contemporary Works of Art." In H. Westgeest (ed.) (2009) *Take Place: Photography and Place from Multiple Perspectives.* Amsterdam: Antennae Valiz.

8

From Private Pain Toward Public Speech

Poetry Therapy with Iraqi Survivors of Torture and War

Shanee Stepakoff, Samer Hussein, Mariam
Al-Salahat, Insherah Musa, Moath Asfoor,
Eman Al-Houdali, and Maysa Al-Hmouz

INTRODUCTION: THE CLINICAL SETTING AS A SITE FOR REGAINING WORDS AND RECLAIMING VOICE

For many victims of ethnopolitical violence, the clinical setting serves as a context for finding words to narrate experiences that seem indescribable and unsayable (Rogers 2006; Van der Merwe and Gobodo-Madikizela 2008). From our clinical work we have developed the view that in the process of regaining words and reclaiming the capacity to give voice to the experience of violation, "victims" gradually become "survivors." Further, consistent with Herman's (1992) assertion, we have observed that for a sizeable portion of survivors, an important component of recovery is the decision to participate in constructive action that contributes to the wider community.

Among the various forms of action that might be considered, we have found that many survivors feel a desire to share their experiences in some type of public forum. Options for public expression include talking with journalists, testifying in post-conflict tribunals and truth commissions, participation in speak-outs and protests, visual arts exhibits, performances of music/drama/dance, and so forth. Likewise, many psychotherapists working in contexts of torture and war feel a sense of moral responsibility to contribute to the promotion of accountability for past violations of human rights, and the prevention of future ones.

Our belief is that as long as the step to speak in the public domain is freely chosen, the forms of self-expression that occur in psychotherapy and those that occur in public venues are not necessarily at odds with each other. In fact, if sufficient psychological support is provided, the benefits of private and public expression can be mutually reinforcing. Public recognition of the reality and impact of experiences of violation can contribute to personal healing; conversely, as individuals achieve a greater sense of wholeness and psychological health, they may feel a deepening desire to draw on their experiences in order to make a difference in the society at large.

Thus, the psychological repair and reclamation of the capacity for speech that occur initially in a protected, clinical setting (e.g. a psychotherapeutic relationship or a professionally facilitated group) can provide a foundation for later truth-telling in public venues. In this chapter we present a variety of specific methods, derived from poetry therapy, by which we promoted self-expression among Iraqi survivors of torture and war trauma who had taken refuge in Jordan. All of the survivors cited in the present chapter were clients in a treatment clinic. The clinic was established and directed by the Center for Victims of Torture (CVT), a non-governmental organization (NGO) established to provide individual, family, and group therapy for survivors of war-related trauma and/or politically motivated torture.

The overall treatment model was based on a combination of psychodynamic, cognitive-behavioral, humanistic, and trauma-focused therapies (Stepakoff et al. 2006, 2010). We integrated these approaches with methods derived from poetry therapy. We found such methods to be particularly salient for our population. More specifically, most torture survivors do not readily find words to describe their experiences and emotions, particularly not in the early stages of recovery. Further, their efforts to describe their ordeal are seldom listened to respectfully and sensitively by others. In addition, larger socio-cultural and political forces discourage – and even actively suppress – the verbal narration of experiences of violation.

This long-term silence about their experiences often leads survivors to feel isolated, burdened, and overwhelmed. One view of clinical work is that "what is mentionable is manageable, what is not mentionable is not manageable" (Stepakoff et al. 2006). That is, finding the words to describe one's experience in the context of a safe, caring relationship usually brings about feelings of comfort, relief, connection (with oneself as well as with another person or persons), and hope.

Although traditional psychotherapy, which indeed in its early days was known as "the talking cure," usually relies on some amount of verbal expression, poetry therapy places a greater emphasis on the significance of words and voice than do mainstream approaches or other creative arts modalities. Moreover, poetry therapy methods allow for a form of truth-telling that can readily be transmitted in the public domain. Namely, in comparison to works of music, dance, drama, or visual art, and in contrast to purely oral expression, poems and other written works are far easier to preserve, reproduce, and circulate.

CENTER FOR VICTIMS OF TORTURE, JORDAN: CLINICAL TREATMENT AND COUNSELOR TRAINING

CVT's Jordan program comprises both direct clinical care in individual, group, and family modalities, systematic training, and live, on-site clinical supervision of the local psychosocial counselors by experienced expatriate psychologists. Along with training and clinical supervision, the expatriate psychologists also work alongside the local counselors as co-therapists for individual and family therapy clients and as co-facilitators of ten-session counseling groups.

The clients were Iraqi survivors of torture and war trauma who had fled Iraq for refuge in Jordan. The first author, who is both a licensed clinical psychologist and a registered poetry therapist, provided specialized training, supervision, and co-therapy to support interested CVT counselors – including the co-authors of this chapter – in the conceptualization and implementation of poetry therapy approaches, and in the integration of poetry therapy with other clinical methods.

From February 2009 to February 2010 the first author together with the co-authors – who were her trainees, co-therapists, and clinical supervisees – developed ways of incorporating poetry therapy methods and techniques in individual, family, and group counseling for Iraqi refugees. Clients embraced these approaches, and derived important psychological benefits from the use of preexisting literature and from the expressive writing activities. Counselors, too, enthusiastically embraced the therapeutic utilization of poetry and expressive writing.

RECEPTIVE AND EXPRESSIVE APPROACHES

Receptive methods of poetry therapy are those that rely on the utilization of preexisting material (Mazza 1999). This usually refers to poems that have been published in collections, anthologies, literary journals, and so forth; it can also refer to songs. The poems or songs to be used in clinical work with survivors do not have to specifically mention torture or war; in fact, most do not. Rather, they capture particular aspects of the experience of suffering, loss, and grief.

There are a wide variety of receptive techniques. The major division, however, is between techniques in which the client selects the preexisting material and those in which the counselor selects the material. Stepakoff (2009) has suggested the terms "client-directed" or "client-initiated" to indicate the former category.

Receptive methods of poetry therapy are usually combined with expressive methods. The latter are sometimes referred to as "expressive writing" (Lepore and Smyth 2002; Mazza 1999) or "poem-making" (Fox 1997), and can be understood as the process whereby survivors engage in their own, original writing. This can take various forms: the most common are journaling, letter-writing, and the creation of poems. It can also include oral and improvisational poem-making (Spring 2003; Stepakoff and Marzelli 2007).

Example of a receptive method: Client-initiated selection of preexisting poem

In a counseling group for men there was a client, "Burhan," whose brother had been brutally murdered in an act of ethnopolitical violence. Burhan had rigid psychological defenses against discussing his emotions about his brother's death, even during sessions when other group members shared about their losses with the group. During one session, about midway through the ten-session cycle, though Burhan still had great difficulty talking about his feelings directly, he shared with the group the following passage from a poem by Al Khansa, a renowned seventh century Arab female poet whose brother had been killed in war in the year 615 A.D. Burhan had committed the poem to memory, and as he read it aloud, it became clear to the counselors and participants that by sharing the poem, Burhan was able to express his own feelings more fully and accurately than he had been able to do on his own:

> *Every sunrise reminds me of my brother, Sakhar*
> *And I continue remembering him until the sun descends*
> *And if it were not for the presence, all around me, of so many other people*
> *who are also mourning their brothers*
> *I would kill myself.*

Hearing this preexisting poem led to a fruitful group discussion of the experience of grief, and of the ways that forming connections with others who are also grieving, and thereby feeling less alone in one's sorrow, somehow made the anguish more bearable. Indeed, this "kinship of grief" (Stepakoff 2009) is a key component of what we seek to achieve in counseling groups for participants who are struggling to cope with traumatic bereavement.

Combining receptive and expressive methods: Example of client selection of preexisting poem followed by expressive writing in response to the poem

In the previous example, the client spontaneously thought of the preexisting poem and opted to share it. Another way of working with a preexisting poem is to specifically ask clients to bring in a poem that they find meaningful or moving. We used this approach in a group of men.

In response to our invitation, one of the clients brought in the following poem by an Iraqi poet:

Reproach

I came to you carrying in my soul
our shared story, intimate and long,
which has been slaughtered.

I came with a tear of longing on my cheek,
with wounded dreams,
and the wish to blame you.

And the arteries of my heart – after you have abandoned me – tighten and release like a swing
as a result of my yearning.

Searching: for whom? and on which door must I knock?
In all the houses of Baghdad, each person is
wrapped up in his or her own calamities.

After briefly reading the poem ourselves, as professionals, to ensure it was appropriate for the group, we suggested that the client read the poem aloud in the session. We were silent for some moments, to allow time for the poem to have an emotional impact on the group members. We then invited them to choose a line from the poem, copy that line onto a fresh sheet of paper, and write some of their own thoughts and feelings in response to their chosen line.

Below are some examples of the clients' written responses, accompanied by the line or phrase they selected:

"Coman"

Phrase selected: "And the arteries of my heart tighten and release like a swing as a result of my yearning."

Written response: This reminds me of my children who are away from me, my children and loved ones and friends who are upset about our departure [from Iraq]...and also, the plight of living as refugees, as foreigners in another country.

"Gadil"

Phrase selected: "With a tear of longing on my cheek, with wounded dreams, and the wish to blame you."

Written response: These words make me think of my ordeal and the time I am passing through like a drowning person..., afloat...in a sea..., not knowing my destiny, so too do I walk toward an unknown fate and I can do nothing about this. I dream about the future, and about the past which my family and I shared, and I imagine a tear falling slowly down my cheek, but it is a useless tear, just as the dreams I dream are useless, because something precious has been broken and smashed.

Therapist-selected poems

Although survivors are quite adept at choosing poems that are meaningful to them and that they feel capture important aspects of their experiences and emotions, there are many situations in which the facilitator or therapist may be better equipped to select poems than are the survivors. In these situations, the facilitator or therapist uses a preexisting poem as a catalyst to increase clients' willingness to talk about their own experiences and concerns. Registered poetry therapists, who have undergone a rigorous process of study, practice, and credentialing, are specially trained to identify poems that are likely to serve as safe and effective springboards for individual and group exploration.

Facilitated or therapist-guided receptive approaches (Stepakoff 2009) refer to situations in which the therapist or group facilitator carefully chooses a poem that he or she feels – based on his or her own life, experiences with other individuals or groups, input from other clinicians, and/or intuition – will help survivors focus on and grapple with particular aspects of their experience. In these approaches, the facilitator/therapist supports the client/group in using the preexisting poem as a springboard for deepening the clients' dialogue and exploration of a designated theme. This method is described in detail in the classic text *Biblio/Poetry Therapy: The Interactive Process* (Hynes and Hynes-Berry 1994).

Poems are selected with the intent of achieving four main therapeutic goals:

1. To describe, in a fresh and creative manner, common aspects of the experience of trauma and violation.

2. To model exceptionally honest and brave self-expression, thereby freeing the clients to express themselves more frankly and fully.

3. To give external form to internal, difficult-to-articulate emotions and perceptions, thereby helping clients contain their psychological pain.

4. To serve as objects of aesthetic beauty, thereby instilling in clients renewed feelings of vitality and hope.

Also, the poems chosen by the counselors or group facilitators are used to stimulate a process of expressive writing in the participants.

Combining receptive and expressive methods: Example of expressive writing in response to therapist-selected preexisting poem

During a time that we were searching for a poem or proverb to use in one of our counseling groups for elderly men, a middle-aged man in individual treatment spontaneously quoted the following rhyming couplet; we decided to use it in the group because we felt that it would have strong resonances for the clients:

> Not all that a person desires does he or she obtain:
> The winds blow without regard for the wishes of the ships.

(Al Mutanabbi, 915–965)

We typed these lines (in Arabic) on a sheet of paper, and distributed it to each of the group members. The Iraqi facilitator (second author) read the poem aloud three times, in order to enhance its impact. Clients were then invited to respond by "free-writing." "Free-writing" is a technique in which clients are asked to write non-stop for a specified number of minutes, without thinking, without censoring themselves and without lifting their pens from the page.

Below are two examples of clients' free-writing from this session:

> *The future was mine and now I am set in oblivion. I do not know where my future lies nor that of my family, and I have a sense of fear, of being terrified and unstable and without safety… My thoughts have become hazy and I have no clue what to do. ("Jalen")*

> *This proverb reminds me of the current situation we live in, where fate plays the larger role in our lives: fate is similar to the strong wind that wreaks havoc and pushes all boats off their course. Despite the ship's plan to reach a shore that had been intended by the captain, the winds lead it to deviate from its course to another shore, which may be a safe shore that one may stay on for a lengthy period, but it may also turn out to be a barren island without water or vegetation and you will be forced to stay there and wait for a glimpse of hope by the passing of other ships or a rescue boat. The proverb makes me think of the plans for the future that we used to imagine, plans for a happy and pleasant life for the whole family, but this is not what has occurred. ("Laith")*

We were struck by the strong responses engendered by this couplet-poem. We have continued to use this proverb and this method in several other groups, with consistently positive psychological effects. We believe that the utilization of a carefully selected preexisting poem stimulates in clients a deep desire to give voice to their own truths.

Expressive approaches

As indicated in the examples above, receptive methods of poetry therapy can be used to stimulate oral or written self-expression. Expressive methods encompass the writing of poems by individuals as well as collaborative writing by dyads, families, groups, or communities (e.g. in which each person contributes a line or phrase). The theoretical foundations of expressive methods include the concepts of catharsis and externalization, that is, the human need to symbolize or represent, via external form, emotions and images that have been purely internal. As with receptive methods, expressive approaches can be self-directed or professionally facilitated.

An example of self-directed expressive writing occurred in an Iraqi family with whom we worked, in which the mother, who had survived a severe episode of politically motivated torture, was accepted for resettlement in a Western country, while her teenage daughter was forced to remain behind as a refugee in Jordan for over a year. "Cantara" (the mother), a sensitive woman with a natural literary inclination, began to regularly compose brief poems in which she expressed her love for her daughter and her hope for their eventual reunification, utilizing text messaging on a cellular phone. It was clear that composing and sending these poems helped Cantara to cope with the painful feelings resulting from her having had to leave her daughter in refuge in Jordan. The daughter seemed to gain strength from reading these message-poems, and often shared them with the therapist during her individual counseling sessions.

In contrast to this kind of spontaneous, self-directed poetic expression, "facilitated" or "guided" expressive methods take place in the context of a formal therapeutic relationship (Stepakoff 2009). The particular clinical approach may vary, as long as writing and other expressive verbal techniques are employed. Such techniques have been used effectively in mutual support groups, cognitive-behavioral therapy and psychoanalysis, but are most closely associated with the creative arts therapies, which, indeed, are also known as the "expressive therapies." In many instances, intermodal approaches are utilized, in which survivors combine verbal and non-verbal techniques (Levine and Levine 1999; Rogers 1993).

In therapeutic work with survivors of torture and war trauma the goals of expressive writing essentially parallel those for the receptive approach: reducing isolation, encouraging free expression, giving form to painful emotions, and fostering hope. The writing assignments have varying degrees of structure and guidance. It is common to integrate expressive writing with the utilization of preexisting poems. More specifically, after devoting a portion of the session to dialogically exploring participants' responses to a preexisting poem, they are given a writing exercise, after which they are provided with an opportunity to share what they have written. A common exercise is to ask the group members to choose a subjectively meaningful word, phrase, or line from the preexisting poem and to use that as a starting point for their own writing, that is, as the title or first line of a new poem. This is, essentially, the method used in the above-mentioned examples of clients' responses to the proverb by Al Mutanabbi.

Example of an expressive method: Client-generated poems as a springboard for group exploration of areas of clinical concern

Below is an example of a poem written by "Kalila," a client in a women's counseling group. The client generated this poem during a session in which the clients had been invited to compose poems on themes that had been emerging in the counseling group over the course of the preceding sessions:

To The Lovely Baghdad (excerpt)

You will be high as a tree.
You will be who you are with all your great history.
You are the land of Harun al-Rashid...
Your light will continue to shine and will not be extinguished
because you are a land of education and science...
Your name will stay present in all times
And you will be the love of all Iraqis.

After Kalila read her poem aloud, the other group members shared the memories and feelings that the poem evoked in them. This led to a rich discussion about the deep and passionate ties that many Iraqi refugees feel for their homeland, and, concomitantly, the feelings of sorrow and longing they must contend with daily as refugees in Jordan.

Example of an expressive method: Therapist pre-structuralization as a means for supporting clients in writing poems

Another common method of promoting the creation of poems is to provide group members with a page that contains a preliminary structure to guide their expressive writing. Usually, this consists of word-stems or sentence completions, which leave a substantial area blank so that the clients can fill in their own words. We utilized this approach successfully in several groups.

The preliminary structure should be created with a theoretical rationale and/or a specific therapeutic goal in mind. In groups for Iraqi survivors of torture and war, we found it helpful to find ways of supporting clients in reflecting on the psychological impact of their victimization. This view was rooted in the idea that traumatic experiences change people, and that one component of recovery is the ability to constellate a new sense of self that encompasses the reality of the trauma but is not completely dominated by it.

As a first step in such a process, we felt it would be useful for clients to be able to bear the painful consideration and verbalization of the differences between who they are today and who they were before they were subjected to torture. Thus, we listed a sequence of four couplets on a sheet of paper, each with the phrase "I used to" [blank] (first line) "but now" [blank] (second line). The provision of this type of preliminary structure can serve to create a sense of containment, while at the same time allowing for honest exploration and self-expression. Further, honest self-disclosure on the part of clients about the psychological impact of torture and war trauma is a prerequisite for supporting clients in finding ways to attenuate some of the more difficult components of that impact.

Below is an example of a poem created by a client when we used this method in a counseling group for Iraqi women.

"Dirran"

I used to go out in the street to go anywhere without thinking about what time it was

but now I have to think about each hour and each minute, and about whether it's a good time to go out or not.

I used not to think about what would happen to my children during the school-day,

but now I'm afraid for them – I worry about them from the time they go to school until the time they return.

I used not to think so much and not to be ill,
but now I am ill in my body and mind.
I used to be a calm person,
but now I lose my temper easily.
I used to be happy on every occasion, even with the simplest things,
but now I feel a sadness inside, even when I'm happy.
I used to be open and self-confident, talking with my family and friends
but now I can't be that way anymore, because I don't know the people I'm talking with
or how much of what I'm saying they will understand.

As this method worked well in the women's group, we subsequently utilized it in a group for elderly men, and found that it was similarly effective with that population:

"Jala" The Life I'm Passing Today (excerpt)

Before the war, I was close to my relatives and visited them often
But now I'm far away from them, and I wish that they were nearer.
I used to go each morning to my job.
But now I don't work, I just sit at home…
I used to have warm, caring contact with my neighbors
But now I am in a country where I don't have friends.
I used to not think much about the present turning into the future.
But now a hundred times a day I wish the day would end.

Example of an expressive method: Therapeutic letter-writing

Letter-writing is another expressive technique that can be systematically incorporated into therapy sessions (Vance 1998). Usually, the counselors give the client(s) a suggestion regarding to whom the letter should be directed and/or what issues it should explore. In counseling groups for Iraqi survivors of ethnopolitical violence, we used letter-writing in a variety of ways, particularly as a tool for working with traumatic grief. It is important that clients not only write a letter in which they express their own thoughts and feelings, but also that they imagine how the person receiving the letter would reply.

There appears to be an archetypal healing function in the psyche that is activated during the imagined reply. More specifically, the responses are almost always reparative and life-affirming. Typical messages include remarks such as "Take good care of the children," "I want you to be happy," "I forgive you," "I'm sorry," "I am not with you physically but I remain with you spiritually," and so forth. These reply letters, and their healing messages, are in some ways similar to the kinds of replies that occur when a client switches chair in the Gestalt/psychodrama technique known as "the empty chair."

Below is an example of a letter that a client wrote to her deceased father, who had been tortured and killed in Iraq. After composing the letter and the imagined reply, the client read both letters aloud in the sixth session of a women's counseling group:

Dearest Father:

How I miss you, I have wished that you were by my side, but fate hastened your demise. I have gone through many difficult and frightening days in my life: they kidnapped me, kidnapped my son, and he is still missing. How much I am in need of you, need to hear your voice and speak with you. I have been through difficult times, but your death has been the most difficult of all. May God have mercy on you and reserve a place for you in paradise.

"Myiesha"

IMAGINED REPLY LETTER FROM CLIENT'S FATHER

My Dearest Daughter:

Although my body is not near yours, my soul is with you wherever you go.
I know what you are going through; try to be patient.
I know how much you need me. May Allah help you.
Take care of yourself and your children and I will be satisfied and at peace.

Father

A WAR-TRAUMATIZED CHILD'S LETTER TO HIMSELF

We also used letter-writing in counseling groups for child survivors of torture and war trauma. In one such group, the children were invited to use the letter-writing as an opportunity to address anyone to whom they had something to express. Some of the children chose to write to their perpetrator, articulating in the letters their feelings of anger and betrayal. Others chose to write to their lost loved ones, giving voice to their feelings of grief and longing. In one group, a particularly creative and precocious 12-year-old boy decided to write the letter to himself:

Dear "Talib,"

You've lost everyone who you like, toys, love, freedom, and friends, you've lost the person who was the most beloved and important to you. You have been beaten, and cursed, and you've been made to feel ashamed...You've been displaced, you had to leave your country, and your heart was very close to your country... I wish for you a pleasant life, and to overcome all the obstacles and problems, and for you to find someone who can help you to solve those problems... I wish for you new friends, like the friends you have found in this group. I wish you a happy life, and I wish peace and renewal for your country, and I wish you success in your hobbies. Thank you my secret friend, I know that you live in my heart.

Example of an expressive method: Collaborative poem-making

Another expressive technique, used in group treatment modalities, is referred to as "collaborative poem-making." This technique can be helpful at various stages of a group's existence, but is particularly empowering at the end of a group cycle. It is a technique that is widely used in poetry therapy, and empirical research has indicated that it enhances group cohesiveness (Golden 1994; Mazza 1999).

In this technique each member of the group is first asked to write about his or her own feelings and thoughts. Then, each member looks over what s/he has written, and selects a line or phrase that is particularly meaningful to him or her. Next, one by one, according to readiness, each person contributes his or her line or phrase, such that one "group poem" emerges.

The group poem weaves the participants' diverse feelings into one coherent whole, and serves both as a container in which the full range of feelings can be "held," and as a transitional object that participants can keep with them after the group has ended. As with any form of creative expression, there is usually a sense of satisfaction and wonder at having been able to successfully transform inner truth into outward form.

We used this technique in the final session of a ten-session counseling group for Iraqi men. The resultant poem is provided below. Most of the line-breaks, as well as each place where there is a double space, indicate a different client's contributions. The title was generated by all of the clients together after a few minutes of discussion.

For the Sake of Life

The future –
> *but I do not know where the future is.*

I still have the hope of building a better future for my family and myself
to make up for the days and years we've missed out on and to forget the past

I wish to sit with my family and children, I wish to see them and hear their
news in a place far from violence, terrorism, and bodily needs

A safe shore where I feel at peace and out of harm's way
> *where I can think of a bright future*

a future with happiness, security, and love
Human capabilities are limitless
> *if the will is strong.*

CONCLUSIONS: FROM PRIVATE PAIN TOWARD PUBLIC SPEECH

In the aftermath of large-scale, ethnopolitical trauma, recovery entails not only the healing of the individual psyche but also repair of the individual's relationship to the larger society. The latter goal usually requires public recognition of the reality of the human rights violations and the suffering that resulted from these violations. Such recognition can only occur if a subset of survivors are willing and able to share their stories in public domains. Poetry therapy methods can contribute substantially to this process by helping survivors regain the words to describe experiences that have felt indescribable, and in developing the psychological capacity to bear and give voice to private pain. We believe that in the act of permitting their writing to be published in the present volume, the survivors with whom we worked have taken an important step toward enhancing public awareness of the realities of suffering and resilience among Iraqis who have been forced to seek refuge in other lands.

AUTHORS' NOTE

The first author would like to dedicate this chapter to the memory of her cherished mentor, Dr. Kenneth Paul Gorelick (1942–2009), who instilled in her an appreciation for the transformative power of poetry, and who, by his kindness, supportiveness, and generosity of spirit, gave her both the desire and the confidence to share this power with others.

Major portions of this chapter were presented by the first author as part of an invited lecture arranged and hosted by the Center for Victims of Torture, Amman, Jordan, on August 6, 2009, under the title "The utilization of poems, stories, proverbs, and expressive writing in the psychotherapeutic treatment of Iraqi survivors of torture and war trauma," for staff of NGOs providing psychosocial care for Iraqi refugees in Jordan.

Contributions to this chapter by the fourth, fifth, sixth, and seventh authors were approximately equal. Thus, the order of authorship among the fourth through seventh authors was randomly generated.

The authors would like to acknowledge CVT's staff at headquarters in Minneapolis, MN, as well as in Jordan, for supporting the development of innovative treatment approaches and for enriching our thinking about ways to serve and empower survivors of torture. Special acknowledgment is due to the Iraqi refugee clients who not only permitted but urged us to publish their writings so that the experiences and feelings of Iraqi survivors of torture and war would be more fully understood.

Notes

All client writings contained in this chapter have been used with the permission of the clients who produced them. The letter by the 12-year-old boy was used both with his permission and that of his parents.

Throughout this chapter, all client and clients' relatives' names have been replaced with pseudonyms. The pseudonyms were randomly drawn from a list of male and female Arabic names. Any connection between the pseudonyms used here and actual individuals from Iraq, Jordan, or elsewhere in the Arab world is purely coincidental.

Harun al-Rashid (763–809), referred to in the poem by "Kalila" that appears on p.137, was the fifth caliph of the Abbasid Dynasty. Under his reign and that of his son, al-Mamun, the Abbasid empire reached its apogee. During his reign Baghdad stood as a rival to Byzantium in both splendor and power. Harun was a munificent patron of the arts and his court became a center of learning and culture (Nissen and Heine 2009).

Arabic-to-English translations of the preexisting poems and client writings used in this chapter were the product of shared efforts among the seven authors, with additional input provided by Dr. Yousef Al-Ajarma, except for the poem entitled "Reproach," which was jointly translated by Marwan Al-Rawi, Shanee Stepakoff, and Samer Hussein.

References

Fox, J. (1997) *Poetic Medicine: The Healing Art of Poem-making.* New York: Tarcher/Putnam.

Golden, K.M. (1994) "The effect of collaborative writing on cohesion in poetry therapy groups." Doctoral dissertation, American University, 1994. *Dissertation Abstracts International, 56,* 867–968A.

Herman, J. (1992) *Trauma and Recovery: The Aftermath of Violence: From Domestic Abuse to Political Terror.* New York: Basic Books.

Hynes, A. and Hynes-Berry, M. (1994) *Biblio/Poetry Therapy: The Interactive Process.* St. Cloud, MN: North Star Press.

Lepore, S. and Smyth, J. (2002) *The Writing Cure: How Expressive Writing Promotes Health and Emotional Well-being.* Washington, DC: American Psychological Association.

Levine, S. and Levine, E. (1999) *Foundations of Expressive Arts Therapy: Theoretical and Clinical Perspectives.* London: Jessica Kingsley Publishers.

Mazza, N. (1999) *Poetry Therapy: Interface of the Arts and Psychology.* Boca Raton, FL: CRC Press.

Nissen, H.J. and Heine, P. (2009) *From Mesopotamia to Iraq: A Concise History.* Chicago, IL: University of Chicago Press.

Rogers, A. (2006) *The Unsayable: The Hidden Language of Trauma.* New York: Random House.

Rogers, N. (1993) *The Creative Connection: Expressive Arts as Healing.* Palo Alto, CA: Science and Behavior Books.

Spring, J. (2003) "Therapeutic soulspeak: The use of ancient oral poetry forms in therapy." *Journal of Poetry Therapy 16,* 4, 199–216.

Stepakoff, S. (2009) "From destruction to creation, from silence to speech: Poetry therapy principles and practices for working with suicide grief." *The Arts in Psychotherapy (Special Issue on Creative Arts Therapies in the Treatment of Trauma) 36,* 2, 105–113.

Stepakoff, S. and Marzelli, C. (2007) "Oral poem-making techniques for use in workshops with Sierra Leonean victims of war atrocities." Unpublished manuscript.

Stepakoff, S., Bermudez, K., Beckman, A. and Nielsen, L. (eds) (2010) *Group Counseling for Survivors of Torture and War Trauma in Refugee Camps and Post-Conflict Communities, Facilitated by Paraprofessional Psychosocial Agents Under the Supervision of On-Site Professional Clinicians: A Manual Based on the First Decade of CVT's Africa Programs.* Minneapolis, MN: Center for Victims of Torture.

Stepakoff, S., Hubbard, J., Katoh, M., Falk, E., Mikulu, J., Nkhoma, P. and Omagwa, Y. (2006) "Trauma healing in refugee camps in Guinea: A psychosocial program for Liberian and Sierra Leonean survivors of torture and war." *American Psychologist 1*, 8, 921–932.

Vance, T. (1998) *Letters Home: How Writing Can Change Your Life.* New York: Pantheon.

Van der Merwe, C. and Gobodo-Madikizela, P. (2008) *Narrating Our Healing: Perspectives on Working through Trauma.* Newcastle, UK: Cambridge Scholars Publishing.

PART III
Projects

9

The Choreography of Absence

(In)habiting the Imagination after War

Carrie MacLeod

Haw di bata de bit – na so di dans de go.
As the drum beats, so the dance goes
(Krio Proverb)

In the northern hills of Koinadugu District in Sierra Leone, West Africa, the remote community of Kabala is rewriting a narrative that promises an alternative point of view to dominant, conflict-laden headlines. Certain stories refuse to be overshadowed by subtexts of recrimination and cross-border insurgencies. New scripts are rising up from the war-torn legacies that have marked this region, and the youth are fueling the creative fire for this momentum. Their crude proximity to over a decade of violence makes this burgeoning vision even more poignant, as the war is often referenced as a crisis of youth (Richards 1995). What is lost between the lines is how "poverty and marginalization in Sierra Leone have not only fostered violent rebellion but also great resourcefulness, whether in respect of livelihood opportunities, political ideas, or associational life" (Fanthorpe and Maconachie 2010, p.272). On a third visit to Sierra Leone since the signing of the Lome peace accord in 1999, my previous assumptions around peacebuilding and reconciliation are realigned by a youthful resilience and an irrepressible imaginative force.

Over the past ten years, while working with Sierra Leone communities both in Canada and West Africa, I have engaged with artists who have been upstaging conventional leaders as they reshape oppressive political, social, and economic systems. Their capacity for creative ingenuity comes from their repeated need to respond in the face of unknown circumstances. My relationship with Sierra Leone performing artists has taken the shape of a call and response song, with opportunities to

147

work with those who have been caught in the crossfire and with African youth who crossed borderlands and cultural boundaries to make a new home in Canada. More than a decade of violence in Sierra Leone has created unexpected chasms in local and global communities. The post-accord period has left unresolved testimonies dangling in political arenas and social forums. Amidst the mayhem of international peacebuilding agendas, artists are positioning themselves on the frontlines of these dialogues. They are courageously exposing key symbolic values that often remain hidden amidst prescriptive "solutions" for pre-war nostalgia and post-war trauma.

It is impossible to calculate the true toll of war on any generation, as perpetual upheaval is difficult to decode through any rational explanation. Even rituals like birthdays and funerals become lost amidst the grinding urgencies of survival. Extreme violence reverses the chronological rhythms of daily life. How can one possibly make "sense" of an imposed reality when primary senses have been literally amputated? The youth in Sierra Leone unabashedly proclaim that everything becomes utterly unrecognizable after war. Home, in every sense, is nowhere to be found. The same Motherland is not there waiting to receive just anyone with open arms. Longings and be-longings are transported into waiting rooms, and familiar homelands become foreign territory. Yet despite outer discord, the younger generation yearns to reshape visions of transitional justice at the center of loss and longing. They must take on the difficult task of re-inhabiting spaces where layers of betrayal have taken place. The medium of performance can help make sense of a legacy of turmoil, as it offers an intimate dwelling place in a wider culture of displacement. This medium has the potential to raise the general public's awareness of the complexity surrounding conflicts within communities and nations as a whole (Goldberg 1996). To dwell is to live fully with all of the senses in relationship with others, and the arts attend to this basic human need even in the center of displacement. Shared sites of imagination mark what is inherently known, but cannot be named.

STAGING COMMON GROUND IN SIERRA LEONE

Almost ten years after the ceasefire, narratives that live in the red African soil pull me back to engage in community art-making once again. In response to an invitation to create performances with emerging young leaders in northern Sierra Leone, I arrive to find a fury of contrasting views on peace and reconciliation. There is overt dissension around what really constitutes a "fair" justice system when so many other systems of livelihood have fallen apart. In the hopes of remaining open and in a place of inquiry, I pose a question to the student body that has circled around in my mind for the past five years: *How can peace be a creative act?*" Not a moment lapses before waves of eager voices fill the room with a succession of ideas. The excitement bounces off the concrete school walls, and I lean forward to decipher the words that continue to resonate. "*Let's create theatrical plays on forgiveness, a giant puppet show on the rights for education, songs that promote anti-corruption in elections, a large cultural dance for peace...*" There is uproar in this process as multiple priorities collide. In the midst of this lively negotiation, their enthusiasm does not dwindle or seep out of the crumbling school walls for one second. Ambivalence and resignation are not welcome here and could never survive amidst the fervor that lives in this untapped potential. The links between youth and post-accord peacebuilding are nowhere more apparent than in Sierra Leone (Wessells and Davidson 2006), and this becomes palpable as compelling visions for a peace festival begin to take shape. Unsettled notions of reconciliation become a catalyst for this exchange, as underlying social and cultural issues begin to resurface without apology. This becomes prime source material for plotting out site-specific performances that will encircle a multi-ethnic festival.

Amid the frenzied brainstorming and eruption of ideas, there is consensus that the theme for the festival will be *Ensembles of Peace: A Celebration of Culture in Sierra Leone.* We decide to explore why the lyrical energy around the notion of "celebration" ignites such a strong response. Before the adjournment of this first gathering, concrete plans are in place to produce an inter-ethnic festival that combines cultural art forms, traditional practices, and expressive arts. By weaving together these three modes, the participants hope to offer a multi-faceted social commentary for a complex peace process. The very next day, their creative ideas translate into a voluntary daily regime of rehearsals and peer-directed filming. The youth insist on documenting their "Peace Ensembles" through the medium of film, with the intention of showcasing their work to extended relatives and families who left Sierra Leone during the war. In Krio the concept of "fambul" (family) stretches beyond blood relatives; it is a familial offer that can reach as far as complete strangers. They are inviting the world to witness a new paradigm for peace from disturbed dis-positions.

Local elders affirm that cultural celebrations have always served as primary catalysts for peacebuilding, but acknowledge that they have not resurfaced in their full capacity since the war. Sitting patiently under the canopy of trees amid the chaos of rehearsals, some of the nation's wisest voices generously offer their aesthetic analysis over the following weeks. Many elders recall instances where peace initiatives brought by outside interveners only exacerbated conflict dynamics. Offering poignant lessons from ancient arts-based practices, griot storytelling circles can embed peacebuilding principles, transmitting them with reverence and care. This artistic exchange solicited between generations can be the beginning of a new partnership, as ancient insights meet contemporary art forms. Having tasted cultural exile, they warn that cultural roots cannot be compromised and ought to be woven into the fabric of reconciliation if peace is to prevail.

The fluctuating momentum towards peacebuilding has been influenced by an undercurrent of fatigue that in part stems from years of media overload. External, international perspectives often emphasize what *isn't* working in Sierra Leone. However, the weight of this derogatory drone creates just enough resistance to catalyze a deeper drive to invert this perception. The youth assert that they want Sierra Leone to become globally known as a nation that upholds the values of peace against all odds. Their conversations highlight the fact that this particular region in Sierra Leone is home to several ethnic and religious groups who currently live alongside one another in peaceful coexistence. The Limba, Kuranko, Mandingo, Yalunka, Fulla, and Susu groups all participate in this lively exchange, and jump at the chance to engage with the theme of "celebration" from different cultural standpoints. The dark fog created by years of sensationalized media begins to lift with the prospect of revitalizing artistic peacebuilding, which can stretch across centuries and cultural boundaries.

THE OUTSIDE PERSPECTIVE

Not everyone is content to embrace the same joyous storyline. Several youth approach this overriding enthusiasm with a critical stance, and choose to deliberately situate themselves outside of idealist peace-filled antidotes. Those who pride themselves on being self-proclaimed "outsiders" refuse to be coerced into premature peacemaking. In their eyes, forced forgiveness and reconciliation is an abhorrent crime that is rarely investigated. They argue that lingering hostilities cannot be casually bypassed and warn that idealism is nothing but another form of violence in disguise. A deeper sense of injustice fuels their movement beyond hypocritical and superficial positions. They hold the strong conviction that an imposed closure on unforgivable actions is simply unacceptable. The connection between ethics, context, and aesthetics is not something to be ignored in this shared human story.

A resistance to an "all arts heal" discourse abounds as these youth position themselves outside of the celebratory dynamic. Their arguments are compounded by tangible examples of highly patronizing arts-based interventions over the years. They reject the looming hints of pathology that surround "war affected children" discourse. Their deeper instincts propel them to imagine ways of living beyond static labels and presumptive stigmas. Creating a more politicized public archive that speaks to complexities *and* international complicities is their top priority. However, the size of this challenge is not to be underestimated. There are very few who choose to live at the intersection where imagination encounters the unfathomable. Certain questions are simply unanswerable in a history that cannot speak for itself. In a nation where both voice and mobility have been voraciously attacked, this courageous ensemble of outsiders carves out peripheral spaces of agency in the center of some of the world's most haunting absences.

The body is the prime language of peacebuilding for the outsider ensemble. Their choreographic thinking challenges others to reexamine an oversimplified analysis of the roots of the conflict. Their shared kinesthetic intelligence adds another dimension to the diamond-trading dialogues that focus solely on economic corruption. This aesthetic inquiry extends even further, becoming an investigation into the art forms and cultural rituals that survived during the war. In this form of living re-search, juxtaposed stories of forced conscription and cultural celebrations begin to unfold. Unscathed vignettes of cultural wisdom still live beneath the surface scars. The body in motion offers a solid frame for exploring key rituals that were previously lost, stolen or dispossessed.

EXPRESSIVE ARTS AND PEACEBUILDING
Several of the other youth ensembles explore peace and reconciliation through expressive arts modalities. Drumming, spoken word poetry, dance, and improvisational theater all offer new vantage points for old perspectives. Each art modality informs and reflects the essence of the other, and fiction finds a place to flourish somewhere in between. Although disillusionment still lingers in Sierra Leone, undertones of joy and play serve as a reminder that celebrations hold a pivotal place in

society. The youth insist that living beyond the refuge of cynicism involves living *into* celebration and performance, rather than solely relegating the arts to special occasions. An undeniable strength emanates from the levity that comes from this discovery. There is a mutual consensus amongst the performers that creating a culture of peace must encompass both celebration and a healthy dose of creative revolt.

The first phase of rehearsals involves collecting stories, rhythms, dances, and scripts that speak to a wider narrative around historical and present-day dynamics of conflict. This process is met with significant challenges, as we all work with one another against an inexpressible backdrop. It is almost impossible to articulate visions for peace in a haze of events that still sits on the skin like an unwanted, filmy residue. The shared experiences of conflict are embedded in the surrounding social and physical landscape, but they cannot always find a form through conventional language. Aesthetic sensibilities that have survived in extreme conditions assume a place-making quality, which can often be found through symbols, metaphors, and rhythms. Outside of the confines of language, improvised gestures offer up an alternative vocabulary that can speak to the extreme distortions witnessed and experienced during the war. Such offerings do not promise easy resolutions, but rather become invitations to live with greater dignity in the midst of tension. There is a potency that comes from simply being alive to shuddering contradictions that are not easily resolved. A question asked by one of the youth becomes central in this collective inquiry: *Who will give us back our stolen years?*

Such a brazen question unleashes an unexpectedly fiery response after a prolonged period of silence in the group. Although it is impossible to know how to answer such a haunting question, the youth are not content to reduce their experiences to a hidden place of silencing. They are up against a formidable challenge as they oscillate between memory, uncertainty, survival and hope. Conflict interveners have pushed many of these youth to "simply" name their issues. There has been little momentum dedicated to moving beyond what the mind and body already know. Willing to completely reverse this paradigm, youth instinctively embody the multiple violations they have lived through before framing them with language. The subtlest gestures expand compressed knowledge systems that have been accumulating in the body for years. Non-verbal responses alleviate the pressure to remain fixed on the literal version of "what happened," while offering a opening onto a much larger story.

Reorienting the senses around what is possible is a first step toward encountering the unimaginable.

In response to this reversed aesthetic ordering, non-verbal points of encounter create openings between the fierce truth of what is known and what can be told. What is omitted in language can still find a home in the body. In this place of embodied composition, a third narrative emerges that is much wider than a mere clash of personalities or political agendas. As intimate, cultural, and universal dynamics are negotiated and re-imagined here, hints of meaning begin to emerge from an era of meaningless death. Each gesture interrogates the physical legacy of a shared global politics and offers ideas for an alternative legislation. This ensemble work suggests that fair governance begins first with a politics that has an inherent knowledge base in the body.

The youth literally begin to take up residence in the arts. Loose debris is reconfigured for stage props. Broken Coke bottles become percussive treasures. Amputated limbs that know the storm of physical silencing are able to find new starting points in multi-part harmonies. Shocking streams of beauty are remapped on bodily ground. A few weeks into the process, an array of metaphors and poetic lines start to act as a blueprint for a cohesive festival script. In the most unlikely locations throughout the community, aesthetic spaces begin to overcome the social stigmas related to the war. The multiplicity of lenses offered through this artistic response challenges the fixed positions and reducible identities that have perpetuated social isolation. The process of producing a communal festival disrupts the protective enclaves formed by this degenerative trend. The festival framework also sends out a collective invitation to become more attuned to reassembling relational dynamics in the present.

In determining the location for rehearsal spaces, there is a strong pull to gather in public areas that intersect with rhythms of daily life. Living soundscapes inform choreographic choices in fields of maize, behind roadside cooking stalls, beside woodcutters toiling in the sun, and at bustling entrances to the main markets. Interruptions seamlessly support a continual flow of ideas. Carving out aesthetic pathways through the clamoring mechanics of daily life is both startling and reassuring. We have no choice but to pay exquisite attention as the mundane and extraordinary encounter one another in real time.

Site-specific rehearsals have a place-making quality to them, as the free play between artists and community members transforms neutral spaces into generative places of belonging. As roving ensembles move their way through Kabala in preparation for the festival, at every new turn there is a living inquiry waiting to unfold. The rigor and discipline of the arts temporarily lift up the dead weight of injustices that blanket the area. The performers intimately know what it means to be caught in between longing and belonging. As late-afternoon market smells waft through expressive arts rehearsals, it is clear that finding common ground is literally just this: collectively imagining new alternatives in common spaces, and welcoming the awkwardness that prevails. Common ground is not a theoretical concept based on consensus, but an invitation to dwell with one another in the midst of collapsing relational fault lines.

THE CHOREOGRAPHY OF ABSENCE

One of my greatest dance teachers is a young man who intimately lives between the lines of resilience and defiance. Although the toll of conflict has left him with permanent scars and amputated legs, he daily inscribes his vision of peace into the unoccupied space around him while resting his entire body weight on the palms of his dancing hands. As he positions himself "upside down" to transpose the muted language in his absent feet, I begin to understand for the first time how embodied agency extends beyond conventional language. Trying to keep up with his contorted acts of strength, many of us flounder while awkwardly attempting to learn from his ingenious choreography of absence. As absent limbs confront the elusive space that holds the collision between biography and history, freedom within limitation takes on a whole new level of meaning. In his physical precision, carrying both elation and mourning, unspoken gratitude emanates through the group as we all clear the field to make room for this master dancer. His dance refuses to be pinned down by politics that are not his own. Phantom nerves still drive the kneading and pulling together of a living archive that speaks of many truths not yet known.

With this inexhaustible momentum in the foreground of our experience, we begin to see that the architecture of peace calls for a sensitive scaffolding of the senses. It becomes clear that altering the center of conflict in the body can alter, in turn, the center of conflict in a community. We are shown again and again how mutable history can find a cohesive physical form in the midst of multiple paradoxes. Carefully crafted movement has the capacity to unravel years of silent agreements. Working in tandem with what isn't yet known provides a training ground for understanding space and time in ways that unhinge habitual responses. The smallest gestures become large achievements in the weighed-down legacy of warfare. Our shared task is not to interpret the literal meanings emanating from the movements, but rather to live more fully into the forms that are moving us. From this we can sense that freedom of mobility is not something to be taken for granted, but should be approached with wonder and an incessant curiosity. The gift of momentum becomes heightened in a context where many have lost mobility before ever knowing what it means to dance.

The vocabulary of choreography offers up an inviting language for peaceful negotiations. Peace is multidimensional, and in turn calls for an embodied polyphony of responses. The arts-based ensembles are designed to support a fluid exchange of roles between directors, choreographers, dancers, and interested community members. Footwork, spinal positioning, and hand gestures become prime threads of connectivity across social and cultural divides. Pedestrian patterns taken from the rhythms of everyday life are infused into the festival choreography. Because the rebels strategically targeted highly esteemed social and cultural values, simple daily rituals were dismantled. Familial greeting rituals are just some of the relational markers that were obliterated in the harsh reality of rebel invasions. For the festival, these lost rituals are sensitively reintroduced into the texts and subtexts of poetry, rhythm, and dance. The reinsertion of social norms into the festival script becomes a way to reclaim what had been stolen. Even though years of conflict have unraveled the cultural fabric that is intricately woven into daily practices, inner impulses of welcome and invitation cannot be killed.

Working with varying degrees of proximity to "hot" issues creates heightened tensions within the groups. In living through fluctuating cycles of radical dissent and acceptance, dance and movement offer a fluid axis that allows oscillation between the two. While the group members boldly confront many limitations, they often find themselves living precariously between the unlived dreams of their elders and daily demands of their peers. The mass displacement from the war and disintegration of traditional family structures has left only fleeting moments of intergenerational inclusiveness. As ancient gara fabrics become interlaced with contemporary art practices, rigid storylines around restitution and compensation slowly expand into a wider socio-historical narrative.

As the expressive arts weave their way through ethnic traditions, new entry points emerge that make it possible to move closer to irreconcilable issues. For instance, memories evoked by the textures of dance do not necessarily lead to a direct translation into a linear text, but rather create vital cues to re-imagine an unwritten history in fragments of theater, dance, and spoken word poetry. The expressive arts principle of de-centering (Knill 2005) creates spaciousness around rigid patterns that need to be shifted. The living narratives and embodied metaphors of this artistic montage refuse to be tied down into fixed positions. Patterns of history begin to come apart at the seams, as domination, submission, and inscription are reshaped into tactile responses in the body. The result? Absurd contra-dictions of war-torn lives are pieced together one word at a time. Each physical utterance evokes new questions, choices, and possibilities. However, even with layers of embodied evidence to back up stories that never make the headlines, subtle forms of resignation occasionally resurface. Waves of disillusionment offer a reminder that conflict does not simply end once peacebuilding begins. Some stories may never be discovered. In extreme circumstances of systematic oppression, certain memories simply fall out of space and time.

Coherent storylines slowly emerge as illusive histories become crystallized into lines of spoken-word poetry. Word association games leading up to poetic compositions bring more focus to scattered ideas. "Simple" words like peace and democracy spark raucous sentiments of both antagonism and cooperation. There are very few places where both celebration and protest can coexist, but poetry offers a frame where they can be malleable together. Gaps in understanding open a space for simple images that intervene into fraught debates. When heated reactions eventually fall into the syncopated rhythms of gritty poetic riffs, displaced memories, for years relegated to the margins, begin to resurface. Poetry invents as it disintegrates, reminding us that peacebuilding is not always graced with a happy ending.

The words rising out of embodied responses become leaping-off points for the creation of call-and-response poetry between the ethnic groups. This physical momentum follows from two simple words: "Peace is…" From this starting point, each ethnic ensemble offers up one stanza of poetry, recites it in a unified voice, and then invites other ethnic groups to respond in similar stanza form. The interchange of voices reclaims what is lost between the lines: "Peace is lost to power gone wrong/ Our names not known in days long gone/ We live today with words to give/ This song becomes our way to live…" Through a bold exchange of body and text, physical gestures complement each song line. While discovering pure delight in getting lost in the improvisation, one youth responds in a declarative tone: "*I will rehearse until I die!*" The younger generation that has lived through the war intimately knows the connection between inertia, resistance, and recovery. For many, daily survival is the most demanding creative act.

To add another dimension to dancing, poetry, and text, the youth from the "outsider group" insist on integrating the spectacle of giant puppets into their theatrical offerings. Their skillful gestures tap into a playfulness that is met with infectious laughter, as larger-than-life movements dare to amplify and mock common mannerisms in the community. Beneath provocative puppet antics, new elements of risk are permitted under this "faceless" guise. Stagnant social ideologies are challenged by the magnitude of this animated force, and everyone is given a generous taste of freedom through proposed political fantasies. Slipping under draped fabric into a limitless imaginal realm, the puppeteers enter into an uninhibited zone where anonymity confronts authority. In a series of original vignettes entitled "Peace on the Streets," these living caricatures bring an ironic life force to the most arduous and unbearable policies that exist within structures of governance. Play-by-play accounts of uncanny "truth and reconciliation" protocols offer an alternative social etiquette that breaks down predictable conventions. The puppets are not out to appease others, nor do they seek approval for their highly politicized viewpoints. Poised somewhere between absurdity, comedy, and tragedy, the puppets speak from a place of freedom that dares to counter the testimonies that are demanded on command. Through the combined vocabularies of spectacle, expressive arts and traditional practices, the limiting binaries of "victim" and "perpetrator" are challenged, as more complex cultural and social narratives emerge.

As outdoor basketball courts transform into spaces of cultural celebration, I am reminded of the significance of this moment. Watching students diligently comb the ground to clear debris and rusted-out bullet shells in preparation for the culminating festival, I realize that cultural celebrations are not irrelevant utopian gatherings. In a fragile political climate, this gathering is an anchor that honors linguistic, ethnic, and artistic lineages. As hundreds of people from Kabala gather to witness the culminating series of performances, they watch incomprehensible lines of history being rewritten for the local and global stage. These multidisciplinary offerings create paradigms for peacebuilding in uninhabited spaces. The arts give us a glimpse, from new sight lines, into how we can start living from a place beyond what we already know. While choruses of feet pound down on red African soil in response to waves of unstoppable applause, the deeply held views of both performers and audience members become unsettled. New inscriptions of hope are alive in places where debilitating conflict has left its mark.

More than anything, there is life here.

It is here where memory, identity and imagination begin to converge. It is here on this simple makeshift stage in the back of a schoolyard, where our shared global dance finds a new choreography in the absence.

It is here where narratives of peace begin to unfold.

References

Fanthorpe, R. and Maconachie, R. (2010) "Beyond the 'crisis of youth'? Mining, farming and civil society in post-war Sierra Leone." *African Affairs 109*, 435, 251–272.

Goldberg, R. (1996) "Performance Art from Futurism to the Present." in M. Huxley and N. Witts (eds) *The 20th Century Performance Reader*. London: Routledge.

Knill, P.J. (2005) "Foundations for a Theory of Practice." In P.J. Knill, E.G. Levine, and S.K. Levine (eds) *Principles and Practice of Expressive Arts Therapy*. London: Jessica Kingsley Publishers.

Richards, P. (1995) "Rebellion in Liberia and Sierra Leone: A Crisis of youth?" In O.W. Furley (ed.) *Conflict in Africa*. London: Tauris.

Wessells, M. and Davidson, J. (2006) "Recruitment and Reintegration of Former Youth Soldiers in Sierra Leone: Challenges of Reconciliation and Post-Accord Peace Building." In S. McEvoy-Levy (ed.) *Troublemakers or Peacemakers*. Notre Dame, IN: University of Notre Dame Press.

10

Creating Space for Change

The Use of Expressive Arts with Vulnerable Children and Women Prisoners in Sub-Saharan Africa

Gloria Simoneaux

In 2000 I received a letter from a young man in Eastern Ghana saying, "I read about your work in an Amnesty International newsletter. I work with orphans. Please come to Ghana and help me with the children." I wrote back immediately and said, "Of course. I'm coming." That is how my work with the children of Africa began.

At the time I was the Executive Director of DrawBridge, an arts program for homeless children in the San Francisco Bay area. The creative process provides a gentle way for children to tell their stories, ground and organize their thoughts and feelings, communicate their experiences to others, and begin to recover a sense of value and well-being. Since the program's inception in 1989 we have worked with more than 10,000 children in shelters and transitional housing sites.

During the past ten years I have returned to Africa many times, and worked with children in Ghana, Eritrea, Ethiopia, Zimbabwe, Tanzania, Kenya, and South Africa. What continues to move me is the extraordinary resilience of children who have suffered unspeakable losses through poverty, illness, and violence. They still laugh, play wildly, tease each other, and dance. They have fun with the simplest of objects. For example, I saw ten children wrestling with a large sheet of black plastic, pulling, falling, and laughing joyously. At the same time they need support and encouragement to verbalize their internal turmoil.

In August 2008 I was awarded a Fulbright scholarship to teach and conduct research in Nairobi in affiliation with the Kenyan Institute of Education (KIE). My job was to reintroduce art into the primary school curriculum, using self-expression to help reduce violent outbreaks among students.

The Kenyan educational system is exam-driven, and teachers and students are focused on achieving high grades in order to pass to the next level. Teaching is done in lecture form and memorizing from the outdated textbook is the accepted method of learning. Art is not part of the curriculum, and therefore the teachers have no interest in supporting art classes. So from the very start I felt as though I was swimming up a rocky creek against a strong current.

Before I began my association with KIE they had initiated a plan to organize an art competition for primary school students, and my participation as part of the judging team was expected. This posed quite an ethical dilemma for me, because non-judgmental expression is central to the DrawBridge philosophy. The process of creating art and the relationship that develops between the counselor and the child is what is valued, not the final product. For us, artwork is a doorway into a child's world, an opportunity to express what can't be verbalized. All self-expression is positive.

At the judging, there were three piles on the floor, labeled "good artwork," "medium good" and "poor." Poor artwork by children? Not in my world! I told my "boss" that I couldn't be a part of this judging, and I left. The "good artwork" consisted of very detailed renderings in pencil, a great deal of it politically inspired – drawings of Kenya's president, prime minister and Kofi Annan. The hundreds of expressive, more imaginative paintings that I had done with children at three schools were discarded. Why, I wondered? Maybe they were too childlike.

Merab, a teacher at the Muslim Girl's Primary School, asked me if I was familiar with the work of Carl Rogers, and told me that she was studying counseling at the Kenya Association of Professional Counselors (KAPC), located a few blocks away from the KIE offices. KAPC is modeled after the work of Rogers' client-centered approach, identical to the DrawBridge (and my own personal) approach. She invited me to accompany her to the center to meet the staff and have a look around. Ten minutes later I met Cecilia, the director, with whom I ended up working for more than a year. I was able to shift my Fulbright affiliation to become a trainer of counselors (focusing on expressive arts and play therapy) at KAPC's four centers throughout Kenya. In addition I initiated three community arts projects as part of Harambee Arts (www.harambeearts.org), my small non-profit organization. Informed by DrawBridge's 20 years of experience in building sustainable arts programs for homeless children, Harambee Arts collaborates with local African grassroots organizations and individual artists to improve the well-being of vulnerable and traumatized African children.

I went to Kenya as a white North American woman with an agenda based on my cultural norms. I had a great deal to share and I was confidently and energetically looking forward to training counselors in the DrawBridge methodology. My vision included an effortless transferring of information and passion. Even though I've traveled and worked all over the world and consider myself culturally sensitive, teaching art therapy to adults in Kenya was not easy. It confronted me with many of my own cultural assumptions, of which I was often unaware.

Kenyans are very polite and normally won't speak up if they don't understand or disagree, as opposed to American students who generally have no problem disagreeing loudly. Every single day of teaching I repeated at least a dozen times, "Are you following me? Am I making sense? Do you understand? *Tuko pamoja* ("Are we together" in Swahili)?" This was followed by nodding, smiling, and the earnest shaking of heads. Later, at the end of the month-long course, at least half of my students included in their final evaluation, "I couldn't understand your accent." One man waited until the very last five minutes of a month-long intensive to say, "Don't you think that directive art therapy techniques work better than non-directive?" He had apparently accepted little of what I had been teaching for an entire month, but waited until the very end to speak up. I was probably not reading their cues very well. Counseling in Kenya consists of giving advice and telling the client what to do. This made teaching client-centered therapy remarkably frustrating and very challenging for me.

For example, during one role-play, the trainee playing the child was very engaged with her drawing and only used the color orange. At one point she placed the crayon on the table and stared at her drawing. The trainee role-playing the counselor took the orange crayon and hid it. Later, I asked my student what she was trying to achieve by hiding the crayon. She said, "I wanted the child to use other colors." To me, this was an example of a therapist directing the child's self-expression instead of grasping the notion of the child knowing what she or he needs. Their ways of thinking about change meant that they had difficulty not trying to control what was happening and simply allowing the child to lead the creative flow.

In Kenyan culture children are not encouraged to speak up or to share their wisdom. In short, children are told what to do and their opinions are not solicited. They have little choice and are expected to fit into a mold, which leaves hardly any room for differently challenged or highly gifted children to excel. The word "respect" is reserved for elders, and I was forced to create a new language to describe the development of trust and the building of relationships with children. This challenged me to clearly articulate my own way of working, based on ideas that I believe to be universally held.

Counselors often receive little training, but once a certificate is bestowed they feel qualified and commonly refer to themselves as "counselor." Those who completed my one-month certificate course were already known as "art therapists" among their Kenyan colleagues. In the United States art therapy students are required to complete years of self-therapy and practicum in addition to strenuous class work.

Most of the Kenyan tribes (there are 47 in total) believe that curses are put by one person upon another. I always include my collection of small animal and monster replications as teaching aids, since they elicit strong responses from children and help them explore their own demons in a safe and playful way. In Kenya the little purple snakes and black rodent characters elicited tremendous fear from some of the trainees. One woman jumped onto the table screaming uncontrollably when she saw the snakes, believing that she was being cursed. I was shocked and quickly had to make her feel comfortable. The other students watched me carefully as I reassured her.

Every trainee had to take time off on a regular basis to attend funerals. It was common and maddening, as I tried to create group cohesion, any type of cohesion. This proved to be one more opportunity to go with the flow and stop being a "rigid American" who needed things to conform to a schedule.

During trainings, I often asked the students, "Were you beaten during childhood? Did it help you to grow up to be a better person?" Many hands shot up… "Yes, I finally realized that I had to stop throwing rocks at cars. Those beatings really made me change my mind about that and I became a better person." I thought to myself, "How can I possibly get my point across that violence against children is always unacceptable?" Children are regularly punished through beatings in Kenya, at school and at home. One of the trainees had a ten-year-old girl with serious learning challenges. She hated to go to school because the teacher beat her. Whenever possible, she returned home after her mother left for work and hid in the house all day. When her mother (the trainee) discovered her at home, she beat her. According to the mother, "It's not beating… it's discipline, a cultural thing."

Logistics and timing were always a source of great irritation. No one showed up on time and they came and went as they pleased. No amount of pleading, cajoling, or bribing helped. Asking Kenyan students not to use their cell phones during class is the same as asking them to stop breathing. In desperation, I said, "Only keep your cell phone on if it is an emergency." Life in Kenya is one big emergency.

Some of my students were unwilling to deal with their own issues. Even though they considered themselves to be trained counselors, they had never talked about a personal rape experience or a severe accident. At the beginning of the course I would gently say, "We can't work effectively with children if we're not willing to look at our own pain." I tried to influence them into changing. By the end of the course I had switched gears, "You must deal with this issue if you want to continue working with children. To do otherwise is not fair to the children, and if you don't have clear boundaries you can harm them."

All of these cultural tensions posed challenges to my way of working. My method is non-directive, and I regard art and imaginary play as the therapeutic process itself. By taking a non-directive point of view, the facilitator tries to ensure that the play will be child-centered; it will flow from the child's own experiences, rather than be directed by the facilitator (Schaefer and Cangelosi 1993). The therapy is in the telling of the story (through art, drama, re-enactment of experiences with puppets, etc.) and in the listening to the story, not in its interpretation or analysis. The facilitator learns to listen without judgment to painful material and to allow children to express themselves at their own pace and in their own time. The client knows what hurts, in what directions to go, which problems are crucial, which experiences have been deeply buried (Rogers 1961). These fundamental principles were often difficult to apply in the Kenyan context.

While I was in Kenya I frequently received text messages from local psychologists or counselors who were interested in my work. One afternoon I met with a young woman who was working toward a master's degree in psychology at a local university. She talked about one of her professors, a psychiatrist who taught art therapy, and she wanted us to meet. Her professor was teaching art therapy, but had no credentials, training, or experience. To help his students he created a detailed list of items that may appear in a drawing and their meanings. For example, he taught that an image of someone drawn with eyelashes means that the client is suffering from such and such, and someone drawn with a big nose means so and so. This mechanistic list of meanings trivializes and misrepresents the field of art therapy and takes away all the magic and opportunity for self-actualization. While teaching, I often repeated the following words: "Understand the dangers of interpretation and judgment."

Most of my trainees had never played as children, nor had they created art. In Kenya, imagination is not encouraged *in school*. Children learn to paint the sky blue, the sun yellow, and to color within the lines. In my workshop, however, the trainees expressed tremendous joy while they painted with their non-dominant hand and drew using unpredictable colors. They painted while dancing and swaying their bodies to the music. They played with balloons, puppets, clay, and masks. They were asked to paint something that they could never imagine painting. The room immediately filled with sexual images and boisterous laughter. The trainees loosened up and had fun, and didn't want to stop. Winnicott (1971) says that if the therapist cannot play, then he is not suitable for the work. Slowly they began to express themselves; over an intensive month-long course many sides of each of us were revealed. Trainees learned to be non-directive and gentle without being passive.

HARAMBEE ARTS
The time that I spent with the children and women of Kenya was a joy. Our ongoing projects included:

- art expression and dancing with HIV-positive women prisoners at Nairobi's Langata Prison

- art groups at the City Primary School's "special unit" for children with autism and Down Syndrome.

Langata Women's Prison
Langata Women's Prison is a dismal place. Prisoners waiting to be sentenced commonly sleep on the cold hard floor for two years or more before going to court. The sentenced prisoners wear black and white stripes with a small colored patch on the front, indicating the length of their sentence. Those with mental health issues ("They are mad," according to the other women) are singled out by the bright yellow

stripe on the front of their uniforms. The 24 women living on death row, waiting to be hanged, are not allowed to do anything. They are deprived of the human dignity that doing mundane chores provides. They yearn to scrub, sweep, cook – anything that would give them a shred of normalcy. They are banned from any self-improvement or skill-building sessions, which are considered a waste of resources as they are never going to return to society. Their grey uniforms set them apart. Many of the condemned had been convicted of murder. They commonly murdered their husband's girlfriend when they could no longer stand the infidelity. In Kenya there is an enormous stigma attached to having an incarcerated family member, and the prisoners have no visitors. The women's biggest sadness is thinking about their children on the outside and the complete lack of information and communication they receive from others.

The Harambee Arts expressive arts group for the women prisoners who are HIV positive is nothing short of miraculous. They are allowed to cook food that we donate, dance to loud music as they play with brightly colored veils, paint whatever they choose to paint, and laugh! The fact that they are allowed to have fun, lots of fun, is absolutely and outrageously strange and wonderful. Of course, we have to take the wardens out for beer and meat on a regular basis, and bring them gifts, in order for this to happen.

The group was initiated in May 2008 when one warden "came out" as HIV positive and was granted permission to start a support group for the prisoners who had the courage to come out publicly. The original group consisted of eight women. The last time that we met, there were more than 60 prisoners attending. Now they ask to be tested, just so they can join our support group.

Occasionally we discuss the actions that landed them in prison, although we don't ask about this. Harambee Arts' goal is to provide time for the women to experience their humanity and their beauty, without having to explain the reasons for their incarceration. We see beyond the prison uniforms. Narrative therapy is one of the techniques that we utilize, viewing the problem as the problem, and not the person as the problem. Within a narrative therapy approach, the focus is not on "experts" solving problems, it is on people discovering through conversations the hopeful, preferred, previously unrecognized and hidden possibilities contained within themselves. This model presents an opportunity for "re-authoring" people's stories and lives.

Narrative Therapy

EXAMPLES OF EXERCISES THAT WE HAVE DONE WITH THE
WOMEN

- Draw yourself in any way that you want. Describe feelings, smells, sounds, colors, etc.

- Draw someone who had a sad thing happen but had the strength to move on.

- Draw a sad or challenging time in your childhood and what helped you through it.

- Draw a happy time from your childhood.

- Draw yourself in the future, in a safe place, in an unsafe place, in a pretend place.

- Draw yourself with your family, as an animal, as the weather, as a nightmare, as someone scary, as wishes.

- Draw your favorite food, the strong parts of your body, the weak parts, the parts of yourself that you value and love the most.

The women particularly enjoy drawing themselves in the future, running their own businesses and living as role models for positive living within the community. "I want to be a good mother to my son."

BODY MAPS

Body mapping was our first large-scale project within the prison. The first day that we met, the women were quiet and shy, and huddled closely together on wooden benches in the outdoor courtyard of the prison's HIV voluntary testing center. That was to be our meeting place for the week, in the blazing sun, beneath threatening storm clouds and in the torrential rains. In addition to the 28 prisoners, our group consisted of the "Madam" (head warden) and several assistants, who were all HIV positive. Occasionally another woman warden would visit and take me aside to comment positively on what she noticed: the change in the women, the beauty of the artwork, and the fun they were having. She said, "You brought out so much courage in those women. The women have changed. They feel appreciated. This is something that nobody ever did before."

I was busy taking care of logistics, running around answering questions, providing encouragement, hoping that it wouldn't rain, refreshing paint palettes, taking photos and video footage, teaching the women how to use my camera, trying to make my voice heard, trying to make my language understood, and most difficult of all…trying not to have favorites.

Normally a body-mapping workshop starts out with half the participants lying down on paper, and partners outlining their bodies in whatever pose they wish to strike. Then the pair changes roles and the other one is outlined. This time we had no room for such large paper – and it was windy.

To break the ice and demonstrate that we would have fun, we started with a game. Everyone stood in a circle, and as we went around the circle, each person called out her name while making a corresponding movement. Each movement and sound was mimicked by the rest of the group, and instantly the atmosphere shifted and the women relaxed. They moved, gyrated, whooped, and laughed wildly. After the game, I passed around a number of brilliantly colored veils and turned on African music. Everyone began to dance. Within seconds, the colored veils were being thrown around, worn on heads or torsos amidst brilliant smiles and constant laughter. The women danced and laughed, their striped uniforms set off by the gorgeous colors of the airy veils.

And this was how we began every morning of the week-long body mapping workshop: dancing alone, in pairs, in groups. Sometimes a pair would dance holding each other close, as in a disco.

I found strong white cardboard, 5 foot by 4 foot, and sketched individuals as each stood in front of me in a pose "that made me feel strong." Sketching 28 women, outdoors, in the wind. It was a commitment, but together we managed!

And as the days progressed, so did their creative use of the veils – they made elaborate head coverings, skirts, and belts.

Historically, body maps have been used in sub-Saharan Africa with HIV-positive individuals to track the virus in the body and to increase self-awareness. I focused on the strengths of each woman, the love in their lives, how they help others and how they have been supported by loved ones. They were single-mindedly focused on their paintings. The women relaxed and felt good about themselves; they enjoyed themselves immensely.

Over the past two years Harambee Arts has also hosted yoga workshops, recyclable art-making workshops, salsa dancing, meditation, and a hero book-making workshop within the prison. Hero books provide an opportunity to examine how a problem has power over us, and where we have power over a problem. The participants create a book in which they are the main characters having "shining moments" during which they have power over their problems.

And the project continues.

Figure 10.1 Author (Gloria Simoneaux) with HIV-positive women prisoners in Nairobi. The yellow stripe indicates "mental health issues." The grey uniform indicates "condemned to death and waiting to be hanged"

Figure 10.2 Women prisoners celebrate life

The City Primary School Special Unit

Autistic children in Kenya are commonly brought up in isolation, kept behind locked doors, and tied to a bed or a table while parents are at work. There is an African belief that the mother who gives birth to an autistic child is cursed. Shame and stigma surround the family, marriages rarely last, and many women are forced to take their bewitched child away with them, ostracized by the husband and his family.

In September 2003 a "special unit" opened at the City Primary School in Ngara, Nairobi, which now serves more than 60 students. The Harambee Arts staff paint with them in two separate groups every week. The children with autism and Down Syndrome who are fortunate enough to attend the City Primary School's special unit display a natural tendency to care for each other. Despite the hardships and the stigma they endure, the bonds between them are remarkably strong and nurturing.

From the beginning, the teachers made it clear that we were very welcome to paint with the children. "You can draw forms and they will color them in." My response: "We would like to try something different. We will give the children colors and let them paint anything that they would like." We received quizzical expressions and went ahead with our plan.

The children's concentration was unexpected and extraordinary, as was their growth as artists. They are commonly seen as having nothing to offer, yet we experienced just the opposite.

The 25 children in teacher Margaret's group, with whom we have been painting for more than a year and a half, are transformed – every single one of them has changed dramatically. Jeff was rigid as a board when we first met; he avoided eye contact and would not allow himself to be touched. Now he jumps up and down and laughs as we enter the classroom. He approaches me with a big smile and outstretched arms, for a hug and a kiss. It feels like a miracle.

One of the most striking changes has been in Fahima, a young Muslim girl who had been severely burned over a large portion of her body. When we first met, she was withdrawn and enveloped by sadness, and rarely smiled or made an effort to paint. Now she is bright and lively. Her eyes sparkle and she reaches out to others with a big smile. Fahima is thrilled with her creations and regularly screams, "Ona! Ona!" which means, "Look! Look!" in Swahili.

Marvin, who had previously been left alone when his parents went to work, is so excited and overjoyed to see us that he is practically jumping out of his skin. He hugs me joyously, and repeats my name (pronounced in the Kikuyu fashion), "Groria, Groria." He also repeats, "Painting, good! Painting, good!" throughout the session. He adores using my camera and says, "picture, picture," as soon as I enter the room. He is asking to use the camera. Noor, a beautiful boy, holds the camera in the middle of his forehead with the lens pointing at the ceiling. He takes such delight in having the camera strap around his neck and holding the camera in his hands. And he has taken some unusual ceiling and window shots.

Most of the "special children" have limited or no spoken language, but they communicate through their painting and in so many other inventive ways.

Adash is a young Indian boy who can be dangerous. He sometimes attacks and pinches at unexpected moments. While he paints he says, "Adash, good boy," throughout the session. Recently, I discovered that his father often says, "Adash, bad boy." Now the parents have a better attitude. They can see that their children can do something, even excel.

Simon sometimes eats the paint (his lips turn green or pink) and flicks his wet paintbrush in my direction (laughing) every time I walk by, so that my clothes and hair are filled with paint by the end of the morning. I say, "No, Simon, that is bad manners," but he doesn't care.

In May of 2009 a collection of the children's artwork was exhibited at the RaMoMa Museum of Modern Art in Nairobi. The children attended the exhibit and saw their paintings hanging carefully on long white walls alongside paintings made by well-known Kenyan artists. Several people expressed an interest in purchasing the paintings. Since then, a few of the children say, "Museum, museum!" on a regular basis. Painting has given them a sense of purpose and a sense of place. What we have done is to allow them to express feelings that were previously deeply hidden. They have found another way to communicate and are bursting with a sense of success and dignity.

What would I say to people who want to work in Africa or another developing country? Even though there are many cultural differences and challenges, it is possible to make a difference in individual people's lives. All you need is paper, a crayon, a playful attitude and an ability to respect children. You don't need fancy supplies, use locally available materials when possible (dirt, local dyes, bottle tops, burlap bags, and cooking charcoal). Making artworks magic.

Figure 10.3 Painting by an autistic child

Figure 10.4 Children affected by autism and Down Syndrome proudly exhibit their artwork at the Museum of Modern Art in Nairobi

Figure 10.5 Simon with green lips about to eat pink

References

Rogers, C. (1961) *On Becoming a Person.* New York: University of Chicago Press.

Schaefer. C.E. and Cangelosi, D.M. (1993) *Play Therapy Techniques.* Northvale, NJ: Jason Aronson Inc.

Winnicott, D.W. (1971) *Playing and Reality.* London and New York: Tavistock/Routledge.

11

Beauty in the Rough Places

Karen Abbs

Darfur's people are resourceful and resilient.
(Flint and de Waal 2005, p.1)

INTRODUCTION

As I sit here at my desk, far away from Darfur, far away from the chaos and horror that happens each day, I struggle with how to present the story of my time there. How do I capture the work, the stories, and at the end of it the beauty that I found in the Sudanese people? How do I show you their incredible ability to cope and to find hope despite the destruction of their villages and their lives? Perhaps I will use what I know, use the expressive arts and start with a story and an image to show the contrasts of life in Darfur, this interplay between the rough places and the beauty.

THE ROUGH PLACES

The incident occurred on our return from the field to Nyala. After spending the night in a small village we communicated with the base and got the green light to drive to Nyala. Seven kilometers from the village we found ourselves in the middle of an ambush. There were five or six armed people. They stopped us.

The whole time in the field, we had a bad feeling that something was going to happen, but we didn't know what it would be. We could not escape our fate. They ordered us out of the car, made us lay face down on the ground, and beat us with sticks. They stole everything, but they were convinced there was more. We didn't have more; we had already spent all our money in the field. The whole incident lasted about an hour and a half. In the end they let us drive away, but without anything. It was very frightening.

Mohammed, international non-governmental organization (INGO)
national staff employee

BEAUTY

Figure 11.1 Beauty

> This is what I remember about my village. It was a beautiful place filled with life and animals, and I could sit and watch the sun. It's gone now, destroyed, and now I live in the city. I never give up hope that one day I can return there, and that one day this conflict will end. I hold this image in my mind, I remember the beauty and I continue to hope.
>
> *Suhil, non-governmental organization (NGO) national staff employee*
> *(painting created during a training session)*

Stories of horror and images of hope: these are the two things that I carry with me after Darfur. Throughout my time there I was struck daily by the ability of the people to hold onto these images of beauty and to hope for a time when things could possibly be different. From February 2008 to December 2008 I was employed by RedR UK, an international non-governmental organization (INGO), to set up a program in Darfur addressing the psychological needs of aid workers (both local and international) after critical incidents such as car-jackings, robberies, and assaults. The purpose of the program, which will be described in detail later, was to provide pre-incident training on the impact of trauma and stress to local and international staff working in Darfur as well as post-incident counseling support.

Mohammed's "rough places" story above is just one example of the incredible number of stories and incidents that affect humanitarian workers, especially local staff, during the course of their work. My main goal in writing this chapter, however, was not to write another account of the horrors that happen in Darfur. While such horrors of course exist, and both Darfurians and humanitarian workers are subjected to unspeakable acts of violence, another story stood out for me. While Darfur is by far one of the "roughest" places in the world to live and work, one can still find images of hope, resilience and beauty within this chaos and destruction, in a place filled with injustice and war. This chapter will explore this interplay of the rough and the beautiful, and show that through the use of the arts the potential for social change exists, and that places of beauty that can eventually emerge through the use of expressive arts therapy.

THE ROUGH PLACES: THE CONTEXT AND HUMANITARIAN SITUATION OF DARFUR

In Darfur, a small region in Sudan, war had been brewing for decades, but it wasn't until 2003–2004 that the conflict deteriorated into something the world couldn't ignore. The root of the conflict is too complex to detail here, but it stems from racial and religious extremism that eventually resulted in what the United Nations called "the world's worst humanitarian disaster" (Flint and de Waal 2005, p.xii). With the International Criminal Court's indictment of Sudanese President Bashir for crimes against humanity and genocide in 2009, it was clear that the situation in Darfur was one defined by "ubiquitous abuse and human suffering" (p.xiii). Despite these declarations, and despite international organizations moving in to provide assistance to the population, the situation in Darfur has remained bleak, with little hope of improvement.

The heart of the story in Darfur, however, is not the conflict itself but the impact it has had on the local population. Through the conflict, more than 2 million people have been displaced, more than 200,000 have become refugees, and hundreds of villages have been destroyed, with thousands living on the edge of survival in IDP (internally displaced persons) camps. From this destruction, one of the real impacts of war on the population that emerges is that conflict destroys positive social capital. Once conflict erupts, it undermines interpersonal and communal trust, destroys the norms and values that underpin cooperation and collective action, and diminishes the capacity of communities to manage conflict without resorting to violence. The outbreak of conflict, in turn, tends to generate increased forms of negative social capital, as affected communities strengthen intergroup bonds as a way of coping with external threats from the state, rebel forces or opposed groups, at the expense of intragroup relations and trust (Baingana, Bannon and Thomas 2005, p.19).

Once this social capital is destroyed, once the society and traditional coping mechanisms begin to break down, we begin to see greater incidences of mental health issues such as depression, anxiety, suicide, and post-traumatic stress disorder. These problems are then amplified when local populations play a dual role: as both survivor of the conflict and employee within the conflict. What I mean by this is that local or national staff employed by international organizations have experienced the impacts of the conflict directly, and have seen the positive social capital of their villages destroyed. For many, their villages and communities have been devastated; families are then forced to live in camps, and social support networks that may have mitigated the impacts of the conflict have often all but disappeared.

Where this situation becomes compounded, however, is when survivors are employed by INGOs who come to Darfur to offer assistance to the population in the form of medical or humanitarian aid. Not only are the local staff then directly impacted by the conflict on both a past and present basis, they are now put at even greater risk because of their employment. This risk comes as a result of rebel groups or government forces potentially seeing the national staff as "collaborators" with international groups. In addition, local staff are also on the frontlines of delivering aid, and are often working in the most insecure and dangerous regions of Darfur. The result of this is that the staff are very likely to experience violent incidents caused by actors in the conflict (rebels and/ or military) during the course of their employment, which compounds the impacts of the past trauma that they had experienced.

THE IMPACT OF THE CONFLICT ON STAFF IN DARFUR

The RedR UK Staff Welfare Program in Darfur, by which I was employed in 2008, was created in response to the needs of these approximately 17,000 national and international humanitarian workers working to assist the population affected by the current conflict. As detailed above, the nature and personal impact of the work for staff in Darfur had become increasingly dangerous, and aid workers were faced with insecurity often becoming intentional targets in the conflict. The result of working and living in this environment was an increase in both cumulative and traumatic stress, and many were suffering from numerous stress symptoms.

Statistics collected by the United Nations in Darfur show the deterioration of the security situation for staff and the increased insecurity that they are facing on a daily basis. Table 11.1 details the security situation for aid workers in the past three years.

Statistics collected by the Humanitarian Policy Group show the deterioration of the security situation for staff and the increased insecurity that they are facing on a daily basis in Darfur. From 2007 to 2009, there were 34 aid workers killed, 82 wounded and 11 kidnapped (Aid Worker Security Database 2010). These statistics demonstrate the level of risk that NGO workers face and the reason for Darfur being the highest incident country of the three most violent contexts for aid work with the others being Afghanistan and Somalia (Stoddard, Harmer and Didomenico 2009, p.4).

Darfur is one of the most difficult and dangerous places in the world to work, which has had a remarkable personal impact on both national and international staff. In 2008, the Headington Institute was asked to conduct a research study in Chad and Darfur on the impact of living and working in insecure environments on humanitarian staff. Their findings included the following:

- 45% feel emotionally stressed

- 51% feel physically stressed

- Two-thirds feel they do not have a good work/life balance

- 18% have been victims of highly traumatic events

- 28% worry actively that such an event may happen to them

- Only 5% of staff felt supported by their NGO

- 82% felt they could benefit from a stress-management training program.

(Augsburger 2007)

What stands out most from the statistics is that the challenges for staff in Darfur are twofold:

1. Most staff in Darfur are local or national staff. This means that the majority of staff have experienced previous trauma as a result of the conflict, and they and their families are dealing with the impacts of surviving in a war zone.

2. Because staff are from the Darfur region and they are working in volatile and insecure areas, they are often subjected to increased violence during the course of their work.

Imagine what it must be like. Perhaps your village has been destroyed and you have witnessed and personally experienced horrendous acts of violence. You are able to find work with an organization, only to face increased violence during the course of your work. On top of that, you may feel that you have no support in your workplace and that your organization doesn't care about you.

As one staff member said:

> I do not feel that my organization has any real support mechanisms in place for staff here, despite "lip service" about the importance of taking care of oneself etc... One of the most challenging aspects of the work here is the lack of any true support structure... (Augsburger 2007, p.27)

THE STAFF WELFARE PROGRAM

The above statistics present a disturbing picture. Not only do staff face increased security risks during the course of their employment, but they also feel less and less able to cope emotionally and psychologically. In response to this overwhelming need from the NGO community, a program was set up to address the emotional needs of the staff, especially following traumatic incidents during the course of their employment. The primary focus of the program was on training staff in understanding the impacts of stress and trauma, helping them to support themselves and others, and providing post-incident counseling support.

While this program was to be delivered to both national and international staff, the primary participants in the program were Sudanese national staff. It was essential, therefore, that the program be culturally sensitive and appropriate. This is where the arts would begin to take center stage. As Loughry and Eyber (2003, p.10) have indicated, "Western models themselves may be at odds with the experiences, cultures, and needs of most non-Western societies. In order to plan effective interventions, the way that distress and suffering are conceived and manifested in diverse societies must be understood."

One of the initial goals of the program, therefore, was to understand the local context and to understand what interventions would be most effective. In addition to this, the program faced another complication, in that the recipients of the training and support would be both national and international staff. Providing training and support to both national and international staff is challenging, because of the different conceptions of mental health, wellness, and expressions of suffering. Within the international community alone there were many different nationalities represented, from African to Asian, European, and North American. It was thus important to develop a program that was flexible in nature, and to offer a variety of responses, especially non-Western, to those impacted by critical incidents.

For the Sudanese staff, the concept of mental health, counseling, and psychology was a relatively new one, and there was some stigma about accepting assistance from a psychiatrist or a psychologist. For this reason, all of our psychological work or counseling after critical incidents was called "support." The concept of support is very accepted within Sudanese culture, and it is very common for groups of people to sit together after difficult incidents and discuss what has happened. In this way we hoped to build on existing support structures and beliefs, and find a model of the program that would be accepted by the participants in the training programs as well as those receiving assistance after critical incidents.

STRUCTURE OF THE STAFF WELFARE PROGRAM

The Staff Welfare Program in Darfur was developed to address the psychological and social impacts of stress and trauma that humanitarian workers faced during the course of their employment. The program, for which I was the Program Manager, offered a three-day Critical Incident Stress Management (CISM) training program, as well as support after a critical (traumatic) incident and follow-up. The education and training was offered to national and international staff of NGOs, and focused on the effects of both cumulative and traumatic stress as well as how to support others after a traumatic incident. In order to reach as many people as possible, training was adapted to the local context, using local psychologists as part of the team. These local psychologists conducted the trainings in Arabic, and all materials were translated into Arabic. In this way the program was accessible to all humanitarian workers and ensured that we were reaching the most vulnerable group in aid work, the national staff.

One of the most innovative aspects of the program was assisting the humanitarian community to put into place a Critical Incident Support Network. This network was made up of volunteers, mostly local staff, who had taken the CISM course and who had received further training in supporting staff impacted by traumatic events. By focusing our training and volunteer program on local staff, we were able to build capacity in the region and to leave behind a program that would function and grow in the absence of expatriate assistance. The hope was that this program would be the first of its kind to offer global psychosocial support to a humanitarian community, and that it would lessen the impact of critical incidents on aid workers.

Another key aspect of the program was that of social change. In this context when we speak of social change, it is not a change in the Darfur context or the current situation. The conflict in Darfur is complex and, as discussed above, has been going on for years. When I speak of social change in Darfur in the context of this program, what I am referring to is the potential for social change within an organization. We were seeking to achieve change in how staff were treated in regard to their physical and emotional well-being. Social change also refers to the potential for humanitarian workers to experience a change in the perception of their emotional and psychological well-being during the course of their work. Too often, the humanitarian workplace is filled with people who believe that all staff are there to perform a duty and that critical incidents are part of the risk of working in this environment.

In order to facilitate this social or organizational change, one of the key elements was to train staff from each organization working in Darfur to cope with the impact of stress and trauma. In addition, staff were provided basic listening and supportive counseling skills in order to be able to emotionally support others after critical incidents. In this way employees could return to their organizations and act as a focal point for change. They could be a voice within the workplace for treating staff differently, with caring and kindness, on a day-to-day basis as well as after critical incidents.

BEAUTY

When we first set up the Staff Welfare Program in Darfur, one of the key tasks was to ensure that the program was culturally appropriate and acceptable for the local context. What I quickly learned through the training programs that we were offering was that words weren't enough.

If we were seeking to create change in organizations around how staff were treated and supported, we needed a training methodology and a support mechanism that was accepted by the local staff. As de Nobriga and Schwarzman have written:

> If we want respect and love and beauty among us and all our many communities, we must actively and systematically promote it through art and through our teaching of others. Teaching, in this sense, becomes a political act, a conscious effort to build a movement of people prepared to facilitate and participate in social change. (2009, p.1)

In the expressive arts, Paolo Knill *et al.* speak about the quest for beauty as part of our "aesthetic responsibility" (Knill, Levine and Levine 2005, p.120). It became clear that the training courses that we were offering needed to be engaging; they needed to capture people and give them energy to move forward with creating change. What was also clear was that the workers attending the training courses were both physically and emotionally exhausted. As detailed previously, the majority of the national staff had experienced trauma on multiple levels and were suffering from numerous personal and professional impacts. Because my background was in expressive arts therapy (EXA), it was decided that EXA was the perfect place to turn for inspiration.

For millennia, we have turned to and utilized the arts (movement, drama, visual art and poetry to name a few) for expression and as a way of making sense of both our inner and outer worlds. As Nathalie Rogers indicates, "They [the arts] are ways to release your feelings, clear your mind, raise your spirits…" (Rogers 2000, p.1). The arts also allow us to give form to the images that haunt our souls, and to find strength and hope. Rogers expresses this process beautifully: "As our feelings are tapped [through the arts], they become a resource for further self-understanding and creativity. We gently allow ourselves to waken to new possibilities" (p.2). It was thus decided that the arts would be an excellent tool to weave into the training process. In this way we hoped that the participants in the training would begin to give voice to their experiences and find new ways of coping with their situation.

As the training courses developed we began to use increasing amounts of art, play, music, and dance as we discovered that all were welcomed and accepted by the Sudanese and international communities. The art-making allowed training participants a new voice around what they had been experiencing, and allowed us to be able to explore past trauma in a safe way. As Rogers writes, "art helps us to accept ourselves and self-acceptance is paramount to compassion for others" (Rogers 2000, p.2). Countless others have echoed the same sentiment, specifically Mariam Nabarro, who worked with Sudanese street children. She found that "even when difficult situations could not be resolved, … the arts gave the children the opportunity to transform it into something else, taking control of their lives, at least on paper" (Kalmanowitz and Lloyd 2005, p.xiv).

We thus began to use the expressive arts in the training in order to allow participants an opportunity to explore difficult situations, and hopefully find some strength and hope as a result. In one art exercise participants were asked to draw a time in their lives when they had a problem or when something difficult had happened to them. They were then asked to trace their hands and write down who had supported them during this time and how. In this way participants could be connected to difficult events in their lives and to support mechanisms. Through this we then taught participants about effectively supporting others and what qualities were most important in a supporter.

One example that emerged through this exercise is as follows (Figure 11.2).

Figure 11.2 The rough places

> We were traveling from Nyala to a field location when our cars were stopped by armed men. We were taken from the cars at gunpoint and then forced to walk for hours through the hills. I was so afraid and the

men were discussing whether they should rape me or not. Luckily, one of the commanders intervened and we were let go, out in the desert somewhere. We were all so afraid. After the incident, we all supported each other, we sat together and we talked. Friends and family also listened to me, and what was most helpful was people just "listening." No one judged me or told me that I had done anything wrong.

Aska, INGO national staff employee

Music and dance were also regularly used throughout the training program to introduce elements of play, and to allow participants periods of freedom from speaking. Often, the group would choose a piece of music together and we would sit and listen. What began to emerge was that the participants felt that the training offered them space and time to re-establish a connection with themselves and their feelings, to relax and to begin to think about how they were personally responding to stress and trauma.

One example of an exercise with music and dance was for participants to choose a partner and then dance on a piece of paper. With each round, the paper was folded into smaller and smaller pieces, and the participants were instructed that they needed to keep dancing, as a couple, without their feet going off of the paper. This exercise was designed to illustrate how, in times of stress and trauma, we can feel that our "space" is being taken away and we can feel confined. Figure 11.3 shows two women participating in the exercise.

Figure 11.3 Dancing for decentering

As you can see, the arts allowed for laughter and a decentering, or moving away, from the stressors they were experiencing on a day-to-day basis. This "decentering allows an 'exit' out of the narrow situational and personal restrictions" that people were experiencing (Knill *et al.* 2005, p.84). Also, "By decentering, we move away from the narrow logic of thinking and acting that marks the helplessness around the 'dead-end' situation in question" (Knill *et al.* 2005, p.83). This decentering, this moving away into "using imagery, storytelling, dance, music, drama, poetry, movement and visual arts together in an integrated way, fostered growth, development and healing" (Kalmanowitz and Lloyd 2005, p.161). Over the course of the training, we could observe a transformation in the participants and, through the arts, a moving away from trauma into an ability to play, laugh, and find hope.

Another important element of the training was the use of play. Games and toys were woven into the training and participants were encouraged to use them as they wished. On the last day of the training, the groups were asked to use building blocks to create a structure that would represent the group cohesiveness they had developed, and act as a reminder for them of what they would take away from the training. This particular group built the structure pictured in Figure 11.4. They said that it showed a sense of play and fun, and that the clay figures represented the fact that they felt joined together in their journey.

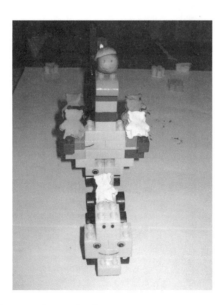

Figure 11.4 Bringing strength to each other

RESULTS

After eleven months in Darfur, my team and I had created a training program and a critical incident support system that was valued by the entire NGO community. The program conducted 15 training programs in many regions in Darfur, including Nyala, South Darfur, El Fasher, North Darfur, and Khartoum, with 193 people attending from local and international NGOs. As research has shown that national staff are most often the direct targets during critical incidents, one of the main goals of the program was to reach out to national staff. This was incredibly successful with 124 of the 193 participants being national staff.

As part of the program, participants were asked to evaluate what was most important to them. The participants identified:

1. Use of music and the arts

The participants most enjoyed the use of music and art throughout the training. They indicated that one particular music video, a song by Mattafix which showed aspects of hope in Darfur, was most impactful because it lead to discussions of coping with and finding hope in difficult situations. They also appreciated how the use of the arts gave them space away from their daily stress and allowed them moments of relaxation and reflection. This in turn built their capacity to care for themselves in a healthier way, and to begin to care for others with increased empathy.

2. Coping with stress

The feedback from the course was that participants felt they gained practical skills through the training, managing their own stress as well as assisting others after a critical incident.

Participants made the following comments:

- "This course helped me to identify ways of coping with stress and how to support others."

- "I will commit to myself to apply relaxation techniques into my life."

- "I will take back what I have learned into my organization."

- "The best aspect was learning how to manage my own stress and support others."

One of the most important results of the program was the development of the Critical Incident Support Network, which was well received and utilized by most NGOs. In the 11 months that I was in Darfur, the network responded to numerous critical incidents such as car-jackings, employee death, armed robberies, abductions, and arrests. The most successful aspect of the network was that it was able to provide support to national staff through the utilization of local staff who had been trained during our training courses.

By the time I left Darfur there were 15 active members in the support network who volunteered to provide the support after critical incidents. These volunteers received ongoing training in basic counseling support from my team, and they were able to provide support in the form of lay counseling and psycho-education after critical incidents. The table below details the extensive amount of support that the Network was able to provide in 2008.

Table 11.1 Support provided by the Support Network in 2008

Type of incident	Number of incidents
Car-jacking	23
Shooting	1
General stress (staff seeking support because of the impact of working in a stressful environment)	21
Traumatic injury	1
Armed robbery (compound)	10
Psychiatric evacuation	1
General evacuation due to insecurity	2
Abduction	2
Temporary detention and harassment	6
Employee violent death	1
Sexual harassment	1
Plane hijacking	1
Total number of incidents	**70**
Total number of people supported by the network (group and individual support)	**252**

SOCIAL CHANGE?

It was my feeling, by the time that I left Darfur, that an element of social change was taking place as a result of the trainings and the support network. Employees began to feel able to talk about the stress and trauma they were facing, and they had begun to implement change in their workplaces. Several managers from NGOs came forward as champions of change, and began to look at self-care systems more actively within their workplaces. And, as a direct result of the support network, the impact of critical incidents was taken seriously, and staff were provided with the needed assistance after incidents. Through this model, we were able to provide impetus for local change and to build capacity in national staff who would then be able to create change in their organizations.

Mohammed, whose story is told at the opening of this chapter, sums this up perfectly in an interview after attending a training session:

> The CISM course changed my life. In the past I felt like I didn't have any support to help me in the field. Recently I have felt afraid to go to the field, even though this is my job. I stopped going to the field four months ago because of the last incident that happened to me. Management was thinking about sending me to Khartoum to meet a specialist. A colleague with whom I experienced two incidents had taken this course, and he told me I should go to the CISM course. After taking the course, I felt supported, and I was able to immediately resume my field activities. One week after the course I spent three days in the field. Before I said never again will I go to the field. My wife would not even let me return to the field. After the course I felt prepared for anything that could happen.
>
> We all know the risk of going into the field, but good procedures and a good understanding of how to deal with situations will reduce the risk. I also now feel better equipped to help others who are preparing for a trip in the field, and also those who have had the same experience as me. I like being able to support my colleagues. I have also requested that my organization send many others to this course to prepare them for the insecurity in Darfur. If something happens, it is important that you are ready for it.
>
> Aid workers need support to be better equipped to provide assistance to the victims of conflict. Many of my colleagues have been involved in many incidents and received no support. This training does a great job providing us with the support we need. They are the only NGO in Darfur doing this.
>
> One of the most useful things for me was the coping mechanism that the course taught. I have had a problem with depression because of my work. This course taught me techniques to help to solve my problems.

For example, what you need to do for yourself, and how better to support your family. Before I did this course my wife wanted me to quit and never return to the field, but I have explained the ideas and knowledge I received from the course, and she forgot everything.

Mohammed, International Non-Governmental (INGO)
national staff employee

Thus we begin to see the emergence of hope and the seeds of change, as shown in the first painting by Suhil (Figure 11.1). Through the arts, national staff began to access coping mechanisms and to remember sources of strength. They also began to express and discuss, in safe ways, the trauma they had experienced. By beginning to heal from their own experiences, they were then able to offer compassion and assistance to others. Expressive arts therapy thus became a key training modality, and the result was an installation of hope and the emergence of small pockets of beauty in one of the most difficult places in the world.

References

Aid Worker Security Database (2010) Available at www.aidworkerssecurity.org/search.php, accessed December 2010.

Augsburger, R. (2007) *Staff Wellbeing in the Darfur Region of Sudan and Eastern Chad. Report Prepared for Interaction.* Available at www.headington-institute.org/Portats/32/ resources/InterAction_Report_Final_November_28_2007.pdf, accessed December 2010.

Baingana, F., Bannon, I. and Thomas, R. (2005) *Mental Health and Conflicts: Conceptual Framework and Approaches.* Washington, DC: World Bank. Available at http:// siteresources.worldbank.org/HEALTHNUTRITIONANDPOPULATION/ Resources/281627-1095698140167/BainganaMHConflictFinal.pdf, accessed October 2010.

De Nobriga, K. and Schwarzman, M. (1999) *Community-based Art for Social Change.* Available at www.communityarts.net/readingroom/archivefiles/1999/10/communitybased.phps, accessed December 2010.

Flint, J. and de Waal, A. (2005) *Darfur: A Short History of a Long War.* London: Zed Books.

Kalmanowitz, D. and Lloyd, B. (2005) *Art Therapy and Political Violence: With Art, Without Illusion.* New York: Routledge.

Knill, P.J., Levine, E.G. and Levine, S.K. (2005) *Principles and Practice of Expressive Arts Therapy: Toward a Therapeutic Aesthetic.* London: Jessica Kingsley Publishers.

Loughry, M. and Eyber, C. (2003) *Psychosocial Concepts in Humanitarian Work with Children: A Review of the Concepts and Related Literature.* Washington, DC: National Academies Press.

Rogers, N. (2000) "The path to wholeness: Person-centered expressive arts therapy." Available at www.psychotherapy.net/article/The_Path_to_Wholeness, accessed October 2010.

Stoddard, A., Harmer, A. and Didomenico, V. (2009) *Providing Aid in Insecure Environments: 2009 Update.* Available at www.aidworkersecurity.org/resources/ ProvidingAidinInsecureEnvironments2009Update3.pdf, accessed December 2010.

12

Art as a Gift

Expressive Arts in Bolivia

Sally S. Atkins

Although rich in cultural traditions and natural resources, economically Bolivia is one of the poorest and most underdeveloped countries in South America. Bolivia has a long history of political struggles and unrest, and almost two-thirds of the population lives in poverty. Many are miners or subsistence farmers. Bolivia has the largest percentage of indigenous population in South America, with the two largest groups being the Quechua and Aymara.

The Department of Human Development and Psychological Counseling at Appalachian State University has had a longstanding relationship with Bolivia. My faculty colleagues, graduate student colleagues, and I have traveled numerous times to the country, especially to the city of Cochabamba and to the surrounding countryside. We have worked with the arts in order to cross cultural boundaries, to create meaningful exchange and to support several local programs that aim to help the victims of poverty, in particular street children. Primarily due to poverty, the presence of large numbers of street children remains a persistent problem in many of the cities, including Cochabamba.

Our work in Bolivia has included several different programs. We have been involved in teaching about expressive arts therapy to psychology students and faculty at the Universidad de San Simon, and in providing professional training in expressive arts therapy for the staff of Amanacer, a program that helps street children, young mothers, and orphans. We have also carried books, basic first aid, and medical supplies, art supplies, and other donations to help meet the needs of these populations, visiting orphanages, schools, and community outreach programs. Our purpose has been not only to share our professional expertise, but also to provide learning experiences for our graduate students and ourselves. Through the arts we have had the privilege of engaging in a reciprocal cross-cultural sharing that has taught us much about life in a developing South American country and much about ourselves.

ART AS A GIFT

Our encounters in Bolivia have continued to be complex, multilayered, challenging and beautiful. With this in mind, I would like to offer a collage of verbal snapshots, vignettes of our experiences, within the framework of Lewis Hyde's concept of art as a gift, as developed in his book *The Gift: Imagination and the Erotic Life of Property* (1983). Hyde says that a work of art is a gift, something we do not acquire by our own efforts, but something given to us, bestowed upon us. Hyde further elaborates that there are at least three aspects of this gift:

1. Art comes to the artist as something bestowed. He or she must open to receive the inspiration that comes.

2. Artists must use their gift to make it manifest in the world, a labor of thanks for this inspiration.

3. The artist must give the gift to others.

Our work in Bolivia has been a series of gifts bestowed, gifts made manifest, and gifts given and received. This has taken place within a reciprocal cultural exchange that has taught us about the power of the arts to cross barriers of economics, class, language and culture. We have learned that to be helpful in a strange culture we must stay open and trust that the inspiration for how to proceed in any given moment will come to us. Our labor of thanks is to continue to learn and to practice our work as expressive artists/therapists and, in the case of crossing cultures, to learn a clear and simple language for sharing it with others. Our responsibility is to take our gifts of experience and knowledge of the arts as healing and offer it to those we encounter, and to receive with gratitude the gifts offered in return.

The gifts we have experienced in Bolivia have been more than the art objects and stories exchanged. The gifting has had even more to do with the sharing of art-making, the behavior of art. The gift, what has been bestowed upon us, has been the discovery, for each of us, of our own artistic impulse as a resource to meet and share with those of a different culture by way of the arts. Most especially, the gifting has been about the sharing of our presence as human beings with each other through the arts.

In the sharing of the gift, says Hyde, a social bond is created. In this sharing, as Stephen Levine (1997) points out in *Poiesis: The Language of Psychology and the Speech of the Soul*, there is a convergence between Hyde's ideas of art as a gift and the ideas of anthropologist Victor Turner (1969). Turner discusses the possibility of creative "communitas" among human beings through the process of artistic ritual. Communitas is the experience of bonding as human beings in community, beyond the structure of societal roles and norms.

According to Levine, "Wherever a work of art is given and received in an authentic manner, a community springs into being" (Levine 1997, p.53). Hyde sees the gift of art (and we would say the gift of art-making) as a "liminal" or threshold gift, an agent of transformation from one state of being to another. This idea also echoes Turner's emphasis on the necessity of liminality as the in-between, the transition state in ritual. In some sense, each trip to Bolivia has been a ritual. We leave the world we know, travel through an in-between, liminal space, and we enter a strange new place. We do not speak the indigenous languages. We face situations in which we do not know our roles. Art-making and sharing become the bridge across cultures and the gifts through which we experience "communitas," a sense of true human community. The following vignettes provide a glimpse into the experiences of communitas we have experienced in Bolivia.

THE CHILD IN THE STREET

When I think of my experiences in Bolivia, many images come to me. Quite a few of the images are faces, some smiling, some stoic and sad, women in the market, shoeshine boys in the plaza. One picture that I will always remember vividly is that of a young boy lying in the middle of the sidewalk. His eyes were closed and he was not moving. We wondered if he were dead. Our group of faculty members and graduate students had just arrived in the city of Cochabamba. We were walking toward the market when we saw him. We stopped, unsure of what to do, as others simply stepped over him or went around him. Quickly our Bolivian friend and guide went to him, awakened him, propped him up and spoke to him in Quechua. He had been sniffing glue, he told us. It is a common and very dangerous problem among the many street children. This was our introduction to the streets of Cochabamba. It was, in a sense, an example of the experience of a liminal space. We were in between, in a place where we no longer knew our roles. It was just the beginning.

WEAVING BRACELETS, WEAVING WISHES

Amanacer is a collection of programs begun in 1981 by the Sisters of Charity of St. Vincent de Paul. Its mission is to offer a safe environment and a new start for children and women who live on the streets of Cochabamba. Because of poor economic conditions, many abandoned children live on the streets of the city or in slums at the city's edge amidst high rates of addiction and abuse. Glue sniffing is the predominant addiction among the street children. Amanacer includes an array of assistance programs, including day facilities and residential facilities for children and young mothers from the street, an orphanage, and counseling, vocational, and educational programs. The staff also make regular night visits to the worst parts of the city to give food and milk to children on the street.

Sayaricuy is one of the many programs run by Amanacer. It is a residential facility for young boys who come directly from the street. The children are offered food, shelter, health care, education, counseling, and some structure in what has often been a previously aimless and dangerous life. If possible they are eventually reunited with their families, or if reuniting with family is not feasible then the boys progress to other levels of the Amanacer program. Sayaricuy means "rise up" in the indigenous language of Quechua.

We met the young residents of Sayaricuy in their modest cafeteria. A few of the boys seemed withdrawn or frightened at the presence of gringos, but most were grinning ear-to-ear and full of curiosity. We had brought gifts of art supplies, clothing, first aid, and other personal items. They sang songs for us, accompanied by one of the boys on the churanga, a traditional stringed instrument made from the shell of an armadillo. One boy played a lively solo on the pan flute, another traditional Andean instrument. Soon we adjourned to the courtyard to play games with the boys and to learn about their latest project – making woven "friendship bracelets." They were weaving these bracelets of yarn and string and embroidery thread to sell to help raise money for the program.

One very tiny boy, Juan, came and sat down beside me on a bench at the edge of the concrete playground. At first he just sat in silence. Then he reached into his pocket and took out a blue, black, and white strip, woven of what looked like embroidery thread. I remarked how nice the colors looked, and he grinned shyly. Then, on an impulse, I asked him if he wove wishes into the bracelet. Quietly he whispered that his wish was to find his family and be reunited with them. I learned later that he was one of many children abandoned by families who could not afford to feed them. I asked if he would teach me how to make a bracelet. With great excitement he scurried away and returned with thread. He quickly tied the thread to one end of the bench and we sat down together on the ground while he taught me how to weave a bracelet. We exchanged our bracelets along with many wishes, both spoken and unspoken, and we spent the rest of the afternoon hand in hand. Later our group bought all of the boys' bracelets to take home as mementos and gifts, and encouraged them to continue with their project. That boy's art gift to me was his teaching. Our gift to each other was our genuine presence and attention.

HELPING THE HELPERS: STAFF TRAINING IN EXPRESSIVE ARTS FOR AMANACER

Early in our Bolivian travels, our faculty members were invited to share the use of expressive arts in training with the Amanacer staff. We wondered what we really had to offer these staff members. While some of us had some small knowledge of their culture, and others had experience working with children in situations of abuse and neglect, and with addictions, none of us had lived with the daily trauma of grinding poverty with which these staff members were dealing. Also, while the idea of expressive arts therapy is certainly not part of the standard training for helping professionals in Bolivia, we knew this to be a culture rich in the arts, particularly the arts of indigenous people. Music, dance, ritual, dramatic enactment, and visual arts all hold an important place in daily life in indigenous culture. We wondered how their artistic traditions might already support their professional work, and if we could enhance this resource for them. As with every situation of cross-cultural exchange, we knew we must first learn from them.

We first asked staff members to share stories about their work, about their hopes and dreams, their frustrations, fatigue, and pain. Visual images and symbols elaborated and deepened the storytelling, and the sharing became intense and deeply moving. Many tears were shed as they told heartwarming and heart-wrenching stories of their work. We were inspired by their courage and dedication, despite the many economic, political, and social obstacles they face.

We began to speak about how, in our professional experience, the arts can help in dealing with struggles and trauma. There was an instant resonance between our gringo ideas of expressive arts therapy and their lived experience in their work and culture. As we asked about the arts and their own self-care, one woman spontaneously began to share a song, and others soon joined in. We stood and moved together in rhythm to the music. We sang, danced, shared more stories and more tears. Then, in closing, we stood silently holding hands and weeping while we played John Lennon's "Imagine." Our sharing created a bond and connection that would endure throughout our future travels in Bolivia. Now, when we return, we are returning as colleagues and friends. Art-making as a gift of cultural exchange has made a bridge for us that remains an ongoing connection.

TEACHING EXPRESSIVE ARTS TO PSYCHOLOGY STUDENTS AND FACULTY AT LA UNIVERSIDAD DE SAN SIMON

Our session with the psychology students and faculty of the university began with a formal lecture and panel discussion in a large lecture hall at the university. We lectured mostly in Spanish, assisted by an interpreter when needed. We spoke about the major theoretical approaches to counseling and psychotherapy in the United States, including analytic, behavioral, and humanistic/existential approaches. We also discussed expressive arts therapy as a new and emerging approach. We learned later that the students and faculty were familiar only with analytic approaches, and that they had no textbooks in the field.

The following day we held an experiential session in expressive arts therapy in the lobby of the Museum of Archeology amid displays of historical artifacts. We introduced the ideas and application of expressive arts therapy to about 50 students and professors. Then we opened our space in a ritual way with breath and poetry. We divided into small groups and sat on the floor of the museum. We used simple visual art (crayon drawings) and storytelling to demonstrate how the arts can enhance group bonding, deepen the process of personal sharing, and create a space for new learning and surprises to appear.

We asked all of the participants to draw a picture of their family, then to share something about their image with the group. As we went from group to group, listening and observing, we were touched by the stories and images. Many were images of suffering. One student drew a scene of a recent political demonstration, which in Cochabamba was a common event that we witnessed frequently. The scene showed his brother, injured and bleeding, in the center. Another picture showed a table with the family seated around it, with one empty chair at the head of the table for the father who had recently died.

As we discussed the exercise, it was clear that the students and faculty knew a lot about the power of the arts from their own culture and life experience. At the same time, it was apparent that the idea of using the arts as a part of psychology was a radical shift from what they were learning at the university. Our reciprocal gifts were more than the words we shared, or the images and stories we were privileged to witness. In our simple art-making experience, we were able to show and discuss how using the arts in an intentional way could facilitate sharing and understanding, and how the arts can offer a container to hold the stories of our lives.

PERSONAL EXCHANGE: THE OLD MAN AT THE CATHEDRAL

I first noticed his frail and ragged figure sitting on the steps of the cathedral. He looked ancient. Then I saw the array of tiny paintings laid out before him on the steps, and I sat down to look at them. I picked up each one carefully to look more closely. He smiled. The paintings were of landscapes, mountains, and water. Some were "framed" by toothpicks glued around the edges. Each was about one inch by one-and-a-half inches in size. They were exquisite. He spoke neither English nor Spanish, and I spoke no Quechua, but a woman nearby translated. He was selling the paintings for two bolivianos each, about 25 cents. I told him, through the translator, that I would like to buy all of them, and I quickly gave him double what he was asking. I hurried back to my room, holding my "treasures" in my hand.

Then I began to wonder about the exchange. The tiny paintings were worth much more to me than I had paid. Should I have given him more? Had I given him too much? Had I insulted him by not bargaining, an important aspect of social and economic exchange in that culture? I was left with the feeling that somehow I should have exchanged more than money, even though I am sure he needed the money. I felt embarrassed that my purchase, however helpful it may have been to him economically, still was a commodification of his art. I wanted to give him a gift in return. The next day and several days after our exchange, I took a small journal I had made of watercolor paper, hoping to find him and give it to him, knowing that the paper was especially scarce and valuable. But I never saw him again. The little paintings are treasures that I share with students as I tell the story of the encounter. Telling his story is the gift I give back to him.

REFLECTING WITH OUR STUDENTS

Each evening we spent one to two hours in a group, sharing and processing with our own graduate students. We wanted students to digest and reflect upon their experiences and to share what they were learning about Bolivia, about counseling and about themselves. Such sharing was not always easy. We used the arts to help us hold and honor the emotional complexity of each day's experience. Each evening, students took their journals and colored pencils and created whatever images came to them from the day. Then we shared the images, along with movement or poetry or journal reflections, trying to touch and hold and convey those experiences which went beyond words. This poem was one of my own attempts at an artistic response to my experience.

Mi Cancioncita de Bolivia
para Terry y Al

En esta tierra estoy trabajando,
Una peregrina buscando sanctuario,
Una viajera palida en un pais rico
Y oscuro como los ojos de los ninos
En la cancha vendiendo limones.
Oscuro como los cuentos tejidos
A las trenzas largas de las cholitas viejas
Marchando en las calles de Cochabamba
Pidiendo las pensiones de sus esposos muertos.

Aqui en esta tierra
Tengo una vista nueva,
Escuchando a su musica,
Encuentro caras
Que ya no son desconocidas,
Nuestras vidas entretejedo
En un paisaje de cuentos.

My Little Song of Bolivia
for Terry and Al

In this land I am traveling,
A pilgrim seeking sanctuary,
A pale traveler in a country rich
And dark as the eyes of children
In the market selling lemons.
Dark as the stories woven
In the long braids of old women
Marching in the streets of Cochabamba
Asking for pensions of dead husbands.

Here in this land
I have a new vision,
As I listen to its music,
I see faces
No longer strangers,
Our lives interwoven
In a landscape of stories.

S. Atkins (2004) "Mi cancioncita de Bolivia." *Headwaters Appalachian Journal of Expressive Arts Therapy* 1, 2, 47. Reprinted with permission.

REFLECTION

These small vignettes are a few of many examples of experiences of cross-cultural learning and reciprocal sharing through the arts that we experienced in Bolivia. In each of the vignettes, art-making and sharing were an integral part of the exchange. In our direct encounters with children at Sayaricuy, our appreciation of their art-making was a means of offering respect and affirmation for children unaccustomed to receiving such validation, especially from foreigners.

In our teaching experiences the arts helped us to show rather than just tell about how the practice of expressive arts therapy can be helpful. In these encounters the art-making also opened the possibility of sharing our human stories as a way of crossing cultural boundaries and building community. In my personal experience with the old Indian man, his art touched my heart, as it does those of my students now when I share the story and his tiny artworks in the classes I teach.

In each of these experiences, as in many others, the expressive arts have given us a language within which to communicate the depth of our human stories. Art-making and sharing have helped us to shape and hold the experience of encountering a culture different from our own, and to expand our understanding and appreciation of that culture. The expressive arts have been a primary aspect of our experience of communitas. Our continued relationships with the people and agencies with whom we worked attest to the effectiveness of the expressive arts as a means of crossing cultures. Our students often tell us that the trips to Bolivia have changed their lives, making them much more sensitive and aware of life in developing countries, of the comparative wealth in which we live in the United States, and the capacity of the arts to contribute to the experience of community.

In our travels to Bolivia we did not see ourselves as agents of social change. We saw ourselves as learners. Perhaps this attitude of respect and prizing of what people of a different culture have to offer to us may be an avenue of social change. Perhaps this kind of attitude of genuine interest in those of a different culture may make a contribution toward fostering community in the world.

References

Hyde, L. (1983) *The Gift: Imagination and the Erotic Life of Property*. New York: Vintage.

Levine, S.K. (1997) *Poiesis: The Language of Psychology and the Speech of the Soul*. London: Jessica Kingsley Publishers.

Turner, V. (1969) *The Ritual Process: Structure and Anti-structure*. New York: Aldine du Gruyter.

13

A Black Dog on a Green Meadow[1]

Doing Expressive Arts Therapy in Peru: Some Headlines

TAE Perú (Judith Alalu, Jose Miguel Calderon, Ximena Maurial, Monica Prado, Martin Zavala)

Hasta que sentimos sobre nuestros ojos
Las primeras paladas de tierra
La última caricia inacabable
Y nos reconciliamos con nuestra procedencia.

(César Calvo)[2]

Living in Peru is like stepping into the decentering phase of an expressive arts therapy session without warming up or being aware; it is like appearing suddenly in a reality often felt as alternative, yet not unreal. The informality, the rawness, the abruptness: all are part of its essence. It would seem there is no time to sensitize us sufficiently to face our daily experience as Peruvians. *More than 69,000 Peruvians missing and killed by subversive organizations and State agents during the internal war in Peru (1980–2000).* Sooner or later we become involved in this overwhelming reality, where sometimes we are not fully sure whether what we are living is a nightmare, a parody, a play, or a drama.

This is the kind of violence that has settled into our daily lives. It appears in the form of racism, in arrogant driving in traffic, in the pollution caused by cars, in the feeling of helplessness caused by unfair law enforcement: culprits who skip trials, accused rapists and murderers turned into accusers.

All this surrounding us, enveloping us. *Seventy-five percent of the victims of political violence were Quechua-speaking peasants.* In a public bus, the loud music, the collector shouting out the route, the smoke, the horns, and more than one person wearing headphones, listening to what they choose to listen, trying to choose what they hear without really accomplishing it, as the shouting, the horns, the music that we do not choose is heard anyway. It would seem that we were training ourselves to try to avoid listening to what we don't want to hear, to see things selectively even if they are right before our eyes, or not to see things that leap into view. Is it that the shrillness of everyday life – the day-to-day violence, its harsh nudity – is covered over by our perception, by our senses? Is it perhaps that if it arrived naked it would affect us so deeply, to the point of leaving us painfully exposed?

Regional government of oreto cancels project with TAE Perú

The TAE Perú 5Team (Expressive Arts Therapy Team) spent a week in the City of Iquitos at the request of the Regional Government of Loreto, to evaluate the possibility of starting a community development project through the arts. Iquitos is the largest city in the Amazon forest region of Peru, full of color, diversity, exuberance, and mixed feelings due to its multiple development possibilities, but also due to its many deficiencies, its poverty, and permanent chaos. The regional president himself supported the initiative with great enthusiasm. TAE Perú were already engaged in the preparations to start this initiative, which aimed to strengthen different groups that work with the arts in the city of Iquitos through the principles of expressive arts therapy. However, after several months of paperwork the project was trapped in government bureaucracy.

"Estamos en la calle," one of the collective exhibitors with whom TAE made contact, offers urban concerts where it brings together "heavy metal" and the traditional rhythms, tales, and myths of the Amazon forest. The exhibition seeks to group different urban, traditional, and contemporary artists to offer them greater possibilities for exposure and venues through which their voice and art may really reach the largest number of Iquiteños.

Contact was also made with "La Restinga," which for the past several years has engaged in different artistic activities with children and adolescents in marginal situations. Just recently they organized a procession through different places in the city, with the image of a shoeshine boy (representing little Jesus), which they created themselves. The idea stemmed from the children themselves, who participated in the creation of the entire event. With this they sought to raise awareness in the community with regard to the hardships that working children face in Iquitos.

With them and other groups TAE Perú was able to enthusiastically imagine different joint work possibilities, taking expressive arts gradually to an entire city where the arts have great presence. A first stage would involve the creation of art together with the different institutions, then building on this experience and determining what would be the best way to consolidate the work and strengthen different initiatives that could emerge. Then, little by little, the different activities undertaken by the different groups involved in the initiative would gradually integrate. Thus the arts with all their transforming potential would have greater presence in the city of Iquitos.

"Unfortunately, from imagination and illusion we were rapidly brought back to reality; or maybe it took us too long to accept this reality. Maybe we were never able to understand the qualities of the reality we were facing, so magical, seductive, and frustrating at the same time," the members of TAE Perú stated with disappointment.

Why don't you answer
Why don't you come save me
Show me how to use
All these things
That you gave me
Turn me inside out
So my bones can save me
Turn me inside out

(Lhasa de Sela)

The Expressive Arts Therapy – Peru team has always discussed the way in which we are immersed in our country, trying to read through it and to feel it, joining efforts to stand up to the challenges… And taking into account how we must attend to ourselves in order to do this. *More than 40 percent of the population in Peru lives in a situation of poverty and extreme poverty.* This time, encouraged by the presentation of this chapter, we wanted to make art in order to try to clarify our ideas as to what doing expressive arts therapy in Peru implies. This could well extend to other Latin American countries.

The proposal involved facing the language of our reality as narrated in all the local newspapers and creating a collage with that material. The reality and its fragments appeared then through images, words, phrases, advertising, shapes, colors, different sized letters... *Madman stabs brother to death / Ransom: one million soles / Supreme scandal in Supreme Court / War in town / I was also scammed / Robbery at McDonalds close to the Palace of Government.* The faces of semi-nude cabaret dancers mixed with characters pursued by the law, the look of victory on the face of "our" world surfing champion, and the grief of the family of a murdered teenager.

We then collaged all these images on a large piece of cardboard without any particular order and not all at the same time. It began to take shape. We used tempera to fill in spaces after the first analysis. And so we had the impression we had accomplished unity. However, something was still missing. *Exports will show the best of Peruvian art / Terry's father was selling cocaine* (who the hell is "Terry"?) / *Money for everyone, participate and win.*

We made time for ourselves so that each of us could include phrases, either our own or taken from newspapers. We shared. *Catastrophe. Faith. You decide. Lab representative in just three months. Peru, third-world tourist destination. Have a nice day.*

We placed white tissue paper over the entire collage, with good results. We felt pleased with the final product (even considering that it was not totally finalized). The fragments of news now appeared veiled, a veil that caused the harshness to fade and made the collage beautiful, a veil that did not conceal but made it possible for it to be seen differently.

From there on, we faced some questions that will try to guide our reflections in this article. Was the veil our aesthetic response to the misery displayed in the newspapers? The veil covers; does it also reveal? What role could the veil have in our work as expressive arts therapists in this country? How can this veil help us formulate principles that may guide the work in expressive arts therapy here?

Tissue paper covers and at the same time reveals. The harshness is there and yet the cry is mitigated. The veil, contradictorily, better reveals what is beneath.

Reality is painful in our country. We often find ourselves in the midst of a clash between our desire to deny reality and the weight of reality itself. *In Peru, the expenditure in the education sector amounts to 2.8 percent of the GDP, far below average levels in Latin America.* It would seem that the attempt of many Peruvians to not "believe" what goes on here is more a reflection of a feeling of survival than a psychotic mechanism of dissociation.

Nevertheless, denial has also been conscious and institutionalized. During the dictatorial administration of former president Alberto Fujimori (1990–2000) the State paid for mass media to sell us a "false truth" for years through written press, radio and television. *Vegetables are good for depression.* Closing our eyes to reality became almost a necessity for the population. *Crops for export grow 20 percent.* What then does it mean to look at reality for Peruvians? When is truth real, and when is it suspect? *The vice president of Regional Credit for Latin America of the rating company Moody's stated that the international financial crisis enabled Peru to show its capacity to absorb shocks, and raised Peru's rating to investment grade.*

Thinking of our work as expressive arts therapists, of our task to enable access to the imaginary space, to value imagination, to pursue beauty, we wonder: what should guide our actions if at times it is hard to distinguish between what is real and unreal? On what reality should we stand?

> *Un perro. Un prado.*
> *Un perro negro sobre un gran prado verde.*
> *¿Es posible que en un país como éste aún exista un perro*
> *negro sobre un gran prado verde?*
> *Un perro negro ni grande ni pequeño ni peludo ni pelado*
> *ni manso ni feroz.*
> *Un perro negro común y corriente sobre un prado ordinario.*
> *Un perro. Un prado.*
> *En este país un perro negro sobre un gran prado verde*
> *Es cosa de maravilla y de rencor.*

(Antonio Cisneros)[3]

Our reality starts to define itself based on our purpose to work with the truth. This means accepting what exists, what we have in front of us, what comes up, beautiful or painful. *During the past 33 years, expenditure in education in Peru has not risen above 3.7 percent of the GDP, and instead has been gradually dropping.* It means accepting our contradictions as a country. This also implies accepting our contradictions as members of a community, as a professional team and as individuals. It means accepting a contradictory reality within ourselves. It means accepting the contradictions of the other.

Tae Perú project evidences lack of commitment
of the district authorities in Ica

On August 15, 2007, Peru was shaken by an earthquake measuring 7.9 on the Richter Scale that hit mostly the cities of Pisco and Ica, 400 km from Lima.

In October of that same year, collaborating with Save the Children and Codehica, TAE Perú started to work on the emotional recovery of the population. The project lasted nine months and involved two different stages. During the first stage TAE Perú trained and accompanied three local groups and one group from Lima so that they, in turn, could work directly with the people. The second stage involved the implementation of safe playgrounds as part of the reconstruction of the city. To this effect the entire community participated in the implementation of the parks, from the design, the delimitation of the space, installation, painting, etc. Training of the local groups continued throughout this stage.

TAE Perú arrived in Ica during the first stage of the project. They had to train a drama group made up by adolescent workers, called *Eclipse Total* (Total Eclipse). The group would present a play in the most severely hit areas of the town. The purpose of the play was to help the population deal with the emotional impact of the earthquake.

TAE Perú faced a group made up of teenagers 9 to 17 years old, and commented: "It was amazing to be facing a group of such young people, who had the responsibility to provide support to the population and who were confident they would be able to do so. These kids not only have to face this task, but also their house chores, their school work and their daily work in the street."

TAE Perú members observed the commitment and responsibility of the group towards their work throughout the entire process. During the training sessions, the members of Eclipse Total had, among other things, a space to share their feelings and internal conflicts about their work responsibilities and their deep desire to play and create.

In contrast to this, TAE Perú had to face a series of setbacks and contradictions arising from the poor management abilities, responsibility, and commitment of adults in regard to the project: authorities who were mostly absent and only made an appearance to receive the applause for the results, namely the play presented in their district; teachers who disappeared mysteriously during the training session and suddenly returned to enjoy the complimentary lunch;

local partners with little capacity to guarantee the good quality of the products acquired for the children's playgrounds, materials that were even billed for as if they were first-class; time-frames and deliveries that were not honored; people who due to previous conflicts shut down the electricity and ruined the park inauguration.

The creation and expression processes were violated and attacked by the unstable conditions under which we worked. We wonder how things would have turned out if the authorities had responded with the same commitment and responsibility as the children and adolescents of Eclipse Total.

We long to enter the imaginary space, accepting its own truth and the reality it may bring, without adorning it in order to make it more palatable, without anesthesia. *Peruvians, men and women. . .killed and missing. . .subversive organizations. . .State agents. . .internal war. . .*

The transparency of our role is in making it clear that we will not deny the rawness of reality; this also means that we will not pretend to see it free from distortions, including our own. However, this implies not denying reality, nor converting it immediately into an artistic creation. *Currently, four out of every ten women are victims of domestic violence.* It implies being present in the pain, in the uncertainty, the chaos and the violence, respecting the pace, making sure that it does not dissipate "too fast," so that we may realize that it exists as an indisputable truth.

Being there will allow the real thing to stem from within us, so that beauty may come to face us and bring us closer to the possibility of change.

Si la mitad de mi cuerpo sonríe
La otra mitad se llena de tristeza
Y misteriosas escamas de pescado
Suceden a mis cabellos. Sonrío y lloro
Sin saber si son mis brazos
O mis piernas las que lloran o sonríen
Sin saber si es mi cabeza
Mi corazón o mi glande
El que decide mi sonrisa
O mi tristeza. Azul como los peces
Me muevo en aguas turbias o brillantes

Sin preguntarme por qué
Simplemente sollozo
Mientras sonrío y sonrío
Mientras sollozo
(Jorge Eduardo Eielson)[4]

As expressive arts therapists we seek out the veil not in order to be suffocated, but rather to help us find ourselves in a space with sufficient "air" to create and access the imaginary, to do *poiesis*, to transform the forcefulness of literal reality without rejecting it.

Thus, while the transparency of bonding is something common to all therapeutic spaces, guaranteeing that transparency is especially important in this country... *Madman kills / Currently, four out of every ten women / Money for everyone, participate and win*...that transparency becomes the safe place from which to access imaginary reality.

TAE Perú participated with the Dutch Cooperation Agency in conducting a workshop based on expressive arts

The workshop aimed at strengthening employability skills for students from two Technological Agricultural Institutes. Tae Perú prepared the work proposal, and the Cooperation Agency together with the authorities of the education sector was in charge of organizing and publicizing the event.

A few surprises came up with regard to the coordination of the organization by the Cooperation Agency and the local education authorities. One hour before the scheduled time of the workshop, we were informed that it was the anniversary of one of the institutes. That same morning we received the invitation to attend the event. Given this fact, the teachers who should have been present at the workshop remained at the celebrations until the next day. Meanwhile, the students were under the impression that the training would be on agricultural and livestock issues; the organizers had omitted to inform them about "the subject" of the workshop.

At the beginning of the workshop we had to admit the occasional fragility of established agreements, as well as the surprise and annoyance that this can generate. Making this explicit, putting it into words and not denying the reality and the feelings it generated, gave rise to the possibility of an open and honest exploration with the arts.

An opening ritual, in which each participant was able to bring something to place in the center of the working space, enabled us to take a close look at beauty: green leaves, dry leaves, moist earth, twigs, colorful fabrics, a cricket, a caterpillar, and a book, among other things. Each one was present in the creation of this center; each could be recognized.

Towards the end of the workshop we visited a lagoon, where we baked potatoes in a mud oven prepared on the spot by the students themselves using the earth in the field. The final artistic presentations, prepared during the days of the workshop, took place next to the food. The working place of these agriculture and livestock students is the field, so that is what we chose as the setting for the last meeting.

The closing of the event was attended by the representative from the education sector. Whether due to the impact that the workshop had on them or for other reasons, the students presented to him their criticism about the teaching work in their institutes. Forced by the insistence of the students, the representative had to affirm several times that he would review their requests through the directors of the study centers. The claims were perhaps a means to return to literal reality, a way of effectively modifying it.

During the time we have been doing our work, we have found ourselves recognizing that what is literal may be present in the entire process of doing art. *More than 40 percent of the population in Peru lives in poverty / why don't you answer / turn me inside out.* We want to do everything possible so that this literality does not become an obstacle, but rather draw on its rawness in an authentic manner in order to let beauty emerge. *Twenty-one percent of the population is undernourished.* We must recognize the qualities of our literal reality so that we may begin its transformation. What should our proposal be as expressive arts therapists, in order to achieve this? Should we propose anything? *Is it possible that in a country like this there still may be a black dog on a green meadow?* What conditions do we consider essential to enter the imaginary space? Are there essential conditions? *For the past 33 years expenditure on the education sector in Peru has not risen above 3.7 percent of the GDP.* What does it mean to prepare the ground to do this? To prepare the ground or to be prepared for the ground: this is to be alert, to watch what goes on, to accept what is in front of us, not to deny but to admit it, *because the shouting, the horns, the music we do not choose, is there anyway* and there is the risk of suffering its attack and/or our defense, the risk that we may wish to fight it from literality, from reality itself. *Madman stabs brother to death.* The harshness of reality is present in the space of creation, in the center and everywhere in the air. *More than 69,000 Peruvian men and women killed and missing.* We must not only call out its presence, but also look at it from another shore, with different eyes, in order to be able to start doing something with it. *A black dog, neither big nor small, neither furry nor short-haired, neither tame nor fierce.* Being on a different shore does not necessarily mean moving to a new stage, but rather staying there, next to the literal, with our senses open, with the risk of being invaded once again. *A black common and ordinary dog on an ordinary meadow. A dog. A meadow.* Using the veil allows us to see without intoxicating ourselves, without defending ourselves beforehand. It allows us to wait, wait for the unexpected, to await the unexpected, to be... *until we feel over our eyes / the first shovelfuls of earth / the last endless caress / and we make peace with our source.* Then we might begin to see something new in the horror, something beautiful, something that was always there, faded in its literality, then we might be able *to move in cloudy or clear waters / without wondering why / just sobbing / as we smile and smiling / as we sob.* Perhaps the veil could let us recognize reality, even if half my body smiles and the other half sobs. Perhaps the transparency will help us arrive at a surprise, arrive at the unexpected, find some faith in this catastrophe and see that our catastrophe is present again.

This means paying attention to the way we feel, letting our senses recover their vitality and their original role, to start creating from there. It is about listening to this internal dialogue and doing something with it – without forcing anything, not even expecting anything. Having faith in dialogue as in the rhythm of our breathing. Trusting that every movement brings another one. *It is possible that there still may be a black dog on a green meadow in a country like this.*

> *In our country this may be a necessary first step, and at the same time the starting point for genuine creation on the way towards change and transformation. The starting point that can help us become aware and have the necessary sensitivity to step into our comedy, and see the drama it actually is without turning it into a banality.*
> *So that we may live our drama with sensitivity, let art and humor and truth not be deprived of value. In our country this may be a first step necessary for the probable appearance of the third one, a step prior to a green dog on a black meadow*
> *a blue green dog like the fish*
> *transparent like the black meadow.*
> *Participate and win.*

Notes

1. This phrase has been taken from a poem by Antonio Cisneros.

2. Until we feel over our eyes / The first shovelfuls of earth / The last endless caress / And we reconcile with our source (César Calvo).

3. A dog. A meadow. / A black dog on a green meadow. / Is it possible that in a country like this there may still be a black dog on a green meadow? / A black dog, neither big nor small, neither furry nor short-haired, neither tame nor fierce. / A black, common dog on an ordinary meadow. / A dog. A meadow. / In this country a black dog on a green meadow / It is a matter of wonder and bitterness (Antonio Cisneros).

4. If half my body smiles / the other half fills with sadness / and mysterious fish scales stem from my hair. I smile and I cry / unaware if it's my arms / or my legs that cry or smile / unaware if it's my head / my heart or my glans / that decides my smile / or my sadness. Blue like the fish / I move in custody or clear waters / without wondering why / I just sob / as I smile and smile / as I sob (Jorge Eduardo Eielson 2002, p.191).

References

Calvo, C. (2010) *Pedestal para nadie.* Lima: Mesa Redonda.

Cisneros, A. (1992) *Las inmensas preguntas celestes.* Madrid: Visor Libros.

Eielson, J.E. (2002) "Cuerpo Divido." In J.I. Padilla (ed.) (2002) *NU/DO Homenaje a J.E.Eielson.* Lima: Fondo Editorial PUCP.

Lhasa (2003) "*My Name*" En: *The Living Road* [CD]. Quebec: Audiogram.

Padilla, J.I. (ed.) (2002) *NU/DO Homenaje a J.E. Eielson.* Lima: Fondo Editorial PUCP.

14

These Stories are Burning a Hole in my Brain

Using the Arts to Tell the Stories of the Ethiopian Jewish Immigrant Community in Israel

Vivien Marcow Speiser and Samuel Schwartz

INTRODUCTION AND BACKGROUND

Today, more than 100,000 citizens of Ethiopian descent live in Israel (Tebeka 2007; Wertzberger 2003). Most were born in Ethiopia and arrived in Israel as part of government-initiated rescue missions such as Operation Moses (1984) and Operation Solomon (1991). While Israel is a country of immigrants, and in its 60 years has successfully integrated waves of newcomers from six continents, the absorption of Ethiopia's Jews has been particularly difficult.

Many Ethiopian Jews left their native country under harrowing circumstances, and thousands suffered traumatic events that were not dealt with on a personal or communal level. On arrival in Israel, many faced absorption problems such as economic hardship, social dislocation, and racism. The migration-associated trauma and subsequent dislocation, as well as the socio-economic disadvantages they experienced upon arrival in Israel, have led to high levels of unemployment, crime, alcohol abuse, family violence, academic underachievement, and school drop-out rates (Biton, Eshkol and Bodovsky 1997; Bodovsky, David and Eran 1998; Lotan and Kin 2007; Wergen 2006; Wertzberger 2003). These problems have been compounded by the fact that due both to the Ethiopians' culture and the nature of Israeli society, the immigrants have not been able to give expression to their experiences (Ben-Ezer 2002, 2006, 2007).

THE DIFFICULT ABSORPTION OF ETHIOPIAN JEWISH IMMIGRANTS IN ISRAEL

The absorption of Ethiopian Jewish immigrants in Israel has been more difficult than that of nearly all previous immigrations. They have faced problems similar to those of previous immigrations (persecution in country of birth, dangerous immigration journey, language acquisition difficulties). In addition, the immigrants have had to deal with new challenges (questioning of their status as Jews, a radically different economic and cultural background) unique to their situation.

Like other groups of immigrants to Israel, the Ethiopian Jews faced persecution as Jews in their native land, at least during certain periods, such as immediately prior to the Operation Moses rescue mission in 1984 (American-Israeli Cooperative Enterprise 2009; Parfitt 1985). Ben-Ezer notes that under Haile Mariam Mengistu's government, Jews who even expressed a desire to emigrate to Israel could face a death sentence (2007, p.383). Despite these dangers, tens of thousands attempted to reach what they believed was their promised land (Ben-Ezer 2002).

Ethiopian immigrants endured harrowing and dangerous conditions during each of the government rescue operations that brought them to Israel, like Operation Joshua in 1985 and Operation Solomon in 1991. The approximately 8000 Ethiopian Jews who came to Israel as part of the 1984 Operation Moses suffered from particularly traumatic experiences that have affected their integration into the country (Ben-Ezer 2002, 2006, 2007; Onolemhemhen and Gessesse 1998). For political reasons, the Ethiopian Jews could not be evacuated from their home country and had to travel on foot to the Sudan before they were able to be airlifted to Israel. An estimated 4000 Ethiopian Jews died on the "Sudanese Route" and many others were separated from their families. Those who survived to reach the Sudan were often victimized in refugee camps by Sudanese criminals (Ben-Ezer 2007, p.385).

Like previous immigrants, Ethiopia's Jews have struggled to learn Hebrew. Many immigrants who arrived as adults never acquired a conversant level of the language. This problem interacted with and exacerbated the already-difficult economic and cultural crises that the Ethiopian immigrants faced.

In addition to these problems, familiar from previous immigrant groups, the absorption of the Ethiopian Jews presented Israel with some unique challenges. For many years, the leading religious authorities did not even consider the Jews of Ethiopia to be legitimately Jewish.

Although the chief rabbinate has since changed its stance, and many Ethiopian Jews have undergone symbolic partial-conversion ceremonies, the authenticity of the community's Jewishness is still doubted by some (Ribner and Schindler 1996; Wagner 2006).

The Ethiopian immigrants came from a starkly different economic system as well. In Ethiopia many Jews were relatively well-off. However, they lived in an agrarian society with little access to the technology available in a second-world country like Israel (Joint Distribution Committee and the Brookdale Institute 2001). On arrival in Israel, the overwhelming majority of immigrants were poorly equipped for employment in Israel's economy, which was transitioning from agriculture and light industry to the provision of international services and the export of high-tech products. So since their arrival the Ethiopian immigrants have faced the most challenging circumstances of any of Israel's Jewish ethnic groups, as measured in economic output, education, and social mobility (Israel Association For Ethiopian Jews 2006; Tebeka 2007; Wertzberger 2003).

Partially stemming from their economic orientation, Israel's Ethiopian immigrants were culturally very different from their native-born compatriots. As is consonant with the agrarian economic paradigm, Ethiopia's Jewish families were organized along a patriarchal structure. Women and children played a subservient role to the dominant male family leader. These characteristics clashed with the relative equality enjoyed by Israeli women, and the almost venerated status that Israeli society affords to its children (Kaplan and Salamon 2003).

The immigration of Ethiopian Jews also introduced (according to some, for the first time) specifically racial tensions to the State of Israel. Cleavages always existed between Israel's Sephardic Jews (who originate in Spain, the Balkans, North Africa, and Asia) and Ashkenazi Jews (who originate in Eastern and Western Europe). While these social tensions bore similarities to the racial strife that exists in other countries, most Israeli Jews (on both sides of the divide) considered these fissures to be along communal or ethnic (*Adati*, in Hebrew) but not racial lines. In the national consciousness the more important distinction was always between Jews and Arabs (Kaplan 1999). The mass Ethiopian immigration in the mid to late 1980s introduced a clear racial divide into the society. Israel's Ashkenazi and Sephardic populations were united in viewing the Ethiopians as a separate "black" race. However, as Kaplan notes, this perception was tempered by society's view of the Ethiopian immigrants through the prism of the Jewish/Arab divide in which the Ethiopians were seen as Jewish and hence "not black" (Kaplan 1999, pp.535–536).

THE UNTOLD STORY

Many scholars have noted that the emigration experience has traumatized Israel's Ethiopian immigrant community. In particular, the fact that many of the most difficult stories, relating to the community's traumatic transmigration through the Sudan, have not been told has created a barrier to successful integration. Ben-Ezer (2002, 2007), based on his research into the Ethiopian Jewish emigration, argues that migration journeys are unjustifiably ignored by migration and refugee studies, as well as in traumatology. Powerful processes occur on such journeys that affect the individual and the community in life-changing ways and shape their initial encounter with, and adaptation to, their new society (Ben-Ezer 2007, p.382).

Lester found that the Ethiopians' reaction to their migration trauma expresses itself in "survivor guilt" akin to that experienced by Holocaust survivors (Lester 2005, p.39). Some members of the Ethiopian community refer to their experience as a "shoah" or holocaust (Ante Portas 2009). Ben-Ezer also noted that Israeli society's lack of interest in the Ethiopians narrative of trauma was a particularly important cause of the deep psychological damage that the immigrants suffered (Ben-Ezer 2007, p.395).

The authors' interviews with Ethiopian immigrants to Israel confirmed these hypotheses. Many Ethiopian immigrants noted that they stopped telling their stories once they arrived in Israel because they believed no one wanted to hear them. When the authors pressed their subjects to describe their transmigration through the Sudan in which many of their relatives perished, as well as the persecution they suffered before, during, and after their immigration, they found that many of the community members thought about these experiences as their own "holocaust." This word came up repeatedly. One of our interviewees said, "I have stories to tell and these stories are burning a hole in my brain."

The authors were aware of the above-described difficulties that had thwarted many previous attempts to assist in the integration of Ethiopia's Jews. They were sensitive to the fact that the immigrants' inability to tell their story was particularly painful to the Ethiopian community. They believed that the use of the arts would be important in allowing these stories to emerge as a means of assisting integration, and as a way for individual and collective healing to begin. With this in mind, the authors devised a new model which integrated the arts and allowed for the telling of stories to be applied on a small scale in the town of Nes Ziona. This approach is predicated upon the belief that the expression of these untold stories is intrinsically healing.

MAKING THE CONNECTION BETWEEN LESLEY UNIVERSITY AND NES ZIONA'S ETHIOPIAN IMMIGRANT COMMUNITY

Lesley University in Israel has been operating for 30 years and is well known for its arts-based programs in education and human services. The town of Nes Ziona is known for its creative, comprehensive, and innovative approaches to programming for its diverse populations. Nes Ziona has a population of approximately 30,000 citizens with about 1000 Ethiopian immigrants or their children, making up some 200 families living in the town. A small number of these immigrants arrived in the 1984 Operation Moses. More than half of them came during the 1991 Operation Solomon. Slightly less than half are much more recent immigrants of the Zera Beta Yisrael. This group is made up largely of converts to Christianity who retained a connection to their Jewish roots. The government decided to bring them to Israel only within the past few years, and some tension exists between them and other Ethiopian Jewish immigrants. A significant statistic regarding all three groups is that about a quarter of the families are single-parent households.

Lesley and Nes Ziona joined together to plan several arts-based interventions aimed at the integration of the Ethiopian community in the town. Over several months, the authors, together with other Lesley instructors and administrators, met with various constituencies including the mayor's office, departments of education, human services, the absorption ministry, and representatives and elders of the Ethiopian community. This fact-finding and community-building process was aimed at identifying the needs of the Ethiopian community in Nes Ziona as well as investigating the efficacy of the programs the municipality was currently operating. The process culminated in several network intervention meetings in April 2007. Together with Nes Ziona municipal officials from all branches of city government (the mayor, educators, social workers, community-center directors, etc.) the authors comprehensively mapped every program that was offered to the community's infants, toddlers, pre-schoolers, grade-school and high-school students, post-army veterans, young adults, parents, families, and the elderly. Following the fact-finding meetings the authors created a life-cycle map of Nes Ziona's programs for its Ethiopian community (Table 14.1).

Table 14.1 Life-cycle map of Nes Ziona municipality's programs for Ethiopian immigrants

Life stage	Relevant municipality program	No. of participants
Early childhood	Infant and child day care (3–6 months)	25
Kindergarten	Afternoon day care	50
Primary school	After-school session until 18:00 Grades 1–4 Etgar Program – home visits for parents and children Grade 1 Gamla – home visit grandfathering program After-school session until 18:00 Grades 5–6	50 ?
Middle school	"After the Bell" program Grades 5–7 Integration arts program	30 8
High school	Girls at risk program "We have no other land" program Ethiopian student counselors Counselors in training Breakdance class – Comm. center Running club	25 ? 6 13 15 15
Outside of educational system	Alternative program (Yoni) (DJ, 4X4, Weizmann Inst.)	4
Army		
Higher education		
Vocational education	Women's weaving program	20
Employment	Women's leadership group	15
	Job training 20–30-year-olds	30
Early motherhood	Home-based-program for mothers of children 0–3	14
Marriage		

Parenthood	Social work home visits supervised by municipal social workers	150
	Father's program	15
Academic employment		
Non-academic employment		
Chronic unemployment		
Advocacy	Thursday open house for vocational consultation	1
Elders		

In parallel, Lesley educators met with the leaders of various sub-groups within the Ethiopian community, such as at-risk youth, women's rights activists, and elders. Using arts-based methodologies, the authors facilitated the dialogue amongst community leaders, identifying their core needs and the extent to which they were currently being met. What was striking to the authors was the remarkable concurrence between all the groups as to what was working and not working in the community.

In this process, the authors uncovered an enduring point of friction between the Ethiopian community and the municipality, highlighting a fundamental conflict between competing attitudes toward immigration in Israel. Many, perhaps most of Nes Ziona's Ethiopian immigrants live in the town's Yad Eliezer neighborhood. Consequently, most municipal programs for the Ethiopian community take place in that neighborhood's community center. While the center is used almost exclusively by the Ethiopian immigrant community, Nes Ziona's mayor and other officials were insistent that it not be called the "Ethiopian" community center. This decision derived from their strong belief that segmenting any one community leads to its marginalization and prevents it from fully integrating into general Israeli society.

However, the insistence on not referring to the center as an "Ethiopian" community center deprived the Ethiopian residents of a feeling of ownership and belonging. Many in the Ethiopian community were adamant that the center's name make reference to the Ethiopian residents and several of the elders said that they "refused" to even enter the center till it was properly named. The irony of this situation was that most of our meetings, both with municipal officials and the Ethiopian community, took place in the center.

THE ROLE OF THE ARTS IN THE ETHIOPIAN COMMUNITY

In addition to the difficulties the immigrants face, the authors also became aware of important sources of strength and resiliency within the community. The Ethiopian immigrants have a deep interest and facility in the arts, with a long tradition of music, movement, and handicrafts.

Music and dance have long been a part of Ethiopian life. Apart from their aesthetic and celebratory purposes, they are valued for their healing properties. For instance, many Ethiopian Jewish immigrants participate in the "Zar" ceremony, which uses prescribed music and dance to cure someone suffering from the mental health effects of a ghost-like "Zar." (Al-Adawi *et al.* 2001; Asrasai-Engede 2007). In addition, Afro-Jamaican-American music plays an important part in the development of the self-image of Ethiopian youth (Kaplan 1999; Shabtay 2001, 2003).

Ethiopian immigrants in Israel continue to produce traditional Ethiopian handicrafts as well. Ethiopian-Israeli men and women engage in traditional wickerwork, weaving, smithery, embroidery (Figures 14.1 and 14.2), and pottery. These activities provide a connection to their previous culture as well as creating marketable goods (Israel Association for Ethiopian Jews 2009).

Figure 14.1 Example of embroidery by a woman in the community

Figure 14.2 Example of embroidery by a woman in the community

The authors hypothesized that building on these artistic traditions inherent in the culture could strengthen resiliency and improve self-esteem. Based on these meetings with the constituent groups in the town and the identification of the most pressing needs, the authors conceptualized a series of interventions that might assist the Ethiopian community in areas that the municipality was not yet addressing. These interventions included a storytelling workshop and leadership training seminar for post-army youth, a middle-school program on the subject of imagining the future, and an art therapy support group for young mothers.

The storytelling workshop for post-army youth

The mayor of Nes Ziona was instrumental in identifying a pressing need in Nes Ziona's Ethiopian community. He noted that the most alienated communal sub-group was post-army youth. He explained that from birth until their early twenties, Ethiopian youth maintain a connection to the society at large. There are numerous early childhood pre-school programs as well as after-school activities for Ethiopian children that run till the end of high school. Israel's mandatory universal military service ensures that Ethiopian youth will continue to be involved in an organized social framework for the next 2–3 years. However, after Ethiopian soldiers are discharged from the army, many lose all contact with general Israeli society. Without employment or educational opportunities they return to their communities and simmer in feelings of alienation and rejection.

In an attempt to provide a continued social connection for this sub-group, Lesley established a storytelling and leadership development workshop in spring 2007. The seminar was led by Lesley faculty member and drama therapist Avi Hadari, who endeavored to facilitate the development of leadership skills on the personal, interpersonal, and group levels.

The workshop took place over 12 sessions in the spring of 2007. About 15 Ethiopian youth participated in the seminar, which was co-facilitated by Mr. Hadari and a municipal social worker of Ethiopian background. The workshop used visual arts, storytelling, and drama therapy to explore the participants' strengths and fears.

At the beginning of the workshop, Hadari asked the participants to create an illustrated map of their family's journey from Ethiopia to Israel. Using various art materials, the Ethiopian youth explored the importance of their family's migration across numerous axes including:

- The immigrant journey – some traveled by plane, others walked on foot for miles; some went through villages while others emigrated from the capital city of Addis Ababa; some came directly to Israel while others spent long periods in a transmigration camp. All suffered dislocation, hardship, and family disruption.

- Generational – some immigrated themselves while others were the children of immigrants. All were exposed to first or second generation traumatic memory.

In another session the participants drew a tree that traced their family's roots, as far as they could recall. Hadari encouraged the students to envision what kind of tree their family would constitute. This sparked conversations about the importance of preserving the family, and the way in which some families came apart on arrival in Israel. It is a common theme in working with the next generation born in Israel that there is considerable conflict between the "old" and "new" societies, and some generational embarrassment about cultural differences and disparities.

Another session integrated additional art forms such as storytelling and drama. Hadari (2009) related that the participants used these modalities to address particularly painful issues such as the intense "strength of Ethiopian women in relationship to the weakness of the Ethiopian men." The participants described the important role of mothers and grandmothers in holding the family together. Other issues that were raised included discussions about the effect of immigration on religious observance, and the ensuing struggle between religious and non-religious branches of the family.

At the conclusion of the intervention the Ethiopian youth drew a map representing the road that lies ahead of them. Hadari said that this project highlighted a dilemma that is common to Ethiopian youth. He said, "Some of the participants desired to re-root themselves and create a totally different way of life. Others wanted to stay with the traditional Ethiopian way of life. They dealt with these issues in their artwork."

Hadari believed that the workshop was challenging but successful in its aims of developing participant resiliency, sometimes in unexpected ways. He noted that:

> *The workshop introduced challenges that came from the diversity of the participants. There was a group that was born in Israel, went through the educational system and the army. However, another group consisted of people who came to Israel in the last seven years. These groups had very different needs. The group consisted of both men and women and youth of a variety of ages. (Hadari 2009)*

The most unanticipated benefit for participants was the way it allowed the Ethiopian participants to forge new connections among themselves. Some of the members of the various sub-groups described by Hadari connected to members of other sub-groups for the first time in the framework of the workshop. He observed:

> *The complexity and the fascinating parts of the sessions were the dialogues within this community, particularly around the gap between the newcomers and the veterans. All of them were interested in climbing up the social ladder. Their primary goals were to get access to education, find jobs and settle down in life. The painful struggles came with the notion that progress means giving up on some of the traditional ways of living. Many expressed the feeling that the older generation does not understand the modernity that comes with this new ambition of progress. (Hadari 2009)*

At the conclusion of the workshop, Lesley solicited written evaluations of participant satisfaction. A majority (86%) found the workshop to be a positive experience. Most noted that the seminar was useful and offered opportunities for expression and creativity, and 90 percent wished to continue with similar seminars in the future (Schwartz 2007).

Imagining the future: Building dreams

The next project that Lesley implemented was a day-long program for 200 middle-school students entitled "Imagining the Future: Building Dreams." In the fact-finding meetings it emerged that many Ethiopian students suffered from a lack of self-confidence and an abiding embarrassment about their origins. Lesley and the Nes Ziona municipality prepared a program designed to strengthen the Ethiopian students' self-image and resiliency, while exposing all the students to the beauty of authentic African culture. The authors worked with a team of artists and therapists/ educators to provide large and small group arts-based experiences and activities. The school opened its doors to the Lesley University team that engaged the students in a full day of programming.

The event was structured around a musical opening and closure, with morning and afternoon arts-based workshops aimed at helping the participants to identify and begin to work toward their future goals. The centerpiece of the seminar was the performances and workshops of the Peace Train, a South-African singing duo comprised of Jewish guitarist Sharon Katz and Zulu singer Shophi Ngidi. The Peace Train social movement was founded by Katz in 1993 in order to promote a peaceful transition from Apartheid to democracy. Katz organized a "Peace Train" of 150 musicians who traveled South Africa by train bringing members of nine diverse ethnic and racial groups together and using music to dissolve conflicts and violence. Since then Katz has taken the Peace Train to many other conflict points around the globe. Katz and Ngidi, confident black and white African women working together, celebrating authentic African music and dance, endeavored to serve as role models for the participants. (More information about Katz and the Peace Train can be found at the website www.sharonkatz.com.) It was hoped that exposure to their performance would contribute towards breaking down barriers and increasing all of the students' appreciation for African culture.

The seminar began with a performance by the Peace Train. Following the opening, the students broke up into small groups and participated in morning and afternoon workshops using the following artistic modalities: visual arts, African music, movement, mandala creation, songwriting, drama, and hip-hop. After the workshops, the large group reconvened to share the songs, poems, dances, artworks, and mandalas they created.

The event was a very successful. In their evaluations the students noted how much they enjoyed and learned from the event. The workshops led

by Katz and Ngidi brought Ethiopian and non-Ethiopian students up
to the stage, dancing and singing together. The arts served to start a
conversation, and soon the students were speaking about their origins,
backgrounds, and parents.

A songwriting workshop led by Dani Robas, one of Israel's premier
singers, gave many students new tools for expressing themselves, as
he allowed them to improvise new lyrics for some of his songs. The
mandala workshops, led by Eitan Kedmi, a noted Israeli mandala artist,
were particularly moving. The creation process provided an outlet for
expression and freed the students to "imagine" and think about their
future based upon their skill sets as identified in the mandalas. The
music and hip-hop workshops connected with the Ethiopian students'
fascination with Afro-Jamaican-American music and elicited a lively
discussion. In the sessions using rap music it was interesting to observe
that many of the Ethiopian children identified their roots as "Jamaican"
and several of them thought that Jamaica was in Africa.

Drawing together, singing together, dancing together, faculty and
students alike joined in common rhythms and generated new harmonies.
The event generated much interest in the community and a segment was
broadcast on Israel's main news program.

Art therapy for single Ethiopian mothers

Lesley's survey of the needs of Nes Ziona's Ethiopian community identified
the town's single mothers as another segment of the population that could
uniquely benefit from an arts-based intervention. Single mothers living
alone with their children in Israel represent one of the most exposed
groups in Ethiopian culture. Ethiopian society has historically been male-
dominated, with households governed by a strong patriarchal figure.
With the immigration to Israel and the relatively quicker acculturation of
Ethiopian women, social norms have broken down, leading to abnormally
high rates of divorce, single-motherhood, and violence against women
(Lotan and Kin 2007). In addition, Ethiopian single mothers in Israel no
longer have the communal structures to support them that had existed
in Ethiopia. Lesley researchers found that many Ethiopian Israeli women
did not engage in the communal and self-help activities that the town
offers, and that this further isolates them and causes distress both to them
and to their young children.

In order to assist this segment of the population, in the spring and
summer of 2008 Lesley conducted an art therapy support group for

young Ethiopian single mothers with small children. The first goal was to provide these single mothers with a creative outlet, as many of them tended to remain in their apartments, detached from other communal involvement. Second, the meetings were geared to provide support, guidance and an opportunity for airing their problems. The modality of visual arts was chosen in the hope that it would be the most non-threatening. In contrast to singing, movement, and drama, work in the visual arts required less Hebrew-language ability and less perceived exposure. Most of the participants were shy and frightened of the Israeli establishment, and did not speak Hebrew well. This in turn contributed to their unwillingness or inability to access available social services.

The workshop was led by Lesley graduate and art therapist Keren Askayo together with a municipal social worker and an Ethiopian-Israeli assistant. It was held at the Yad Eliezer Community Center in Nes Ziona's Ethiopian neighborhood. The group met weekly for two hours over the course of 12 weeks.

With Askayo's guidance the Ethiopian women created works of art that related to their daily ordeals. Askayo used art therapy techniques in order to talk about and assist the women in addressing issues such as parenting, immigration, culture-shock, and gender. Askayo noted that the women were only willing to create aesthetic objects that they could use in a practical fashion to decorate their houses, or that could serve other utilitarian functions.

Askayo was struck by the fact that the group members were dependent upon her as a leader and would not choose colors unless she approved of them. For example, if she told one participant that red beads would work well in their artwork, all the participants would then use only red beads.

The program served not just to help the participants process their issues through the arts; it also helped bridge the gaps between the Ethiopian immigrants and the Israeli establishment. For instance, Askayo began the first session with beadwork, familiar to the participants from their experiences in Ethiopia. Many of the immigrants continued to work in this medium on arrival in Israel, either at home or in workshops at the community center in their neighborhood. The use of beads did not raise the participants' anxieties and allowed them to have informal discussions that later focused on significant issues in their lives.

After the participants were comfortable in the setting and with the materials, she worked with the women in the creation of classical Israeli art forms (such as Hamsas, Mezuzas, and Hallah covers) that bridged the divide between Israeli and Ethiopian-Jewish culture. Askayo made sure to choose projects for each meeting that could be completed within one session. She believed that it was important for them to be able to produce a concrete work of art with ornamental value that they could share with their families.

Moreover, like Hadari, Askayo observed that the workshop participants did not have extensive communication channels among themselves or with other segments of the Ethiopian community. The workshop helped to change this situation. The previously reticent women coalesced into a group as a result of their joint participation in the arts-based activities. They opened up to each other and shared stories about both pedestrian and highly traumatic experiences. They shared life-management tips as well as pointers for dealing with specific aspects of Israel's society and establishment. They frequently discussed memories of Ethiopia and, according to Askayo, were able to process their experience of the immigration in ways that they had never done before.

The participants explicitly recognized the benefits they derived from participation in the group. They spoke of their hope to continue such projects in the future as well as the joy they received from the creative art process. They specifically noted how much they gained from speaking with one another on both the practical and emotional levels.

CONCLUSIONS

Lesley's experiment in academic and municipal cooperation towards integrating the Ethiopian immigrant community in the town of Nes Ziona has been fruitful and rewarding. This "town and gown" collaboration had to overcome a number of obstacles in order to succeed. After analyzing the success and failure of these programs, the authors have formulated some conclusions about the nature of the Ethiopian community's integration problems, and about future directions for successful intervention and research.

The problems faced by Nes Ziona's Ethiopian community are severe, and Lesley needed to be realistic regarding what it could accomplish within the scope of its interventions. The authors realized that their resources only permitted them to engage in a small number of target interventions, and they chose areas that promised to provide the best match between their arts-based programs and the most urgent needs of the community.

While Lesley is known for its practical arts-based outreach programs, it needed to adapt its models to the particular conditions that applied in Israel. The Nes Ziona municipality was very helpful in guiding the authors toward interventions that stood the highest chances of success. In the absence of a budget that would allow interventions targeting every stage of the Ethiopian community's life-cycle, the authors recommend continuing to engage in specific interventions designed to assist the most vulnerable segments of the immigrant population.

Telling the "untold" story

The authors confirmed the findings of Ben-Ezer and Ante Portas that the Ethiopians' inability to recount their traumatic immigration narrative caused community members significant distress. The participants in the programs expressed their gratitude for having the opportunity to discuss these issues. They appreciated having a mainstream Israeli audience interested in hearing this narrative, sometimes for the first time. Lesley's researchers and clinicians believed that these opportunities were helpful in developing expressive capacities that increased the participants' resiliency and could be important components of future interventions.

Opening channels of communication

Lesley's initial fact-finding work indicated that a central problem facing Ethiopian immigrants was the conceptual distance between their community and Israeli society in general. An insight arising from each of the interventions was that an equally problematic situation exists within Nes Ziona's Ethiopian community itself. Hadari and Askayo found that the participants had not developed efficient channels of communication among themselves. One of the signal contributions of their workshops was to enable these sub-groups to develop intra-communal networks which could then branch out to other sub-groups within the Ethiopian community, and from there to Israeli society at large.

For the future, the authors hypothesize that establishing intra-communal connections will be an important first step in connecting the Ethiopian immigrants to the larger Israeli society. The authors also believe that the arts are particularly effective channels for creating and sustaining these connections.

The centrality of the arts in the building of resiliency

The authors' findings strengthened the claims of previous researchers about the centrality of the arts to Ethiopian culture. The arts-based programs built on the already existing connections between the Ethiopian community and the arts. While the Ethiopian participants initially viewed the arts as commercial or artisanal tools, it was not a great leap to allow them to see the arts as a means of self-expression.

This familiarity with using the arts, alongside the unfamiliarity with employing them in a therapeutic context, proved to be especially successful in developing the participants' capacity for creative expression. The arts served as a buffer that allowed the immigrants to engage non-verbally with the traumatic events that distressed them while separating themselves from the most painful aspects of their experience. These media allowed the participants to give expression to the encounters that would otherwise "burn holes" in the brain.

References

Al-Adawi, S.H., Martin, R.G., Al-Salmi, A. and Ghassani, H. (2001) "Zar: Group Distress and Healing." *Mental Health, Religion and Culture 4*, 1, 47–61.

American-Israeli Cooperative Enterprise (2009) "The history of Ethiopian Jews." Available at www.jewishvirtuallibrary.org/jsource/Judaism/ejhist.html, accessed October 2010.

Ante Portas, H. (2009) "The Great Holocaust of Ethiopian Jewry" (Hebrew). *Forum of the Israel Association of Ethiopian Jews* (October 4). Available at www.iaej.co.il/newsite/forums_viewMessage.asp?forumID=2&msgID=1768, accessed October 2010.

Asrasai-Engede, S. (2007) "Music Encompasses the World – the Disease of the Zar" (Hebrew). *Forum of the Israel Association of Ethiopian Jews* (June 25). Available at www.iaej.co.il/newsite/content.asp?PageId=524, accessed October 2010.

Ben-Ezer, G. (2002) *The Ethiopian Jewish Exodus: Narratives of the Migration Journey to Israel 1977–1985*, Routledge Studies in Memory and Narrative 9. London and New York: Routledge.

Ben-Ezer, G. (2006) *The Migration Journey: The Ethiopian Jewish Exodus, Memory and Narrative.* New Brunswick, NJ: Transaction Publishers.

Ben-Ezer, G. (2007) "Trauma, Culture and Myth: Narratives of the Ethiopian Jewish Exodus." In L.J. Kirmayer, R. Lemelson and M. Barad (eds) *Understanding Trauma: Integrating Biological, Clinical, and Cultural Perspectives.* New York: Cambridge University Press.

Biton, M., Eshkol, E. and Bodovsky, D. (1997) "Criminal and Detached Youth Among Ethiopian Immigrants (Hebrew)." Kiryat Gat Seminar For Parents of Detached Ethiopian Youth. Available at www.iaej.org.il/newsite/content.asp?PageId=513, accessed December 2010.

Bodovsky, D., David, Y. and Eran, Y. (1998) "Drinking Alcohol: Dilemmas in Providing Information to Ethiopian Immigrants." In N. Michaeli & O. Naor (eds.) Alcohol and Information. The Efshar Organization, Ministry of Labor and Welfare.

Hadari, A. (2009) Personal communication.

Israel Association for Ethiopian Jews (2006) "Current State of Affairs: The Ethiopian Israeli Community." (Unattributed report.)

Israel Association for Ethiopian Jews (2009) "Ethiopian Jewish Culture – Handicrafts." Available at www.iaej.co.il/newsite/content.asp?pageid=403&lang=he, accessed October 2010.

Joint Distribution Committee and the Brookdale Institute (2001) "The Integration of Ethiopian Immigrants into Israeli Society: Challenges, Policy, Programs and Action Directions." (23 April). (Unattributed report.)

Kaplan, S. (1999) "Can an Ethiopian change his skin? The Beta Yisrael (Ethiopian Jews) and racial discourse." *African Affairs 98*, 393, 535–550.

Kaplan, S. and Salamon, H. (2003) "Ethiopian Jews in Israel: A Part of the People or Apart from the People." In U. Rebhun and C.I. Waxman (eds) *Jews in Israel: Contemporary Social and Cultural Patterns*. Hanover, NH, and London: University Press of New England/Brandeis University Press.

Lester, D. (2005) *Suicide and the Holocaust: David Lester*. New York: Nova Science Publishers.

Lotan, O. and Kin, H. (2007) *Data Regarding Violence against Women among Ethiopian Immigrants* (Hebrew). Jerusalem: Knesset Center for Research and Information.

Onolemhemhen, D.N. and Gessesse, K. (1998) *The Black Jews of Ethiopia: The Last Exodus*, Atla Monograph. Lanham, MD: Scarecrow Press.

Parfitt, T. (1985) *Operation Moses: The Untold Story of the Secret Exodus of the Falasha Jews from Ethiopia*. New York: Stein and Day.

Ribner, D.S. and Schindler, R. (1996) "The crisis of religious identity among Ethiopian immigrants in Israel." *Journal of Black Studies 27*, 1, 104–117.

Schwartz, S. (2007) *Feedback on Avi Hadari's Group Leadership Skills Workshop for Ethiopian Army Graduates in Nes Ziona*. Netanya, Israel: Lesley University.

Shabtay, M. (2001) *Between Reggae and Rap – Music and Identity among Ethiopian Youth* (Hebrew). Tel Aviv: Tcherikover.

Shabtay, M. (2003) "Ragap: Music and identity among young Ethiopians in Israel." *Critical Arts Journal 17*, 93–105.

Tebeka: Advocacy for Equality and Justice for Ethiopian Israelis (2007) *Going to the Top: Excellence and Industrial Leadership Ethiopian Immigrant Academics*. 1–11. Israel, February.

Wagner, M. (2006) "Shas's Ethiopian rep may finally take Knesset seat." *Jerusalem Post*, February 7.

Wergen, Y. (2006) *Integrating Ethiopian Immigrant Students into the Educational System* (Hebrew). Jerusalem: Knesset Center for Research and Information.

Wertzberger, R. (2003) "The Ethiopian Immigrant Community: A Situation Report, Gaps and Claims of Discrimination" (Hebrew). *Knesset Background Paper* (July). Available at www.knesset.gov.il/MMM/data/docs/m00799.doc, accessed October 2010.

Afterword

The Power of Poiesis

MaryBeth Morand

As a relief worker I have seen interventions that respond to wide-scale humanitarian emergencies evolve over the past 20 years. In the 1980s and early 90s, responses to disasters and displacement were organized in a quasi-colonial fashion. International experts swooped in and decided what communities needed, and then distributed aid. The affected community was not usually consulted. The people involved were systematically referred to as "beneficiaries," "the caseload," or "the victims of…" Humanitarian work was associated with charity; the power rested with the munificent foreigners. Little thought was given to the community's need to recover as a vital element in its social reconstruction, or to the fact that self-determination would allow the community to re-align and become more adroit in obtaining resources for itself. In this way, some post-conflict or post-emergency populations became "protracted situations," and "foreign aid dependency" and "donor fatigue" became frequent topics of discussion. A positive outcome of the relative failure of these efforts has been an overhaul of the attitude of most humanitarian organizations toward the communities they serve. Since the mid to late 1990s, needs assessments amongst all segments of the community – including the elderly, youth, women, and minority groups – are conducted at the onset of an emergency. The "beneficiaries" and "victims" of yesteryear are now "survivors" and "stakeholders." As such, they are now relied upon to identify short- and long-term solutions to the crisis at hand. Humanitarian relief has become more focused on the strengths, rather than the deficits, in the communities. Of course, we still report on morbidity and mortality, sexual and gender-based violence, single female heads of household, war-affected youth, etc., yet we now concentrate on helping the community find resources to envision new possibilities, rather than reinforcing the problems themselves.

Having witnessed the paradigm of delivering humanitarian relief shift over the past two decades, it has been fascinating to read the authors in this volume recount the evolutionary process in the maturation of expressive art therapy itself. Many of the key principles that they espouse mirror the transfer of disproportionate power away from the service provider (therapist/relief worker) and onto the creator(s) of the artwork, who is no longer seen as the "patient," "client," or "beneficiary." Honoring this empowerment of the creator(s) is crucial to grasping the power of *poiesis* as a transformative process. Just as providing tents, blankets, and sacks of food without adequate initial inquiry can actually make a bad situation worse (e.g. when the aid goes to militias, when vulnerable groups in the community do not receive the aid), an overly hasty approach to community art-making can actually deepen wounds. Thus, I am grateful that these pioneers have laid the groundwork for a respectful and resource-based expressive art facilitation process, in which humanitarian workers can interact with communities and address their complex and disturbing issues without doing harm or prolonging suffering.

Although tents, blankets, and sacks of food are necessary for survival, they do not provide the sustenance that individuals and communities need in order to reinvent themselves after they have been ripped asunder and irrevocably changed by traumatic events. The necessity of this healing and reunification has been recognized in humanitarian relief in the last decade. As a result, psychosocial interventions, especially those using the arts, have moved forward as a primary response to crises, not as a leisurely postscript provided when time allows. Nowadays, the arts are widely used to work with communities during or immediately following an event that has displaced or traumatized a community. As well as setting forth a framework for practice, this book provides a rich collection of realistic and poignant examples of the responsible use of expressive arts while communities are in turmoil. Every chapter adds a different and indispensable dimension to facilitating art with precarious communities. In each instance the art that was created epitomized the community at that specific place, in that particular time, and under those special circumstances in a way that no statistics or prescribed standards and indicators ever could. This is the amazing power of art.

If there is anything that we have learned in the past two decades in both humanitarian relief work and in the practice of the expressive arts, it is to handle power with care. This book carries out that task, and is essential for anyone who wants to make the arts available in the service of social change.

Contributors

Karen Abbs has worked internationally for more than five years after spending eight years in Canada as an expressive arts therapist/clinical counselor specializing in trauma counseling. She has worked for Médécins Sans Frontieres (Holland) in Kashmir (India) and the Central African Republic implementing psychosocial programs in conflict and emergency settings, as well as a mental health advisor for nine countries worldwide. Ms. Abbs has also developed RedR UK's Psychosocial Program in Darfur, focusing on providing training in Critical Incident Stress Management and support to humanitarian workers after critical incidents. Ms. Abbs is currently a psychosocial advisor for Columbia University (ICAP) in Swaziland.

Maysa Al-Hmouz has been employed as a psychosocial counselor with the Center for Victims of Torture since February 2009. She spent two years as a psychologist in a program designed to treat nicotine addiction.

Eman Al-Houdali has been employed as a psychosocial counselor with the Center for Victims of Torture since March 2009. She also worked as education specialist and sensory room coordinator at the Al Noor Family Institute in Amman, and as a teacher at YMC, Al Mashreq School.

Mariam Al-Salahat has been employed as a psychosocial counselor with the Center for Victims of Torture since February 2009. She spent a year as a psychologist with The Swedish Organization for Individual Relief, at Sweileh, Jordan, and a year and a half as a counselor with Mercy Corps Comprehensive After-school Project, in Amman.

Moath Asfoor has been employed as a psychosocial counselor with the Center for Victims of Torture since December 2008. His employers have included Care International, where he worked as a Counselor for Iraqi refugees in Jordan; the United Nations Relief and Works Agency (UNRWA) in Jerusalem, where he was a social worker for Palestinian refugees; and an International Development Research Center funded poverty reduction project in Jordan, where he was a community specialist.

Sally S. Atkins is Professor of Human Development and Psychological Counseling at Appalachian State University, where she coordinates the graduate program in expressive arts therapy, and is a core faculty member at the European Graduate School, Switzerland. She is a licensed psychologist, registered expressive arts therapist and a member of the American Academy of Psychotherapists. Her publications include poetry, professional journal articles, books, and book chapters. She has traveled and taught in Switzerland, Canada, Sweden, China, West Africa, Peru, and Bolivia.

Karen Estrella is Associate Professor and Coordinator of Expressive Therapies at Lesley University, Cambridge, MA, where she specializes in multicultural approaches and community mental health. She has over 20 years' experience practicing expressive therapies and mental health counseling in community-based settings.

Ephrat Huss is an art therapist, social worker, and family therapist holding a lectureship at Ben Gurion University teaching creative interventions to social workers in Israel. Her doctorate was on art as a speech act for marginalized Bedouin women in Israel. She has published widely in the area of arts-based research, and on the connection between social work and art therapy.

Samer Hussein, originally from Iraq, has been employed as a psychosocial counselor with the Center for Victims of Torture since December 2008. Prior to this he was employed by several different non-governmental organizations that provide psychosocial support for Iraqi refugees in Amman.

Debra Kalmanowitz is a HPC registered art therapist (UK). She has worked extensively in the context of trauma, political violence, and social change, locally, internationally, and in countries of conflict. Debra is the co-editor of the book *Art Therapy and Political Violence: With art, without illusion,* and co-author of *The Portable Studio: art therapy and political conflict: Initiatives in the former Yugoslavia and Kwazulu-Natal, South Africa.* Currently based in Hong Kong, Debra works with refugees and asylum seekers. In addition to working as an art therapy supervisor, consultant and lecturer, she continues to co-direct ATI (Art Therapy Initiative) and to make her own art.

Paolo J. Knill is Professor Emeritus at Lesley University (Cambridge, MA) and Rector of the European Graduate School (Switzerland). He is the author or co-author of numerous works in English and German, including *Minstrels of Soul: Intermodal Expressive Therapy,* and co-author of *Principles and Practice of Expressive Arts Therapy: Towards a Therapeutic Aesthetics.*

Michelle LeBaron is Professor of Law and Director, University of British Columbia Program on Dispute Resolution, Vancouver, BC. She has done foundational work in the conflict transformation field and has directed research/practice initiatives applying arts-based methodologies in a wide range of contexts both domestic and international. She is the author of three books on conflict transformation across cultures and is currently Principal Investigator of the Dancing at the Crossroads project, a Canadian government-funded initiative involving Canadians, Europeans, South Americans, and South Africans in collaboration on the culturally appropriate use of dance, movement, and other expressive arts practices in reconciliation processes.

Ellen Levine is co-founder of and faculty at ISIS Canada, a three-year training program in expressive arts therapy, and a senior staff social worker at the Hincks-Dellcrest Centre for Children's Mental Health in Toronto. She is Dean of Individualized Studies in Expressive Arts Therapy and core faculty at the European Graduate School in Switzerland (EGS). She was the founding director of the program in Expressive Arts Therapy and Social Change at EGS. She is an author, co-author, and editor of a number of books in the field of expressive arts therapy, including *Tending the Fire: Studies in Art, Therapy and Creativity* and *Principles and Practice of Expressive Arts Therapy: Toward a Therapeutic Aesthetics.*

Stephen K. Levine is Professor Emeritus of Social Science at York University (Toronto), Vice-Rector and Dean of the Doctoral Program in Expressive Arts: Therapy, Education, Consulting and Social Change at the European Graduate School in Switzerland and Co-Director of ISIS Canada, a training program in expressive arts therapy. He is the author of *Trauma, Tragedy, Therapy: The Arts and Human Suffering,* and *Poiesis: The Language of Psychology and the Speech of the Soul,* co-author of *Principles and Practice of Expressive*

Arts Therapy: Toward a Therapeutic Aesthetics, and co-editor of *Foundations of Expressive Arts Therapy: Theoretical and Clinical Perspectives.* He is editor of *POIESIS: A Journal of the Arts and Communication.*

Bobby Lloyd is an artist and HPC registered art therapist, supervisor and lecturer based in London. She has worked for many years with children, young people, and families who have experienced trauma, political violence, social upheaval, and deprivation, in the UK and in countries of conflict. Bobby is co-author of the edited book *Art Therapy and Political Violence: With Art, Without Illusion* and is co-author of *The Portable Studio: Art Therapy and Political Conflict, Initiatives in the Former Yugoslavia and Kaw-Zulu-Natal, South Africa.* Her current practice focuses on community-based settings, including schools, Traveller and Gypsy sites, and housing estates where she is exploring the role of mobile studios. She continues to co-direct ATI (Art Therapy Initiative).

Carrie MacLeod has used an arts-based approach to education, advocacy, and social action for over a decade. This work has focused on peace and reconciliation initiatives in Sierra Leone, West Africa, with social justice projects throughout India and Central America, and in the context of immigrant youth programs in Canada. She is currently Research Director of the Dancing at the Crossroads Project at the University of British Columbia. At the European Graduate School, she is on the faculty of the MA Program in Expressive Arts in Conflict Transformation and Peacebuilding, and is the Director of the International Centre for Arts in Peacebuilding.

Vivien Marcow Speiser is Professor and Division Director of National, International and Collaborative Programs at Lesley University, Cambridge, MA. She is a board certified dance movement therapist. Her interests and expertise lie in the area of cross-cultural conflict resolution through the arts. She has worked extensively with groups in the United States, the Middle East, and in South Africa.

Shaun McNiff is founder of the first integrated arts in therapy graduate program at Lesley University in Cambridge, MA. He is an exhibiting painter and the author of *Trust the Process: An Artist's Guide to Letting Go*; *Art as Medicine*; *Art Heals: How Creativity Cures the Soul*; *Art-Based Research*; the recently published *Integrating the Arts in Therapy: History, Theory, and Practice*, and other books and writings. McNiff has received various honors and awards for his work. In 2002 Lesley University appointed him as its first university professor.

MaryBeth Morand is Director of the MA Program in Expressive Arts in Conflict Transformation and Peacebuilding at the European Graduate School in Switzerland. In addition to working as an emergency responder for international non-governmental organizations, she has worked for UNHCR for over ten years in many conflict zones and disaster areas, including Somalia, Bosnia, Azerbaijan, Darfur, and Aceh. She is currently a senior staff development officer in UNHCR's Global Learning Center in Budapest, Hungary, where she is trying to infuse the arts into many aspects of learning for humanitarian staff, and using expressive arts with refugee men who have been accepted for resettlement in Hungary.

Insherah Musa has been employed as a psychosocial counselor with the Center for Victims of Torture since December 2008. She also worked as the project coordinator for the Jordan Community Centers Association (CCA).

Samuel Schwartz is Associate Director of the Lesley University Extension Program in Israel. In this capacity he has managed arts-based interventions with a variety of populations including Ethiopian immigrants and Arab-Jewish dialogue groups. As Spokesperson and Director of Academic Affairs at the Consulates General of Israel in Boston and Los Angeles in the 1990s, he designed and led numerous conflict resolution outreach projects in 12 US States. He has published journal articles on the topics of conflict transformation, international relations, and cross-cultural community organization.

Gloria Simoneaux is founder and director of Harambee Arts: Let's pull together, a training program for caregivers in Sub-Saharan Africa. In 1989 she founded DrawBridge: An Arts Program for Homeless Children and served as the executive director until December 2007. She is an adjunct professor at JFK University in Orinda, California, and teaches at CONNECT Family Therapy Institute in Harare, Zimbabwe, and at The Kenya Association for Professional Counselors in Nairobi, Kenya. Ms. Simoneaux is a recipient of the Jefferson Award for public service (2007). Currently she is a Fulbright scholar in Nairobi, Kenya.

Shanee Stepakoff is a writer/poet, clinical/community psychologist, and registered poetry therapist. She was the psychologist for the UN-backed war crimes tribunal in Sierra Leone for over two years. In addition, she spent a year as psychologist/trainer for the Center for Victims of Torture's (CVT) program for Liberians in the refugee camps of Guinea, and a year as psychologist/trainer for CVT's treatment clinic for Iraqi torture survivors in Jordan. She has presented, trained, consulted, and published widely on the utilization of the expressive arts with victims of ethnic and political violence. She is presently based in New York City, where she is on the medical staff of St. Luke's Roosevelt Hospital.

TAE Perú, Terapia de Artes Expresivas Perú (Judith Alalu, Jose Miguel Calderon, Ximena Maurial, Monica Prado, Martin Zavala) is a training institute in Lima, Peru, associated with the European Graduate School. The authors are members of the teaching staff of the institute and practice and teach expressive arts therapy in Lima and other parts of the country.

Subject Index

Author Index